A HUNDRED YEARS OF
SPYING

A HUNDRED YEARS OF
SPYING

PHIL CARRADICE

AN IMPRINT OF PEN & SWORD BOOKS LTD.
YORKSHIRE - PHILADELPHIA

First published in Great Britain in 2021 by
PEN AND SWORD HISTORY
An imprint of
Pen & Sword Books Ltd
Yorkshire – Philadelphia

Copyright © Phil Carradice, 2021

ISBN 978 1 52678 141 3

The right of Phil Carradice to be identified as Author of this work has been asserted by him in accordance with the Copyright, Designs and Patents Act 1988.

A CIP catalogue record for this book is available from the British Library.

All rights reserved. No part of this book may be reproduced or transmitted in any form or by any means, electronic or mechanical including photocopying, recording or by any information storage and retrieval system, without permission from the Publisher in writing.

Typeset in Times New Roman 11.5/14 by
SJmagic DESIGN SERVICES, India.
Printed and bound by CPI Group (UK) Ltd, Croydon, CR0 4YY

Pen & Sword Books Limited incorporates the imprints of Atlas, Archaeology, Aviation, Discovery, Family History, Fiction, History, Maritime, Military, Military Classics, Politics, Select, Transport, True Crime, Air World, Frontline Publishing, Leo Cooper, Remember When, Seaforth Publishing, The Praetorian Press, Wharncliffe Local History, Wharncliffe Transport, Wharncliffe True Crime and White Owl.

For a complete list of Pen & Sword titles please contact
PEN & SWORD BOOKS LIMITED
47 Church Street, Barnsley, South Yorkshire, S70 2AS, England
E-mail: enquiries@pen-and-sword.co.uk
Website: www.pen-and-sword.co.uk

Or
PEN AND SWORD BOOKS
1950 Lawrence Rd, Havertown, PA 19083, USA
E-mail: Uspen-and-sword@casematepublishers.com
Website: www.penandswordbooks.com

Contents

Introduction vi
Chapter One　　　The Second Oldest Profession 1
Chapter Two　　　Spy Fiction and Spy Fact 16
Chapter Three　　An Advance into War 32
Chapter Four　　　Conflict Comes at Last 50
Chapter Five　　　A Host of Spies – the Interwar Years 72
Chapter Six　　　　A Gathering Storm 97
Chapter Seven　　War! 116
Chapter Eight　　　A Cold, Cold Comfort 142
Chapter Nine　　　The Yanks are Coming 157
Chapter Ten　　　　Colder Yet and Colder 168
Chapter Eleven　　A Continuing Fascination 185
Chapter Twelve　　An End of Spying? 195
Notes 201
Bibliography 205
Index 207

Introduction

To most of us the world of spying is one of mystery and suspense, romantic places, dangerous villains and noble heroes. Nothing could be further from the truth. In reality it is usually hard to differentiate between heroes and villains. Indeed, in many cases they are exactly the same people, spying for both sides at the same time. That is what makes the spy's world so fascinating – if not totally wholesome.

It would be foolish to state that this book can examine every aspect of spying during the 100 years it covers. It would need a volume five, ten, twenty times the size of this one to relate every mood and moment of spying and then, because of the nature of the subject, it would still miss so much. So this is not a definitive survey; it's a sample, a toe in the water, a look at the more interesting spies and their adventures during one of the most fascinating centuries of world history.

The book concentrates on the careers of spies themselves rather than the political machinations that sent them off to glory or death. After all, without the spies there would be no spying. Many spies are mentioned here, many more are not. Readers may lament the exclusion of this agent or that one, but ultimately it comes down to shortage of space and personal preference.

I make no apologies for concentrating largely on the British espionage services, which was where my interest began. But the nature of the spy game demands more. Spies cannot exist in a vacuum, that would defeat the very object of spying, and so the book also contains stories of German, Russian, French and American agents and their relationships with their British colleagues or opponents.

Enough prevarication: this is not the place for long introductions saying what the book is or is not about. Hopefully that will become clear as you read. As the bard did NOT say, 'Read on, MacDuff, and damned be him who first cries "Hold, enough".'

Phil Carradice, St Athan, 2020

Chapter One

The Second Oldest Profession

'Some become spies for money, or out of veracity, or megalomania, or out of ambition, or out of a desire for thrills. The malady of our time is those who become spies out of idealism.'

Max Lerner

There have always been spies, people who watch, clandestinely or openly, the activities of other people and then report back to yet more people. The word 'people' is deliberately over-used in this opening paragraph.

Spying has always been bound up with the lives of people, what they do and why they do it. Spies are individuals who have appeared briefly in our consciousness, sometimes under the radar, sometimes in the full glare of publicity. They are people who have sometimes left their mark on our history and sometimes fallen into well-deserved ignominy.

The art of spying has been glibly and probably accurately termed the second oldest profession in the world. It has certainly been around for a long, long time. And yet there are those who advise forgetting the appellation 'second'. Spying, they say, is actually the first and oldest profession. If so, it is not quite clear where such an acknowledgement leaves large portions of society: the ladies of the Turkish harems, the camp followers of all invading armies since the beginning of time, and the women from the back alleyways of villages, towns and cities across the world.

One thing is clear. Since man first began to covet the land and possessions of others, spies have been used to supply information for the benefit of attacking or defending armies. For governments and politicians spies have helped to inform policy, assist with strategy and, through the validity or ineptitude of their information, helped devise tactics.

Spies have made political and military careers for their associates and then destroyed them with little more than a nod of the head. If envy is an innately human emotion then it is easy to see why the spy, as an entity, has been appreciated by some and yet soundly reviled by others.

A HUNDRED YEARS OF SPYING

The Book of Numbers in *The Old Testament* tells us that after the flight from Egypt the patriarch Moses despatched twelve spies into Canaan, one from each of the twelve tribes of Israel. Their job was to reconnoitre the lie of the land, assess the potential opposition and to analyse the ease with which the country might be conquered.

Unfortunately for Moses, the spies employed in the mission were amateurs, scouts rather than secret agents. Apart from two men, Joshua and Caleb – both ferocious, hard-bitten warriors – the spies were terrified of the region's fortified cities and the 'giants' who supposedly ruled the lands.

They returned with negative reports. As a result Moses turned his eyes away from Canaan and the Israelites were forced to wander in the desert for the next forty years. It was a classic case of a leader listening to the wrong advice. The amateurs got it wrong and while Joshua and Caleb might fume and fret there was nothing they could do in the face of Moses's decision.

The Mogul rulers of India understood the power of insider information far better than Moses. They ruled their vast territories on the Indian subcontinent by a combination of wise judgement and harsh military force. As a result they employed dozens of agents or spies. The Emperor Akbar apparently had over 4000 of them, all employed to scout, observe and report back, telling him exactly what his enemies were doing.

It was a spy or traitor, depending on your viewpoint, whose information enabled the Persian general Xerces to find a hidden mountain track and wipe out the 300 Spartans in the pass of Thermopylae. It might have been underhand but it ended one of the great 'last stands' of history.

Similarly, it was a spy or double agent in the camp of the much-expected and much-feared Jewish Messiah who betrayed Jesus of Nazareth to the Temple Authorities. Judas Iscariot's betrayal price of thirty pieces of silver has been used ever since to represent the treasonous and illicit dealings with which spies have become associated.

King Alfred the Great preferred to keep his own counsel, and instead of sending spies into the opposing Danish camp, he adopted the disguise of a minstrel and went himself. Or so the story tells us. Like the legend of Alfred burning the cakes, the tale should be treated with caution. Would someone like Alfred really risk his life in such an enterprise when he could have employed more easily replaceable agents to do it for him?

The Tudor spymaster Francis Walsingham not only created an effective network of secret agents but used some of them to 'set up' Mary, Queen of

Scots. The story of Mary's downfall is the stuff of legend involving illicit messages being concealed in the false bottoms of beer barrels, secret late-night liaisons by lantern light and betrayal at both high and low levels: cruel but highly effective with double dealing at every turn of the dice.

Elizabeth was unhappy with Walsingham's machinations and the way in which a queen had been treated. The great spymaster was sent away from court and never worked for the Tudor government again. Elizabeth did, however, sign the death warrant for her cousin. Whatever Elizabeth really felt about his actions, Walsingham succeeded both in sending Mary to the block and in making the country peaceful for a while. More importantly, the throne of England and the person of Queen Elizabeth were secure at last.

The supreme use of spies as a political weapon, however, has to come from Nazi Germany. It was the network of spies and informers created by Adolf Hitler and Herman Goering in the 1930s that terrified and browbeat the nation, consigning the German people to fifteen years of terror. During that time fear stalked the corridors of apartment blocks and lurked around every street corner in the Reich. Nobody trusted their neighbours and nobody dared to criticise those in control. It was dictatorship of the spirit and, arguably, the Nazi regime would not have survived without this insidious but highly effective underground network.

Given the examples quoted above – and there are many more – it's small wonder that the analogous position and reputation of the spy has remained so perfidious over the years.

In history, in memory, in literature and in comedy the spy has always been there, open to attack or comment. The writers of the television series *Blackadder* managed to get it right when, in an attempt to convince the reluctant Blackadder to hunt down an enemy agent, General Melchett and his 'toady', Captain Darling, discuss the merits of the spying culture:

> Darling: 'So you see, Blackadder, Field Marshal Haig is most anxious to eliminate all German spies.'
> Melchett: 'Filthy Hun weasels, fighting their underhand war!'
> Darling: 'Fortunately, one of our spies …'
> Melchett: 'Splendid fellows, brave heroes, risking life and limb for Blighty.'[1]

Regardless of how they are viewed spies have always performed a useful and much-valued service. Unfortunately for them, that service and their willingness, as General Melchett had it, to risk 'life and limb' for their country, has not always earned the approval they have deserved.

Death and vilification remain constant threats for anyone who ventures into the spying profession, while the very nature of what the successful spy does to earn his living ensures that public acclaim is both fleeting and limited. Indeed, the best that most successful spies can hope for is a large dose of anonymity.

When that anonymity is removed the result is usually a maelstrom of hyperbole and condemnation. Purple prose doesn't begin to cover it. The media loves disaster, and consequently an exposed or 'blown' spy is an excuse for lurid headlines and weeks of recrimination with fingers of accusation pointed in all directions. Clearly, being a spy is something of a poisoned chalice, so much so that you often wonder why people are prepared to do it.

Ask anyone to name a well-known spy and the reply is usually one of three choices. Ian Fleming's fictional hero James Bond will be first. Quite apart from the fact that Bond never existed, he is also not a spy, he is just an assassin, a killer. As Fleming himself said, a hard object thrown at a problem with the hope that through a combination of luck and brutal determination he will batter his way to a successful conclusion.

For the second response you might be lucky and get something about the Cambridge spy ring of the 1950s. Kim Philby, Donald McClean and the rest have managed to retain a hint of romance, despite the fact that it was Britain they were betraying. There are still people out there who remember them, if not fondly then at least with a degree of admiration.

So, we have James Bond and the Cambridge spies. The third response will inevitably be Mata Hari, although in all fairness that has probably more to do with eroticism than actual spying ability.

That really will be the end of it as far as the public is concerned. There is nothing inherently wrong with that because the very nature of spying is, by and large, its secrecy. Everything about it is clandestine, hidden.

The world's greatest spy could easily be the mild-mannered man next door who seems to spend his time mowing the lawn or washing his car. Or it could be the woman serving behind the grocery counter at the local supermarket. Despite our preconceptions, he is unlikely to be the muscle-bound hulk who works out five times a week at the local gym. You simply do not know, and if you did the spy would not be worth the cost of the telephone call to turn him in.

****

To some extent even the use of the word spy is both limiting and wrong. The dictionary definition will tell you that a spy is simply someone who is employed either to watch others or collect information. In fact spies do a great deal more than that.

Over the years the term spy has become a catch-all for most aspects of undercover dealings and clandestine operations. From the fictional James Bond to Somerset Maugham's equally fictional hero 'Ashenden', and from real life agents like Oleg Penkovsky and Kim Philby to the unknown, unidentified figures who haunt our nightmares, the name spy has been applied and has stuck.

Imagine it: there is secret work to be done, dirty work as some would have it. So the automatic response is to 'call in the Funnies', as John Le Carré declared in one of his Smiley novels, thus glibly bestowing the concept of the spy onto all men and women who fight their battles away from the front lines and without the paraphernalia of glory and fame.

With that in mind it is probably worth spending a few moments thinking about what it is that our spies do actually get up to when they are at work.

There are two basic arenas within which most spies operate. Firstly there is the need to keep the home country safe from the machinations of enemy spies. This, to use the correct nomenclature, is counterintelligence. Then there is the polar opposite, spies or agents who penetrate other countries and organisations in order to confuse, damage and extract information from the enemy. Within these two arms of the service there are a whole range of activities that fall within the reach of the man or woman we call 'the spy'.

Spying creates something of a dichotomy in that it is, by its nature, a lonely and solitary business. The more people who know what the spy is doing the more chance there is of betrayal. And yet spies cannot exist entirely alone. They need allies, assistants who will often carry out much of the spadework for them. They need contacts to carry messages and provide arms and supplies. They need people who know the immediate locale and will help them avoid detection.

As a result, spies build networks of support for themselves and other helpers, both within the country to which they are assigned and outside in the wider world. The resistance networks created, fuelled and funded by the Allies in Occupied France, Yugoslavia and Czechoslovakia during the Second World War are classic examples of this particular aspect of the spy's tradecraft.

Spies engage in acts of sabotage. Again, take Occupied France and the other theatres of war as an example. Blowing up railway lines and factories might be straight out of the annals of James Bond, but they are necessary activities for agents operating in foreign countries in times of war or crisis.

Spies uncover or expose opposition provocateurs and undermine enemy positions. They have been known to assassinate and kill, to steal state secrets and incriminate dangerous enemies. They are, in fact, secret agents who do whatever is necessary to advance their own situation, ultimately for the overall benefit of their country with perhaps a little bit extra for themselves. And of course, as was originally envisaged, spies also collect, collate and pass on vital pieces of information.

The art of spying might be as old as Methuselah but for many years it was very much an amateur profession. That is not to say that all of the undercover agents carried out their work for nothing. Payments invariably remained an ad hoc arrangement. The thirty pieces of silver concept has never quite gone away as far as undercover work is concerned.

Until fairly recently spies were drawn from a wide pool. They were often professional army officers, individuals who had already been paid for their services and were acting on orders. In these cases the spies would have been young men, eager for adventure, happily accepting the challenge of undercover duties when they were offered.

On the other hand they could just as easily have been willing civilians, men and women who were employed for specific activities or the provision of particular pieces of information. Whichever type of 'volunteer' was used, invariably such individuals were dedicated patriots willing to risk their lives for a cause. That motivation was often as much a hindrance as an aid, but for such people payment, like their own safety, was often a secondary consideration.

THE SECOND OLDEST PROFESSION

There have been dozens, probably hundreds, of examples throughout the years of the amateur spy at work. However, the American Revolution provides a classic snapshot of how these early spy systems were used.

After several early defeats due to poor information gathering, George Washington, commander of the American Continental Army, began to realise the need for accurate knowledge of enemy dispositions. There was no shortage of volunteers willing to scout out troop movements and eavesdrop on careless talk in the taverns of New England. Washington happily took them up on their offers of help, but that willingness to assist in the fight actually caused the future American president more problems than he ever imagined possible.

Apart from conflicting reports that varied according to the interests and attitudes of each individual spy, the Revolutionary leader was hampered by the patriotism – to the detriment of military logic – that his agents displayed. They took unnecessary risks and as a result several of the early undercover men were unmasked by the British and executed.

Nathan Hale – America's first spy, as he has become known – was one of Washington's original spies. He volunteered to operate behind British lines but had little understanding of the dangers involved or any real ability in the art of espionage. Undoubtedly brave and fearless, Hale drew attention to himself by asking too many obvious questions about troop movements and dispositions with the result that he was arrested, condemned and sentenced to be hanged. His final words – 'I am only sorry that I have just one life to give for my country' – sums up the motivation of those early American patriots.

Eventually several efficient spy networks were created for General Washington and the rebels. The most famous of these was the Culper Spy Ring which was able to boast of five years operating behind enemy lines without losing even one of its agents. Members of the group developed techniques which have since become the staple of nearly all spy novelists; things like the use of invisible ink, dead letter drops and messages written in code.

The American rebel spies became adept at the use of disinformation. The style and nature of the Revolutionary struggle was actually a civil war: neighbour spying on neighbour, cousins and brothers fighting for different armies. It was ideal for the use of double agents, counter-intelligence operators who took pride and delight in confusing the British forces.

The most famous of these counter espionage spies was Enoch Crosby who became remarkably efficient at infiltrating loyalist groups and then 'blowing' them to General Washington. Posing as a loyalist, Crosby allowed himself to be captured several times by the rebels. He would be flung into captivity with others who had chosen to remain loyal to the British crown. Together in the confines of their prisons they would hatch a plan, perhaps even stage a prison break, and then Crosby would give them up to his real comrades. Much useful information was gathered in this way and Crosby became famous as a double agent, so much so that even his own parents believed him to be a traitor to the cause of American independence.

With spying in its infancy, naivety and ignorance on the part of the British certainly helped the American spy networks. The British commanders seemed unable to accept the fact that this was not a game to be played by gentlemanly rules, where honour and codes of conduct were more important than the final outcome of a battle. It was a misconception that was to hurt them deeply.

Unbelievable as it might seem, Lewis Costign, a captured rebel army officer who was granted freedom of movement on giving his parole not to escape or involve himself in acts of war, was allowed to roam unchecked and without supervision up and down the strategically important streets of New York. Even when it became clear to the authorities that somebody in the city was passing on vital information there was no attempt to put a limit on Costign's movements.

For weeks on end Costign lounged in the coffee houses, drank in the taverns and watched the warships and troop convoys pulling into and out of the Hudson and the other waterways that surrounded New York. Then, in his own time, he returned to his lodgings, wrote his reports and sent everything back to his superiors in the American camp.

As the New England summer slid slowly into winter, Costign continued to stroll unchecked around the city. By now he had become a familiar figure with the British soldiers and merchants who had come to regard him almost as a friend. Nobody believed that such a gentleman would ever stoop to such a low trade as spying.

Soon, as was the practice of the time, Costign was officially exchanged for a British prisoner-of-war, but much to the amusement of those in command of the city he declined to return to his own forces. He was allowed to stay in New York where he was apparently supremely happy.

Not one of the senior British officers even dreamed of questioning such strange behaviour. They simply accepted Costign's decision as natural. But all the while this friend of the British was gathering much-needed information and passing it onto Washington and his Continental Army. In all, Costign spent nearly six months spying for General Washington in one of the main centres for British troops and supplies.

Women, forbidden to take part in the actual fighting, were particularly effective agents. Once again operating from the moral high ground, the British could not bring themselves to believe that the Revolutionaries would dream of using members of the fairer sex to help their campaign for independence. How wrong could they be?

Soldiers, many of them Hanoverians far from home and lonely, were billeted with American families, and under the influence of warm fires and copious amounts of alcohol the need to remain tight-lipped soon faded. The harmless old lady who sat dozing in her rocking chair alongside the fire, the woman of the house bustling into and out of the room with the soldier's food, the young girl who flirted with the redcoats, these were enemy agents working at the coalface of the rebellion. Unknown to the soldiers, they were taking note of everything that was said.

Spies like Lydia Barrington Darragh, from a highly regarded Quaker family, had almost unfettered access to British senior officers, some of whom even lodged with her. None of them expected for one minute that facts garnered from their loose tongues, even down to the contents of official meetings and briefings, were being carefully recorded and reported to Washington by Darragh and her contacts.

Another female patriot, Anna Smith Strong, became one of the most efficient messengers of the whole war, so much so that her name has gone down in American folklore. Posing as a simple housewife and operating under the noses of the British troops, she regularly passed on information to her fellow spy Caleb Brewster. As members of the Culper Spy Ring, she and Brewster developed an ingenious method of getting information to Washington.

It was a simple but, as it turned out, foolproof technique. Anna simply used the washing that was hanging on the clothes line at the back of her farmhouse on Long Island as a signal. A black petticoat meant that there were goods or news to be collected; the number of white handkerchiefs dotted in amongst the rest of the washing indicated which of six remote and carefully chosen caves along the coastline housed the information.

Brewster would see the signal, and as soon as it was convenient and safe, collect whatever was there. He would then take his bounty to the Continental Army.

Anna Strong was never exposed as a rebel spy, spending years working for the cause. The naive British never suspected her. She continued to pass on information until the end of the war and American independence was secured.

It was not just the rebels who used women agents. Ann Bates, a school teacher from Philadelphia, remained a loyalist throughout the war and made several forays into Washington's camp in New York State, disguised as a peddler. The information she gathered during one of these visits was sufficient for the British to reinforce their positions on Rhode Island with the result that the rebels were forced to withdraw.

There is a school of thought that says Peggy Shippen, wife of America's most reviled traitor, Benedict Arnold, was the catalyst in turning him from an American hero into a British agent. Apparently she persuaded Arnold to hand over to the British the fort at West Point and laid plans for the capture of George Washington. If those two schemes had come to fruition they would have changed the outcome of the Revolutionary War.

Peggy Shippen's life as a spy and agent makes a good story, but sadly the only person who could have corroborated it was John Andre, the British spy chief in North America and Arnold's 'handler'. He was later executed by the rebels and therefore unable to comment. There are, however, letters in existence showing there was a relationship between Peggy and Andre, and we know that she acted as a messenger between her husband and the British when techniques like invisible ink and the numbers code (using a dictionary common to both Peggy and Andre) were used.

As the nineteenth century unfolded the use of spies became relatively common. Indeed, the growth of empires made their use almost compulsory. No matter how strong they might be, the whole concept of rival power blocks could instil fear and trembling into any nation that had ideas or intentions of extending its power base. And that, of course, meant that up-to-date information on the strengths and weaknesses of rivals was essential.

For British administrators during this period, Russia, the bogeyman across the mountains from India, was the greatest threat. The thought of the Russian Bear flexing its muscles and casting envious eyes on the jewel in Britain's Imperial crown terrified them all.

The rulers of India needed to know what the Russians were up to, and with that in mind spies in the remote districts of northern India soon became as common as parcels from Fortnum and Masons. As always it was a two-way process. Russian generals needed to monitor British movements and plans so their spies and agents also proliferated on the frontier.

The Himalayas were a significant barrier, but the deep passes and valleys of the border provinces provided a way in and out, with the result that the North-West Frontier became the epi-centre for both British and Russian spying activity. Local tribesmen were used as informers, but it was young British and Russian officers who were charged with going under cover and keeping the passes safe.

The Russian threat to India was grossly exaggerated. Various Czars may have had delusions about seizing control of British territories beyond the Khyber Pass but they never had the resources or the finances to do more than dream. Not that the British realised. The safety of India was a constant concern, one that never quite went away. At the high point of the empire, adventures on the distant edges of British dominions and control of those dominions were an acceptable part of any young officer's life and career.

Wherever the British Empire stretched its mighty paw – at river stations and mountain retreats, at roadside hostelries and in the crowded bazars of the towns – there you would as like as not find some servant of one empire or the other. They would be pale-skinned, eager youngsters waiting to collect and pass on titbits of information that might just be of interest to the puppet masters in Calcutta or St Petersburg.

It was a time of romance and danger. Throughout the nineteenth century and well into the twentieth, in Turkey and Egypt, in Burma and India, the agents of both empires waited patiently and watched. John Buchan, one of the best early spy writers, admirably summed it up when he put into the mouth of spymaster Sir Walter Bullivant the clipped but powerful explanation of the situation in the Middle East. The ever-ready Richard Hannay sat and listened:

> We have had our agents working in Persia and Mesopotamia for years – mostly young officers of the Indian Army.

> They carry their lives in their hands, and now and then one of them disappears, and the sewers of Baghdad might tell a tale. But they find out many things, and they count the game worth the candle.[2]

Hannay, of course, goes on to become one of those young men in a classic example of spy literature from the First World War era, the novel *Greenmantle*.

******

By the end of the nineteenth century world tensions had reached a point where everyone knew that conflict was coming. It was just a matter of when and where it would break out. The 'Great Powers' of the time were all developing their military might. In the mistaken belief that security rested with the strength of their armed forces it was a simplistic response to threats, and the biggest bully with the biggest fists was considered the safest and the strongest ally.

The result was that Britain's navy and Germany's army became two of the greatest forces for destruction that mankind had ever seen. The rivalry between Britain and Germany was intense. Germany's mercurial but mentally unbalanced Kaiser Wilhelm II fretted and cast envious eyes at all British possessions, in particular at the Royal Navy.

The Kaiser's premise was simple. If Britain possessed a powerful collection of warships to protect her coast then Germany would need an even more powerful one to threaten it. It was, to him, a simple case of quid pro quo. As a result the Kaiser and his naval commander, Grand Admiral Von Tirpitz, ordered the building of Dreadnought battleships and battlecruisers to rival anything Britain might possess. The British, of course, replied in kind and the great naval race began.

By 1908, with the surge to create bigger fleets with better warships well under way, there was never any doubt that Britain could out-build Germany in the battleship stakes – as long as the British government, in the shape of the Admiralty, did not interfere and put a cap on the nation's shipbuilding programme. That, as successive First Sea Lords and senior Admirals knew, was always a distinct possibility.

All British governments were conscious of their budgets, particularly in an election year when the amount of money spent on items like

Dreadnoughts could easily bring a government crashing down. The fear of government intervention, therefore, made the reports of spies, now carefully monitoring the German shipbuilding activities, more important than ever.

The Admiralty needed information: facts with which it could batter the ears of the First Lord of the Admiralty and other politicians; facts that would ensure Britain did not sit complacently on her laurels and allow Germany to overtake her. The safety of the nation and the British Empire depended on that premise.

Like most spying interventions it was yet again a two-way process. German spies haunted the dockyards at Chatham and Devonport, at Pembroke Dock and Rosyth, operating as efficiently and effectively as their British equivalents who were monitoring the German building yards at Wilhelmshaven, Hamburg and Kiel.

By 1914 writers like William Le Queux were estimating that there were over 5,000 German spies operating in Britain. To anyone with half an ounce of sense it was an impossible figure, but by then common sense had gone out of the window as raw fear and tension took over.

Le Queux was a novelist with his own agenda and was not always the most reliable of sources but even if his figure of 5000 was to be reduced by half it would still make an incredible number of German agents operating in Britain.[3]

Le Queux was just the tip of the iceberg. Stella Rimington, herself a former head of MI5, has acknowledged the debt we all owe to that curious band of writers and alarmists, the spy authors. The connection between fact and fiction has always been, in this particular case, much closer than anyone ever realised: 'Espionage has attracted many authors. An earlier period of shifting loyalties provided us with Ben Jonson and Christopher Marlowe – both agents; Shakespeare's father, too, worked for the Elizabethan spy machine, as, it has been suggested, did Shakespeare himself.'[4]

Germany's Kaiser Wilhelm was a paranoid and highly disturbed man who suspected treachery everywhere. That paranoia might have begun with the strength of the Royal Navy, but it was not just the British that he feared.

The armies of Russia and France were also carefully watched, and the spying activities of Germany created a wave of reflected paranoia across Europe. That paranoia manifested itself in events like the Dreyfus Affair when, in 1894, French officer Captain Alfred Dreyfus was convicted of high treason and incarcerated on Devil's Island in French Guiana.

Dreyfus had supposedly passed French military secrets to the German Embassy in Paris. He was, of course, totally innocent. It was later proved that the real traitor was actually a man by the name of Esterhazy. It's a name worth remembering. John Le Carré certainly did and was later to use it for one of the possible traitors in his book *Tinker, Tailor, Soldier, Spy*.

Dreyfus, a haughty, distant sort of man, was also Jewish and the scandal raised all manner of anti-Semitic feelings in France. Never a popular individual, either with his comrades or his superiors, it was the anti-Semitism displayed by the French officer class that left many observers with a particularly bitter taste in their mouths.

The real cause of the affair, however – one of the greatest miscarriages of justice ever to taint the French legal system – was fear of Germany and the threat she posed. Memories of the French defeat in the recent Franco-Prussian War remained strong and the military elite were determined never to allow such a humiliation to occur again.

By the end of the nineteenth century French fear and distrust of Germany had reached epidemic proportions, as real and threatening as the British fear of Russia. The country needed there to be German spies preying on its military secrets. Exposure and capture of these individuals could only reassure the French public and Alfred Dreyfus was the chosen victim.

It took extensive investigation by Georges Picquart, head of counter espionage in France, and support from public figures like Emile Zola and Georges Clemenceau to finally free Dreyfus and return him to his family. Even then, despite public opinion beginning to move against the authorities and in favour of the convicted man, it still needed several retrials before justice was done.

Seemingly unscarred, Dreyfus went back into the army, serving with distinction as an artillery officer during the First World War. He survived the conflict and eventually died as a retired and much-respected Lt Colonel. His name, of course, lives on as an example of just how far mistrust in the hands of unscrupulous individuals can actually go.

The Dreyfus Affair created unrest in France and abroad, but more than anything it highlighted the whole business of espionage, and brought it out into the open where it could be discussed and dreaded. Regardless of whether Dreyfus was guilty or innocent, the general public seized on the art of spying, and with a slight frisson of fear, mixed with a delicious hint of excitement, they took spies and their activities to their hearts.

In the years that followed that interest did not falter. Indeed, it could be said to have grown even more intense as the stakes themselves grew higher. Not everyone could be a spy – not everyone wanted to be – just as not everyone could hunt them down and imprison them, but certainly everyone could read about them.

While spying itself remained a surreptitious and hidden business, enjoyment of the process and the results of undercover work became fixed in people's minds as glamorous, fascinating and essential to the safety of the country – whichever country that might be.

Chapter Two

Spy Fiction and Spy Fact

'He's a walking contradiction, partly truth and partly fiction, taking every wrong direction on his lonely way back home.'
                                                        Kris Kristofferson

It is sometimes hard to differentiate between fact and fiction when looking at the motivation for the lives and careers of espionage agents. Indeed, many people will acknowledge that spy fiction can very quickly become spy fact.

The opposite also works – spy fact can almost as easily become spy fiction. Popular from the moment of its inception, the genre has been hugely influential, so much so that writers who specialise in undercover or spy-based fiction have become a major component not just in the literary world but also in the real life world of espionage.

It is not difficult to see why but we should start by eliminating the hack writers who would be paid to write about almost anything and would come up with the goods, as long as the money was right. The product was not always particularly accurate or realistic.

The hacks might produce a story about an American Wild West they did not know or had even thought about until the publisher's offer dropped through the letterbox. They might describe a trip to Mars or Venus, a journey that they would never experience. Such writers were utterly reliant on their own limited imaginations and, usually, pretty poor research. Many of them churned out spy fiction once the genre became popular, and their books and their names have long since disappeared from view.

The upper echelons of spy writers, however, were a different class altogether, and there was one common feature amongst nearly all of them. Out of all the writers who turned their hands to producing quality spy novels in the first fifty years of the twentieth century only

SPY FICTION AND SPY FACT

Eric Ambler – one of the classiest of all spy writers – had not been involved at one time or another in the spying business. It meant that while the plots of these experienced writers might sometimes seem to be fantastic or even improbable they were actually grounded in a degree of reality. The hard, indisputable truth of a man who has been there, seen it, done it, contrasted with the ingenious workings of the fiction writer's imagination are often far closer than anyone can imagine.

The work of the spy has, from early times, been well recorded, not least in the *Bible*. Even before that, however, the spy had been acknowledged in literature when in 510 BC the world's first textbook on spying, along with advice on how to create a secret service, was published in ancient China. This was *Ping Fa*, a book that was so accurate and so useful that it was reprinted in English during the Second World War. Like so many other early recorded instances of the spy's world, this was a factual record of events, and as such it remains a piece of history.

Fiction that concerned itself with spying came much later than *Ping Fa*. Storytelling had been around for thousands of years, ever since mankind began to gather together for warmth and shelter, in the caves or wattle and daub huts of ancient peoples. But it was always an oral or spoken art and remained so throughout what we now, euphemistically but inaccurately, refer to as the Dark Ages.

In the days when illiteracy was the norm rather than an exception, when hand-written books were the preserve of the great abbeys and monasteries, it was tales told around the fireside and in the halls of kings and princes that kept the art of storytelling alive. Storytellers – bards as they were more correctly known – made their way from royal palace to royal palace and retained an honoured place amongst the retinue of the king's servants.

Tales were carefully crafted for the royal ears. However, it was also entertainment for anyone who wished to stop what they were doing, listen to the storyteller's words and allow the wordsmith to transport them for a few minutes into a world of fantasy and magic.

The arrival of the mediaeval printing press, brainchild of Thomas Caxton and Wynkyn de Worde, began to change things, but it was as late as the eighteenth century before novels started to appear from the pens of people like Samuel Richardson and Henry Fielding. *Pamela* (Richardson), *Tom Jones* and *Joseph Andrews* (both Fielding) undoubtedly altered the course of human history, but they did not impinge on the secret life of the spy.

The first true detective stories – to which spy stories are indisputably linked – did not appear until the final years of the nineteenth century when Charles Dickens and Wilkie Collins started to experiment in the genre. Both of them became adept at creating dark, hidden worlds, the ideal environment for any writer interested in secrecy and cunning.

Detective or crime stories, though, while having a similarity to spy tales, are also intrinsically different. Crime fiction invariably centres on the detective and his efforts to solve the crime. Wilkie Collins's *The Moonstone* and *The Woman in White*, and Dickens's *Our Mutual Friend*, not to mention the entire Sherlock Holmes canon, are classic examples of this. Spies did not have the same appeal for the general reader:

> The pure spy story, if not derided was at least ignored. Spying was regarded as something despicable and no spy could be considered as a hero. Nor was it ever considered desirable that the chief villain of a story should be a spy. A thief, yes; a murderer, most certainly; but a spy was the nineteenth century equivalent of a sexual pervert.[1]

Things were beginning to change, however, and although they didn't know it professional writers were waiting in the wings to create a whole new genre. Soon mysterious agents became something of a craze with writers as varied as Baroness Orczy and Alexander Dumas claiming their yard of turf.

The Scarlet Pimpernel and *The Three Musketeers* may not have been traditional spy stories in the sense that we know them now, but they did deal with clandestine happenings and the fate of governments. And they did make passing reference to secret agents and the odd midnight rendezvous or two. It might be justifiably claimed that the two romantic novels were the forerunners of bigger and better things.

As the nineteenth century drew to a close potential writers of spy fiction were quietly sharpening their quills and regularly reading the national press for stories of illicit dealings. It meant that when the time came these men were well informed and, in the main, knowledgeable about their subject.

Recognising the international build-up in arms and weapons as a very real danger to national security many writers were clear that their aims were to entertain but at the same time warn people what was happening under their noses. Some of them even put such an acknowledgement into the front pages of their books.

Clearly, spy fiction remains a relatively new art. And yet, despite being so fresh, the early examples of such literature actually predate many of the intelligence agencies that were designed to manage and manipulate undercover work. In fact, spy stories did not only predate the shadowy organisations dedicated to the management of espionage agents, they had an amazing and profound effect on their development. It was not the other way around, as might be expected.

The spying agencies, free standing and unattributable to any specific government department, were common to all countries, but they began life in the United Kingdom. Inevitably, once Britain had such an agency other countries felt they had to follow – which they did, pretty smartly.

Being home to the first real-life spy agency is appropriate because the spy novel – with the exception of one false start in America – also began in Britain. Perhaps that is one of the reasons why Britain still holds a premier position in the spy-story stakes.

More spy fiction – good, bad and indifferent – has been produced from the UK than any other country in the world. And yet, having made that sweeping statement, we have to look to the United States in order to find the world's first spy novel.

******

What can probably be regarded as the original spy novel was written by James Fenimore Cooper, the American author who also produced the better-known adventure tale *The Last of the Mohicans*. It was called simply *The Spy* and appeared in 1821.

That publication date is far earlier than might be imagined or expected by anyone looking back over publishing history, but it is easy to see why this should be. The Napoleonic Wars had only recently come to a conclusion and the American War of Independence was still within living memory. Both conflicts meant that warfare in all its many guises, including espionage, were still at the forefront of people's memories.

Fenimore Cooper's story was set during America's fight for independence from Britain and much of the background detail would have been gleaned from men and women who had experienced the struggle at first hand. That certainly helped give the book authenticity and realism.

The Spy concerns a British army officer named Harvey Birch who decides to venture behind enemy lines to visit relatives. He is captured, condemned as a spy and sentenced to death. Cooper's hero manages to escape punishment, living to 'spy another day' – or not, as the case may be. Not really a spy story in the way that later examples tended to be, *The Spy* did at least give some literary acknowledgement to the concept of spying on the enemy.

The book was a huge success in both America and Europe. It established Cooper, who had previously spent three years as a junior officer in the US Navy, as one of the most popular writers in the English-speaking world. Cooper followed up his success ten years later with a second spy novel, *The Bravo*. This time he stepped out from America to set the novel in Europe. The book attacked Venice as a ruthless city state which, despite its mask of bonhomie and friendliness, was, in reality, quite Machiavellian in its policies.

Fenimore Cooper became US Consul in Lyon and was an early advocate of creating a Department of Intelligence in the US Navy. He was one of many spy writers who dabbled in real life espionage, both in his later administrative role and during his short-lived naval career when he served on patrol vessels operating along the shores of the Great Lakes. Information gathering was one of the major tasks for such vessels and all young midshipmen like Fenimore Cooper were active in the exercise.

James Fenimore Cooper's two books were something of a false start for the genre of spy literature. After an initial flurry, interest dropped away and Cooper himself moved on to write more popular stories about the American frontier. It needed a dramatic event to rekindle interest in the spy, both as a real-life person and as a hero/villain in popular literature. That event was waiting in the wings, on the other side of the Atlantic Ocean.

The Dreyfus Affair stirred the imagination of many ordinary men and women who could now see spies and traitors lurking behind every curtain or open doorway. And, of course, writers were quick to jump onto what was soon to become an ever-rolling bandwagon. The British Empire and its paranoid stance towards the Russian presence on the North-West Frontier of India was an obvious target and places like Afghanistan were an ideal location to set adventure stories.

Adventure stories they may have been but there was also a clear theme running through virtually all pre-First World War spy literature. To begin with, such stories were nearly all concerned with the rivalry between European powers, centring on the constant jockeying for control of Asia. In line with this theme exotic locations were an essential element.

Running parallel to this was the domestic or 'at home' version of the spy story in which the activities of anarchists and revolutionaries threatened the safety and security of innocent civilians. Finally, all spy stories had to contain the crucial elements of historical romance that were so beloved and expected by the reading public, in particular the female reading public.

The first real spy novel came from the pen of Rudyard Kipling, doyen of the empire, and, as might be expected, was set along the frontier provinces of India. *Kim* appeared first as a serial in *McClure's Magazine* and was published as a novel in October 1901. It is the story of an orphaned boy who becomes an agent for the British, carrying secret messages and keeping watch on Russian activities on the North-West Frontier. It is filled with exotic detail, the smells and sights of India almost pouring off the pages.

Arguably Kipling's finest book, *Kim* was an immense success, hammering home the tinder-like atmosphere of northern India. Nobody who read the book could fail to see the Russian threat or the vital necessity of monitoring Russian activities in what Kipling and the British public were now calling 'The Great Game'.

Kim was a pace setter and was followed two years later by what is probably an even better spy novel, *The Riddle of the Sands*. A sensational page-turner of a read, this was, if not the greatest of all the early spy stories, then certainly the most realistic and the most influential.

Written by the future Irish patriot and martyr Erskine Childers, *The Riddle of the Sands* is the story of two amateur British agents thwarting the plans of the Kaiser – who makes a brief appearance in the book – to build a fleet of barges intended to carry an invading army across the North Sea. The story of a planned German invasion of Britain terrified readers and was an immediate success, with over three million copies of the book being printed and sold.

With a realistic sailing background based on his own yachting experiences around the north German coast, Childers' book was more than a mere piece of fiction. It was a warning against German militarism: an effective warning as it turned out. The Admiralty realised that their charts of the area where the story was set were woefully out of date. The Intelligence Department of the Royal Navy promptly sent out a team of agents and surveyors to make new drawings of the German coast.

People had become more aware of spies as the nineteenth century wore on, but *Kim* and *The Riddle of the Sands* took things a stage further. The two novels provoked an immediate explosion of interest in the genre of spy writing. They lifted spies and double agents, anarchists and revolutionaries out of the doldrums where they had lain for too many years.

The result was revolutionary. Almost any hack writer worth his salt now made an immediate appeal to his publisher – let me write a spy story. Publishers, seeing the financial benefits of the genre, soon had their writers scribbling away in an attempt to produce something that would rival, or maybe even better, *Kim* and *The Riddle of the Sands*.

This led to a significant problem, for the literary historian at least. The two seminal spy books were the product of intelligent, talented men who had the ability to create not just spy stories but worthwhile pieces of literature. They were not simply mindless page fillings by people who knew no better. Unfortunately, much of what now appeared came from writers with nowhere near the level of skill as Kipling and Erskine Childers.

The volumes that were rushed to the bookstalls were the product of mere scribblers, whose only claim to fame came from their ability to produce pulp fiction as quickly as the publishers demanded it. Quality did not come into the equation. Research, familiarity with the topic and even the places to be written about were not things that unduly worried these early spy novelists: 'It was possible for a writer who had never travelled more than six miles from, say, Pudsey, to produce a spy novel that would be acceptable.'[2]

Joseph Conrad's 1907 novel *The Secret Agent* was an exception, and is as much a study in the psychology of marginalised individuals as a tale of adventure and high treason. It takes as its central theme a revolutionary cell of anarchists and an attempt to blow up Greenwich Observatory. The character drawing is excellently done and it is at least the equal of Kipling and Childers. Sadly, much of the supporting cast of writers is not.

Regardless of their quality – or lack of it – the book-buying public seized on the glut of spy novels with relish. Some of the hack writers, commissioned by gleeful publishers, were managing to write five or even six novels a year in a desperate attempt to keep up with demand. The bookstalls on railway stations, in the Strand or almost any large city street were full of spy novels and were bought by everyone from city clerks to Members of Parliament. They were, it was rumoured, the favourite reading matter of Queen Alexandria, wife of King Edward VII.

The spy novels of this era tended to follow a fairly basic formula. Nearly all of them featured beastly foreign agents – mostly Germans – who were busily squirrelling away, building up networks of fifth columnists and spies, ready to attack British communication networks and defence facilities prior to a sneak invasion by a deceitful enemy.

Torture, attempted assassinations, treachery, blackmail and murder, all usually set amongst luxurious living environments – for the heroes, at least – were standard fare. There were very few surprises. Readers knew what they were going to get when they picked up one of these pulp novels, but that did not stop them selling in droves.

Until the outbreak of the First World War the theme of German expansion and military growth dominated the market as far as British spy stories were concerned. It was to be expected: the topic reflected the general disquiet and distrust amongst the public.

For many years France and her ally Russia had been the traditional enemies for Britain, but the posturing of the Kaiser and the alarming growth of German naval and military forces swung the pendulum of hate towards Germany. The Entente Cordiale of 1904 formally bound Britain to France and Russia and thereafter the Germans were fair game.

Interestingly, neither Kipling nor Childers went on to produce more genuine spy thrillers although several of Kipling's Indian tales did flirt around the edges of the subject. Writers like Saki (Hugh Monroe), E Phillips Oppenheim and George Chesney were amongst the better-known scribblers who tried their hand at the new genre, and in the main did reasonably well. Most of the others have now disappeared into well-deserved anonymity.

******

There is one man who, more than any other, was implicit in helping to popularise the spy novel as an entity, and at the same time assisted in the creation of Britain's first secret service organisation: a bizarre, egotistical and self-indulgent spy writer by the name of William Tufnell Le Queux.

In the pre-1914 days Le Queux was a household name in Britain. His books sold by the thousands and at one time he could claim to be the highest paid writer in the country. He, like many others, managed to turn out at least five books a year, most of them anti-German spy novels centring on fifth columnists and bands of enemy agents operating in Britain.

A strange, self-absorbed man, William Le Queux was at best economical with the truth when it came to writing or talking about his own life. He called himself an adventurer, a traveller, a writer and a spy and was happy to boast about his close links with the publisher Lord Northcliffe and with Field Marshal 'Bobs' Roberts of Boer War fame: 'His *Who's Who* entry listed his recreations as "revolver practice, skiing in Switzerland, the study of Egyptology and criminology" and "experiments in wireless telephony."'[3]

On the face of it this was hardly the type of man who would go on to influence several government ministers and help create an institution that has survived until the present day. Yet Le Queux did exactly that, and in the process created for himself a lasting and fascinating legend.

On 30 March 1909 a sub-committee of the Committee of Imperial Defence met at Westminster under the chairmanship of RB Haldane, Secretary of State for War. Other members of the sub-committee included the First Lord of the Admiralty, the Home Secretary and the Commissioner for Police.

The purpose of the committee was simple: to discuss and hopefully find an answer to the enormous amount of foreign espionage that everyone from the lowest household servant to the Prime Minister himself believed was going on in Britain. It was, however, a mammoth task.

One of the witnesses called to give evidence to the sub-committee was Colonel James Edmonds, head of an army unit known as Military Operations Counterintelligence. Even now it sounds like a grand title, but with only two staff and an annual budget of just £200 Edmonds was limited in what he could achieve.

Nevertheless, true patriot that he was, Edmonds would do his bit. He presented the sub-committee with extensive reports and records regarding the nefarious affairs of hundreds of German men and women then living in the country. A large number of these incomers were, Edmonds noted, employed as waiters, barbers or musicians, professions where they could effectively eavesdrop and listen to what their customers were saying.

Edmonds also regaled members of the sub-committee with tales of Germans who had been encountered when they were out sketching or photographing. Dozens of different subjects, from dockyard installations to harmless looking river estuaries, were recorded by these amateur enemy artists. They might be innocent activities, Edmonds said, but the drawings could potentially be of huge value to any enemy contemplating invasion.

It was all interesting enough but unfortunately there was little hard evidence to back up any of Edmonds's claims. Solid facts were called for, not wild guesses. The sub-committee was adjourned and a date set for a second meeting. Edmonds was now desperate for his views to be taken seriously. He knew that he would receive little help from a police force that was already overstretched and understaffed but he needed to find firm evidence to present to the committee. Enter William Tufnell Le Queux.

Le Queux had been born in London in 1861 and educated partly in Britain and partly on the Continent. He was fluent in several languages and knew everyone it was important to know. However, he had not gone to the 'right' school; reason enough for the snobbish upper classes who then dominated the government not to like him.

William Le Queux became a writer and journalist, travelling the world to carry out his duties as a war correspondent for *The Daily Mail*. He grew increasingly fascinated by espionage, taught himself to become an expert shot with a revolver and formed the unshakeable view that the entire German nation was envious of the British way of life. One day he declared – 'The Day' as he called it – German troops would invade Britain.

He, like many other writers, began to produce 'invasion literature': alarmist stories that prophesised disaster if Britain did not do something about the enemy forces that were steadily building up on the other side of the North Sea. Britain's leaders, Le Queux declared, were slumbering over their glasses of port while the German army grew in strength and resolve. In the foreword to his sensationalist novel *The Invasion of 1910* Le Queux chillingly wrote:

> The object of this book is to illustrate our utter unpreparedness for war, from a military standpoint; to show how under certain conditions which may easily occur, England can be successfully invaded by Germany; and to present a picture of the ruin which must inevitably fall upon us on the evening of that not far-distant day.[4]

Le Queux's book was an instant success, selling more than a million copies within a few weeks of publication, and was even translated into Urdu and German. In the wake of the success, he and Lord Roberts formed their own secret service, enlisting like-minded men who were prepared, at their own expense, to gather information about German military plans. All the money Le Queux earned from *The Invasion of 1910* was channelled into paying for this private espionage agency.

The results were spectacular, if not always totally accurate, and Le Queux was soon bombarding the government with reports about German fifth columnists. His warnings, however, were ignored by the Cabinet ministers. He went back to writing novels such as *Spies of the Kaiser*. It was hardly his best work, but like all his other books, was one that was snapped up by the eager British public.

Many people regarded the new book not as a novel but as a piece of factual reporting. That was just what Le Queux had intended. Whether it was fact or fiction, or a mix of both, it was this novel that soon exerted a powerful influence on Haldane's sub-committee.

Le Queux's claim that there were over 5,000 German agents operating in Britain first saw the light of day in this book. It was a figure he had arrived at from the information reported to him by his private army of spies. It was exaggeration fuelled by enthusiasm and it terrified the uninitiated.

The public bought the book in their thousands and believed implicitly in the figures Le Queux had quoted. Spy fever flooded the country, more virulent and anti-German than ever before. Le Queux found himself inundated with hundreds of letters from 'helpful patriots' telling him of suspicious characters in virtually every part of the country. The number count of German spies in Britain rose rapidly.

Le Queux and Colonel Edmonds were already friendly. Now they came together to pool their evidence – flimsy and circumstantial as it might be – on the number of German agents in Britain, all of them watching and waiting for their opportunity to strike. At the second meeting of the sub-committee on 20 April 1909 Edmonds, now armed with 'irrefutable evidence', presented the vast bulk of this information to Haldane and the other committee members.

Deluged by such a volume of material it was inevitable that the committee began to fall under the spell of spy fever. Haldane was, initially at least, inclined to disbelieve the mountains of information that he and everyone else knew had originated from William Le Queux, but like several others he slowly began to change his mind.

One document in particular was instrumental in helping to convert the committee from a neutral and objective group of individuals into what can only be regarded as a fervent anti-German mob. In its own way this document was as significant as the Ems Despatch that started the Franco-Prussian War of 1870, or the Zimmermann Telegram which brought the USA into the First World War in 1917. And like those two spurious pieces of communication, it was equally as ridiculous.

The document was a report that Le Queux had obtained, purporting to come from a French commercial traveller who was journeying through France and the Low Countries by train. During one stage of the trip he was ensconced in the same compartment as an unknown German who was carrying exactly the same type of bag as him. When the German left the train he mistakenly took the wrong bag:

> The commercial traveller opened the bag left behind and found that it contained detailed plans connected with a scheme for the invasion of England. He copied out as much of these plans as he was able during the short time that elapsed before he was asked to give up the bag, concerning the loss of which the owner had telegraphed to the railway authorities where the train next halted.[5]

The document, like the whole story, was as far-fetched as a description of the Dark Side of the Moon and smacked more of Le Queux and his feverish, overworked imagination than it did of careful and considered espionage work.

The idea that a French commercial traveller with no military training could copy detailed war plans, written in German, while sitting in a rocking railway train is frankly ridiculous. So too was the idea that he could then transmit the information to British intelligence without the knowledge of the German owner. Not only that, but the bag that was so conveniently mislaid by the owner, containing this supposedly vital and damning information, was unlocked and left open for the world to see.

Nevertheless, the veracity of the document was acknowledged by the Director of Military Operations and the Director of Military Training, both of whom were serving on the sub-committee. The plans, they declared, had to be the work of a professional espionage agent who had a thorough knowledge of the weak points of British defences.

With the all-important and terrifying idea of a plan to invade Britain written down in black and white – one that was now staring the committee members in the face – the document was accepted as totally genuine. As a result, the sub-committee made a number of suggestions that were rapidly put before the Cabinet and accepted. These began with the creation of more draconian controls over the freedom of movement of all aliens, regardless of who they were and why they had come to Britain. It concluded by granting the police special powers to deal with potential spies. By far the most important statement, however, was something that came in between those two; the recommendation that an independent secret service bureau should be established in Britain.

Britain had, of course, employed spies and agents before. In the main, they had been attached to the army or the navy. This was different. This bureau was to be a free-standing, totally independent organisation with no links to the Foreign Office, the Crown, the War Office or the Admiralty. It was to be a secret intelligence service that, officially, did not exist. In that way government and its ministers would be protected from what was still regarded as the dirty business of spying.

There was no intention of destroying what already existed. The army and the navy would retain their intelligence departments, operating along the lines they had always followed, but they were not to be part of the new secret service. All that was needed now was the legislation to control and give legality to the new organisation.

A new Official Secrets Act was duly hurried through the House of Commons late on a Friday evening in June 1910 when barely a hundred MPs were present to vote. This was done to avoid any undue objections from opposition parties and it worked. There were only two queries from Liberal MPs and the bill was passed to the Lords with almost no opposition.

The new Act was a powerful piece of legislation. From now on lack of evidence was immaterial when it came to the prosecution of spies. As long as there was moral certainty that the accused was actually an enemy agent that was good enough.[6]

It was an amazing shift in attitude, the product of over-stimulated and terrified minds. But it could not have happened without the help of William Le Queux.

Le Queux was undoubtedly a strange individual who clearly had difficulty separating the fantasy of his books from the reality of the world. He was one of those butterfly characters who flutter into view, spread their mischief or their good and then disappear for ever.

He might now be something of a forgotten man, but his part in creating Britain's first independent spy agency should never be overlooked. Without him it is doubtful if such an agency would have come into existence quite so soon. Perhaps in ten or twenty years' time something may have materialised but not in 1909.

A bizarre individual, egotistical to the point of obsession, Le Queux was driven by a rabid fear of German militarism. With his help that fear permeated a whole nation – several nations for that matter – and it did not do his book sales any harm either.

Whether Le Queux picked up on the mood of the country or whether the anti-German sentiments of the nation were created and developed by him remains a matter of conjecture. Either way, it was rare for any writer of pulp fiction to have such an effect on so many people.

The enthusiasm for spy novels did not die away as the world slid slowly into the conflict that was waiting over the horizon. Fear of fifth columnists remained rampant and the 'penny dreadfuls' continued to exploit this aspect of the spy novel.

Apart from the continuing barrage of pulp fiction there was the occasional gem that stood out from the mess of pottage. One of the most notable was Joseph Conrad's 1911 masterpiece *Under Western Eyes*. It was another nihilist tale, this time about a reluctant Russian spy sent to infiltrate a revolutionary group in Geneva. In its own way the story was equally as effective as *The Secret Agent*, even though it appealed more to the intellectual reader than the general public.

The British public had recently witnessed the work of anarchists at first hand. The Tottenham Outrage of 1909 saw two immigrant refugees involved in a robbery followed by a chase across London during which over 400 pistol shots were fired. Twenty-three casualties resulted, with two fatalities, a policeman and a ten-year-old boy. The affair concluded with a faintly ludicrous chase between two tram cars and the suicide of the two criminals.

The Siege of Sidney Street took place in January 1911. Two Latvian refugees, after killing three unarmed policemen during a bungled jewellery robbery, were besieged in an East London lodging house, surrounded by armed police and units of the British army. Winston Churchill, then Home Secretary, arrived to watch proceedings which concluded with the house on fire and the suicide of the two Latvian anarchists.

Both events hit the newspaper headlines as 'anarchist outrages'. In fact they were the end result of botched robberies, admittedly by men who had been forced to leave their own countries because of their revolutionary views, but they were not the nihilist attempts at disrupting British society that the media alleged. The British public chose to ignore that fact.

The two events fuelled the anti-immigrant emotions of the public, Londoners in particular, and made them a willing audience for spy novels dealing with anarchist groups. For a long while almost any foreigner was suspect, particularly foreigners who had chosen to come to Britain to live. Any novel that featured dastardly foreign spies was therefore eagerly snapped up.

GK Chesterton tried his hand at the genre with *The Man who was Thursday* and even Arthur Conan Doyle had his detective hero Sherlock Holmes investigate missing government plans in stories such as *The Bruce Partington Plans* and *The Adventure of the Second Stain*. What was meant to be the final Sherlock Holmes story, *His Last Bow*, was written in 1917 even though the action which sees Holmes operating as a double agent takes place in the summer of 1914.

Writers like John Buchan and Somerset Maugham came later. Buchan's initial foray into the spy world, *The 39 Steps*, was written during an illness that confined him to the house in the year after war was declared, while Maugham's *Ashenden* appeared some time later.

Buchan and Maugham were masters of their craft and while the spy story gave Buchan, in particular, the chance to vent his spleen and a virulent streak of anti-Semitism, their works were masterfully compiled and achieved. However, even they would have to admit that they could not have achieved half of the success they did had it not been for men like William Le Queux.

Spy fact and spy fiction make an interesting combination. Success in the genre was enough to propel John Buchan into the upper echelons of government. His final years of service saw him appointed Governor General of Canada, a post he held until his death in 1940.

Spy fiction and the upper ranks of government often seem to go together. The favourite reading matter of President John F Kennedy and many of his advisors – at least until the CIA disaster at the Bay of Pigs shocked them into reality – was Ian Fleming. Kennedy's decision to back the CIA plan to invade Cuba confirms a gung-ho attitude that smacks of James Bond. The failure of the operation was a sobering slap across the cheek that would have brought even Bond up short. His brother Robert Kennedy's subsequent handling of Operation Mongoose, which saw schemes like presenting Castro with a poisoned cigar and a lethally dosed diving suit, could have come directly from the pages of Ian Fleming. Indeed, for a long while there seemed to be no limit to the influence of spy fiction on government policy.

The appeal of spy stories – and, from the 1920s onwards, spy films as well – continues to this day. Directors like Alfred Hitchcock seized the genre and ran with it, but at no time have the stories ever been as popular as in that pre-1914 period. In this way the fiction reflected the fragile nature of the times when the world stood poised upon the edge of oblivion.

Chapter Three

An Advance into War

'Good neighbours will always spy on you to make sure you are doing well.'

Pawan Mishra

The great advantage of having a secret service organisation which does not officially exist is that every task the organisation undertakes – good, bad or indifferent – is totally deniable. That was one of the major ideas behind the creation of Britain's first independent spy bureau.

In the days leading up to the outbreak of the First World War deniability was a particularly useful attribute to possess if the task or job in hand was badly handled and turned out to be an embarrassing failure. It was certainly not a bad fall back for an embryonic organisation attempting to make its way in the treacherous world of international espionage.

There have been many highs and lows in the life of Britain's secret services. However, there is no doubt that the five years between the creation of the British Secret Intelligence Service in 1909 and the declaration of war against Germany were something of a high water mark for the spying industry both in Britain and abroad, in development and intent if not in results.

There was undoubtedly expectation in the air. The attitude of many senior officers of the secret service, and of the army and Royal Navy in general, varied between the twin peaks of enthusiasm and despair.

Some senior officers and politicians regarded spying as nothing more than a game, an extension of the public school ethos which still dominated military thinking. Others thought of it as a low and coarse profession, necessary but not to be acknowledged in polite company. For these people the information procured by the spy was always going to be questionable.

AN ADVANCE INTO WAR

However, those who were involved in the actual hands-on process of spying knew that great tests lay ahead of them. The future of the espionage services would soon be challenged by war and, despite what many of their leaders might say, a game was the last thing anyone wanted.

The other European nations soon followed Britain's example in creating independent spy services, throwing off the shackles of officialdom and subsequent links to their military and government. By the second decade of the twentieth century the clandestine, unsavoury world of the spy, underhand and dirty as it appeared to many, was firmly established.

Thanks mainly to the efforts of British secret agents and spymasters who were already thinking ahead to a projected future conflict with Germany, the tiny and otherwise unimportant country of Holland quickly became a centre of spying activity. Due to its location, close to the German border and with easy access across its undefended frontiers, a huge organisation of more than 300 British spies and undercover agents was established there.

The Dutch government, although knowing that in any conflict their country would remain neutral, adopted something of a laissez-faire approach, a live-and-let-live attitude that perfectly suited the espionage world. In the years ahead, Holland's shoulder-shrugging was to prove an invaluable factor for Allied agents in particular.

The Belgian espionage service was considerably smaller than the Dutch/British equivalent, but despite being effectively taken out of the war by the German victories of 1914, Belgium continued to play a part in the conflict.

Even those parts of Belgium that were occupied by German forces were crucial in the espionage war. Anti-German feelings were high in these areas and the atrocities committed by the invading armies – never as great as the media claimed but genuine nevertheless – served only to create a huge and willing pool of prospective agents.

The British nurse Edith Cavell, although never a spy as such, was based in German-held Belgium from where she helped dozens of soldiers from both sides to escape back to their own lines. Arrested by the German military and shot by firing squad in October 1915, her execution provoked furore in Britain and America and was as great a propaganda coup for the Allies as the sinking of the *Lusitania*.

Edith Cavell was just the tip of the iceberg. For over four years of warfare Britain made great use of Belgium and Belgian agents.

The French also greatly expanded their espionage service in the years leading up to the First World War. Indeed, in an effort to create a 'better class' of spy the French paid what was universally regarded as the highest wages in Europe to their undercover workers. That was a significant factor as far as the freelance agents were concerned, far more important than any partisan or patriotic emotions they might harbour. The high wages meant that no one was likely to put their employment in jeopardy by offering their services to two or more countries at the same moment in time.

Only the entrance of the USA into the war in 1917 relegated the French to second place in the league table of espionage payers. The Americans, although they remained little more than bit-part players, were happy to throw money at the espionage market, particularly if it helped keep the frontiers and the hinterland of their own country 'spy free'.

Contrary to public opinion, at the beginning of the twentieth century the Germans were no better prepared for espionage work than the other European nations. The vast legions of Teutonic spies and fifth columnists so feared by everyone and so beloved by the fiction writers of the world simply did not exist.

The German High Command had traditionally relied on observations and reports from military attachés and diplomats in order to build up their information dossiers. Semi-official facts, it was felt, would provide a more than adequate picture of enemy dispositions and attitudes.

The Germans began to change their approach when their own Germanic version of William Le Queux emerged. This was General Friedrich von Bernhardi who, in 1912, published a book, *Germany and the Next War*, expressing the same doubts as Le Queux about his country's readiness for the coming conflict. Bernhardi had no qualms about war itself, believing that conflict on a national scale was 'a biological necessity'. Even so, he accepted that if his country was ill-prepared for the inevitable war it would not bring glory or cleansing of the blood, only disaster.

General Bernhardi was the son of a Prussian soldier and a farmer's daughter. He was a confirmed monarchist and supporter of the Hohenzollern dynasty, a professional soldier who rose to become a much-decorated senior officer. Bernhardi was the first German soldier to ride through the Arc de Triumph, at the head of his victorious troops, after the conclusion of the Franco-Prussian War. It was an accomplishment that he cherished to his dying day. He was later to become one of the founding members of the ultra-nationalist Fatherland Party, but in 1912 he was concerned only with the safety of his beloved Germany. He had no pretensions to being a great writer but his book was an immediate success.

The German public became as obsessed as the British with spies and fifth columnists and there was a sense of panic in the country as wild rumours spread. Most of them were ridiculous, some were even inclined to a Heath Robinson-type farce: 'The British were said to have flights of homing pigeons each carrying, fastened to its tail, a tiny camera operated at set times by clockwork [...] British intelligence could [(thus] piece together aerial photographs of German military activity.'[1]

The idea of pigeons, complete with ticking tail feathers, tracing delicate lines above the Rhine and Danube and on across the industrial areas of Germany was so ludicrous that it was almost believable. Huge numbers of Germans were taken in and actually believed implicitly in the fantasy world of spy pigeons. And that was just the start.

Stories of British and French spies traversing the country in large and expensive motor cars – rumours that predated John Buchan's later tales of Richard Hannay and his wild motoring surges across Germany and France – had an immediate appeal in a world where touring cars were beginning to dominate the roads. It was romantic, it was thrilling, and above all it was believable.

Groups of German vigilantes were soon on the prowl, stopping any expensive-looking car that happened to be travelling their way. Some of these vigilante bands even fired on cars that refused to draw to an immediate halt.

There is no record of any fatalities during these dark and deadly episodes but the effect of black-cloaked figures appearing out of the shadows, brandishing shotguns and rifles and issuing gruff orders to stop, must have terrified the upper-class ladies and gentlemen tourists. They were, after all, engaged in nothing more illicit than a brief trip down the Rhine or Moselle valleys.

As German spy fever grew in intensity some of the incidents that took place were nothing short of ridiculous. Perhaps the most inane was the case of one unfortunate lady's maid who was faced by the indignity of being strip searched while she was leaving Germany by train. When examined she was found to have secret messages written in code on her backside! The messages were photographed and sent off for examination and decyphering. As it turned out, the maid had gone to the toilet before the journey began and, for reasons of hygiene, spread that day's *Frankfurter Zeitung* on the lavatory seat before sitting down. The messages were nothing more than that day's front page news rubbed off on her bottom.

As war approached ever nearer the German army took over the responsibility for gathering information about enemy activities, in particular the land forces of France and Russia. It was perhaps too little, too late.

With hostilities pending, Major Walther Nicolai, head of the *Geheime Nachrichtendienst des Heres*, (better known by the considerably shorter and more succinct title of ND) was given unlimited funds for espionage work. Despite this, Nicolai was clear that by neglecting its spies and agents in the pre-war years the Federal government had done the Fatherland absolutely no favours whatsoever.

It was a frantic and frenzied period but the one exception to all of this hurried, stop gap creativity was Russia. In a rapidly dissolving empire, rotten to the core and riven by rival cliques, it was soon discovered that most Russian spies were not only working for Russia but also for whomever they were supposed to be spying on. Britain, Germany, France, they were all grist to the mill of the freelance Russian agents.

By working for both sides the spies could claim double the normal income and inevitably the matter of loyalty came down to who was offering the highest pay packet. It was the very problem that the French had tried to solve by paying abnormally high wages.

Russia had traditionally 'bought in' its spies. They were men of varying nationalities who had little affinity with anything other than money. And while the Russian government might be lacking in credibility and direction it was certainly not short of finances.

In 1905 the Russian Baltic fleet had sailed to disaster at the Battle of Tsushima on the other side of the world, a journey of over 5,000 miles. Its progress was monitored by a wide range of spies hiding along the coastlines and sometimes watching from rowing boats that rocked unsteadily in the waters alongside the Czar's battleships. These spies were reporting the voyage of the fleet on its journey to Japan, informing neutral countries like Britain and France and the newspapers of the world about its progress.

At the same time the spies were also providing the Russians with a constant stream of false news about the waiting Japanese. All of Russia genuinely believed that Japanese torpedo boats were lurking in fiords on the Swedish coast, in the mists of the North Sea and between the palm trees of West Africa.

Any reasoned or objective assessment should have told everyone that such traps were not possible and were simply the stories of highly paid agents. Reasoned and objective, however, were not words that were often used in Russian government and military circles.

In the end it came down to who to believe. By and large the Russians went with the spies, a mistake that led to the Baltic fleet firing on British trawlers in the mistaken belief that they were those damned little Japanese torpedo boats. As a result of this blatant double dealing, and in the face of their crushing defeat at Tsushima, nobody in the Russian hierarchy had a great deal of faith in spies.

Consequently, the Russian secret service was dissolved and espionage was limited to internal affairs where the growing groups of revolutionaries had already become the chief concern of the Russian monarchy and government.

The Okhrana, the Czarist secret police that had been brought into existence as late as 1880, became a much-feared and deadly organisation that did sometimes operate outside Russia but only if such activities were in some way related to the elimination of revolutionary agencies and individuals.

******

As far as the British were concerned, from the beginning there were two categories of people working in the espionage business: there were intelligence officers and there were agents, both of them with very different roles.

Intelligence officers were formal, fully employed members of the espionage service who, in theory at least, were highly trained and schooled in the techniques required. These men were able to operate either openly, declaring that they were operatives of a foreign service, or covertly under cover as diplomats, trade delegates and so on.

As a variation there was also a loosely banded group of individuals, unofficially known by the name 'illegals'. These were trained intelligence officers, men and women, working in 'deep cover' using false names and with absolutely no protection or immunity. If they were caught or exposed they were, literally, on their own.[2]

Agents or 'covert human intelligence sources' as they were known, were the people at the coalface of the spying game. They were the ones who provided intelligence officers with information, usually but not always for financial reward.

Recruited mainly from individuals who were unhappy with the state of affairs in their homeland, or were in urgent need of financial help, they would receive some limited training in methods of espionage. Normally this was restricted to the techniques needed to operate – meeting systems, dead letter drops, communication and liaison with Intelligence Officers and so on.[3]

The new British Intelligence Service was also divided into two, home and foreign. The home section was concerned with counter espionage, catching enemy spies working in Britain. Known originally as MO5 this department would eventually morph into what is now called MI5, and as a perfectly acceptable branch of defence services, did not require the deniable status of its companion service.

The foreign section was intended to be altogether more proactive and was there to gather information from foreign countries. Known as the SIS (the Secret Intelligence Service), it would in time become known as the more famous MI6. This was the covert arm of the spying service that nobody in government would acknowledge or admit even existed.

From the moment of their creation there had always been a degree of discord between the two departments. Spy catching, the work of MI5, was always regarded, particularly by those outside the organisation, as something of a job for glorified policemen with the result that the sanctity of the law remained strong for its members.

SIS, by its nature, had been created to work on the other side of the fence. Its employees often operated outside the law – especially the law of other countries – living lives that were perilously close to the criminal fraternity. They were, in the opinion of many, pirates and rogues, renegades and cut-throats.

The first head of MI5 was Captain Vernon Kell. A commissioned officer in the South Staffordshire Regiment, he had served under Colonel Edmonds

AN ADVANCE INTO WAR

in the original Counterintelligence Department and was recommended by his chief as the best man to head up the new section. Afflicted all his life by asthma, a debilitating illness which limited his army career, he seized on this new posting as the best way to serve his country.

A superb linguist who spoke five languages, including German and Russian, Kell was also a veteran of the Boxer Rebellion in China. And yet he presented as a shadowy, insubstantial character, a man who, it seemed to many, was more used to weekend hunts or shooting parties than he was to the business of catching spies. That was certainly a misjudgement on the part of those who sat and watched his organisation grow.

Vernon Kell was a highly efficient and capable officer who was to remain in charge of MO5/MI5 for more than thirty years. When Winston Churchill did, finally, choose to retire him at the beginning of the Second World War it was the end of an era.

In 1909 Kell took charge of an organisation that was based in just one room at the War Office. Finances were tight and it was not unusual for Kell himself to fund some of the early activities of MI5. It was an act of benevolence that was replicated by several of the other secret service chiefs.

Kell began his career at MI5 with a staff of just fourteen. It was a small group but even so it was still seven times more than Colonel Edmonds had been allocated. By the end of the First World War this figure had grown to a colossal 700.

The foreign arm of the new service, the SIS, was not that much better off. It was headed up by Captain Mansfield Smith-Cumming, a most unusual, even bizarre naval officer who immediately stamped his mark on the new organisation and in the process became something of a legend within the espionage world. A total workaholic, Cumming started with SIS one week before intended. His diary entry for the day read as follows: 'I went to the office and remained all day. But I saw no-one, nor was there anything to do there.'[4]

That would soon change. Cumming, developing his eccentric personality, wrote only in green ink and peered sternly at everyone through the lens of a gold-rimmed monocle. For official meetings and contacts he dropped the hyphenated Smith-Cumming and became known only by the final part of his surname. However, he was universally known by those within the service as C, an appellation that he retained for the rest of his time in charge and one that continued, like the use of green ink, with each of his successors.

Much of what has been written about Cumming has become tinged with fantasy and perhaps that is appropriate for the man and for the job he had been asked to do. Cumming was an eccentric who, people claimed, used to propel himself around the office on a child's scooter, terrifying staff and visitors alike as he hurtled down the corridors towards them. He had a wooden leg and often drove the sharp tip of his paper knife into this leg if he wanted to make his point or intimidate people on the other side of the desk. Like Kell, he too was often forced to dip into his own pocket in order to fund early missions.

In line with the concept of total deniability, SIS was based in the Liberator Building in Whitehall, well away from government interference and from Kell and his 'policing' organisation. Distance, like anonymity, suited Cumming well. The SIS had several other bases, such as Ashley Mansions in Vauxhall Bridge Road, and as early as 1910, with the assistance of the Post Office, Cumming had established it as a bogus address. This was supposedly home to Messrs Rasen, Falcon Ltd, a firm of shippers and importers, and was the beginning of a long association between spying and the import and export business that Ian Fleming was to later take and use in his Bond novels. No such firm or address at Ashley Mansions ever existed and the cooperative Post Office would simply forward to Cumming any mail or material directed to the bogus firm.

The SIS chief occupied a turret room in the Liberator Building, reached via a series of steep steps. The steps must have been difficult to traverse for any able-bodied man let alone one cursed with a wooden leg, but Cumming took it in his stride.

Despite a lack of adequate funding, Kell and Cumming soon began to organise their work loads. Neither of them found their jobs easy. They were faced by duplicity at every turn: 'Stalin said "A spy should be like the devil, no-one can trust him, not even himself." [...] Many wartime spymasters were uncertain which side their agents were really serving and in some cases bewilderment persists to this day.'[5]

Separating the wheat from the chaff soon became part of the daily activities of both MI5 and SIS. The important fact was that now, for the first time in history, Britain had a spy service that was not linked to or shackled by the constraints of government. The future beckoned.

******

From the beginning Kell and his embryonic MI5 worked closely with the civil police, taking most of their referrals from them. It was hardly an imaginative approach but it was understandable.

To begin with Kell was forced to rely on information passed to him and to his agents by the police rather than set out to create his own networks of informers and double agents. That would have been undoubtedly more effective but considerably more expensive, so, for the moment at least, it was not to be.

Kell might fume and fret over the constraining effect of budget restrictions, but he simply did not have the money or the manpower to do more. And so he was forced take referrals, not unlike job applications, from the police and the public.

The case of Wilhelm Klauer, a German dentist from Portsea, is an early example of a 'honey trap'. Klauer bought what he thought were the plans for a new torpedo from a contact who turned out to be a police informer. The dentist was arrested, duly handed over to Kell's eager clutches and in 1913 was sentenced to five years imprisonment.

As well as investigating potential enemy agents, Kell and his men had also been given a preventative role that allowed them to dabble in both sabotage and the subversion of enemy plots – at least as far as their limited finances would allow. However, as war approached this increasingly became the most crucial element in their task, forcing Captain Kell to take an imaginative approach to funding and finances.

Despite the lack of money, there were still successes. As early as 1909 the most important German 'post office' – a centre for collecting and passing on secrets to German intelligence – had been identified by MI5 and marked down as a target. Run by Karl Gustav Ernst from a barber's shop in Caledonian Road in London, it was a massive spy ring. Ernst, the chief German agent, who came to Britain in the 1860s, had been slowly and efficiently building it up for years.

Kell obtained a warrant to intercept all mail arriving at and leaving No 402A Caledonian Road and for several years the activities of the spy ring were carefully monitored. It was a perfect example of how to maintain a watching brief without the enemy realising a thing. More importantly, the identity of every single member of the Karl Ernst spy ring was recorded, all of their movements noted and reported, ready for the time when Kell decided to strike.

That moment came early on the morning of 4 August 1914, the day that Britain declared war on Germany. Before dawn police and MI5 raids took place on the barber's shop and on several other locations. In all twenty-one suspected enemy agents, including Karl Ernst, were arrested and taken into custody. Charged with conspiring to gather information regarding the armament, movement and disposition of Royal Navy ships, Karl Ernst went on trial that November and was sentenced to seven years imprisonment. It was a perfect start to the war for Kell and MI5.

Interestingly, only one of those twenty-one German spies was ever prosecuted; the chief organiser and agent Karl Ernst. The rest were held in custody or interned, as the authorities termed the process, until the end of the war. Such detentions were now allowed under the terms of the new Official Secrets Act.

The rationale behind not taking these fairly low-grade operatives to trial was simply that MI5 did not want to expose all of its secrets, its techniques and the identities of its operatives in a public showcase that would undoubtedly have been carefully watched and monitored in Germany. It was, to say the least, a somewhat bizarre reasoning.

The very nature of rolling up their network and the fact that the names of the spies were even listed in *The Times* would have given the Germans all the warning they needed. It hardly mattered. The spies were out of circulation and the reputation of Kell's MI5 was made.

There were many false moments during the war and arrests of perfectly innocent individuals were fairly commonplace, but they were usually released within a week or so. On the other side of the coin, eleven German spies were executed by firing squad between 1914 and 1919. Many more were interned or imprisoned during the conflict.

The work of MI5 was a significant if unspectacular success. Yet none of it would have been possible without the pioneering skill and enthusiasm of Vernon Kell, Major General Vernon Kell as he became by the end of the war. He was also awarded a knighthood for his work in counterintelligence, which was certainly well earned.

******

SIS, later to become known as MI6, suffered from a handicap similar to the one that afflicted Kell's organisation. This was the level of funding Cumming and his men received.

Inappropriate funding was a factor which, in hindsight, is hard to understand. An awareness of what the enemy or potential enemy was up to was clearly the best way to keep Britain safe. Government had approved the formation of the new secret service bureau but failure to give it even halfway adequate funding was nothing short of errant foolishness. Nevertheless, a criminal lack of money was what Kell and Cumming were faced with and they had no alternative but to make the best of a bad job.

For Cumming, whose role automatically involved activities in foreign countries, this was particularly difficult. With finances tight, he had to find ways to carry out his tasks, but in doing so, not spend too much money. As a consequence his first agents tended to be British nationals living in Germany: men and women who had first-hand experience of the German way of life, German culture and the nation's preparedness for war.

It was an ad hoc system that relied on the honesty and patriotism of the volunteers. Without any hope of reward or praise, these early agents noted down and then passed on reports of troop and ship movements. It was clearly better than nothing, but much could, and undoubtedly did, get missed by this amateurish arrangement.

When Cumming did find himself forced to use professional intelligence officers to gather first-hand information the results were not always propitious. Captain Bernard Trench and Lieutenant Vivian Brandon, two naval spies despatched into Germany in May 1910, were quickly uncovered and each sentenced to four years imprisonment.

The two men served only part of that sentence and returned home to find that the Admiralty and the government had denied all knowledge of their activities, exactly as planned when the bureau had been first set up. The two officers had been on leave, their superiors declared, and whatever nefarious activities they had got themselves involved in was their own business, just as their punishment was their own fault.

The imprisonment of Brandon and Trench meant that any arrested spy was, and has continued to be, entirely on his own. None of the agents expected anything different. It was their lot in life as unsung heroes of the empire.

In the early days one of the main problems encountered by a cash-strapped SIS was monitoring the honesty of those it employed as agents. It was all a matter of trust, relying on gut feelings from the intelligence officers who recruited their own spies and who, in the early stages of the organisation, were as inexperienced as the men and women they were running.

As far as senior military commanders and members of the government were concerned, not to mention the officers of MI5, they simply looked at the SIS and sadly shook their heads in disbelief.

Most of the SIS agents were thought to be little more than scoundrels who were to be distrusted as much, if not more, than the enemy they were spying on. There was probably more than an element of accuracy in this belief.

The business of spying has always meant fighting underhand and underground battles against foes who, very often, do not even know that a battle is being raged. Nothing is ever clear cut or obvious, not even things like payment for clandestine operations.

Unlike military actions where there are clear lines of support, the art of spying involves stealth and secrecy with limited supply and rescue routes. Spies are out there on their own without any obvious signs of support, and as such need to be relatively self-sufficient.

Inevitably this has always meant that the people who spy have to deal with reasonably large sums of money on a regular basis. If their motives are anything less than scrupulous there has always been a clear temptation to misappropriate funds for their own use:

> An Agent in Hungary staged a suicide and went off to the United States with all the SIS cash he was able to lay his hands on. Another shot himself when asked to explain what he had done with the £28,000 that had been sent to him.[6]

Nothing is simple in the world of spies. The nature of counter espionage has meant that the profession has always been shrouded in fog. As Donald McCormick has said, 'It all sounds terribly vague/Spies deal in shadows and whispers.'[7]

Small wonder then that Mansfield Smith-Cumming was such an extrovert whose view of life and the job he had to do was never anything other than sunny. A more sanguine approach would probably have killed him.

To the end of his career Cumming regarded spying as something of a joke, a wonderful bit of fun, and assembled his team according to the basic principle that although counter espionage was a serious business it was also a great sport. One so-called Russian expert was appointed to the team not because of his knowledge base but simply because he admired C's collection of revolvers. Gifted amateurs, as the man once said.

******

The secret service bureau with its two main arms, MI5 and SIS, might have been established in 1909 but there was still considerable confusion in Britain's espionage services. This was largely down to the proliferation of additional intelligence agencies that still existed in the country.

The Foreign Office, officially charged with keeping the country and its people safe, was always interested in and involved with spying. While its officers and managers could appreciate the two new agencies, there was no way that they were going to wind up their espionage arm and hand everything over to MI5 and SIS. In the years ahead the Foreign Office spies would become almost as numerous as those from the two specialist bodies.

The Royal Naval Intelligence section was a long-established organisation run by Admiral Reginald 'Blinker' Hall. Admiral Hall was the brains behind the British codebreaking service operating out of Room 40 at the Admiralty, a forerunner of Bletchley Park.

What became known as Room 40 was a highly effective and essential service, so much so that within only a few months of war erupting across Europe 'Blinker' Hall and his codebreakers were able to read almost every message Admiral Von Tirpitz and his staff sent to the ships of the German Navy. Tirpitz, blithely unaware of the breach in security, continued to send messages that were compromised and accessible to the British.

The British Army also had its own intelligence service as did the War Office under General G. K. Cockerill. Add in smaller units like the Indian Secret Intelligence Section and Admiral Jackie Fisher's own private intelligence network (based on the continent) and it is clear that in the final years of peace, Britain, perhaps more than any other nation in the world, was well equipped with spies and counter espionage agents.

What really interested Cumming and the upper echelons of SIS, however, were not the routine facts and figures that agencies such as naval or army intelligence units were better equipped to provide, but the more esoteric aspects of life in enemy countries. The mood of the people, attitudes to potential conflict and political unrest or opposition to the ruling party, that was what really floated Cumming's boat and was one of the main reasons he helped to establish the spy network in Holland.

Cumming was not alone in his interests. The German ND under Walther Nicolai was equally as desperate to know about the state of public morale in Britain. In this the Germans were largely ineffective, thanks to the watchfulness of MI5.

Even so the thirty German spies who were arrested in Britain during the war can be regarded as a tiny part of a much larger intelligence service. There would have been more German agents who escaped the clutches of Kell and MI5, but even so the general consensus of opinion is that very little information of use was provided for the ND either before or during the First World War. More useful facts, it has been noted, could have been discovered by careful study of Britain's daily newspapers.

Despite the failure of the ND to infiltrate Britain there were some successes on the continent as the clocks ticked ominously towards midnight. What the German ND termed 'tension travellers', people who travelled around Europe and could be employed at times of great stress, were most useful to them, particularly in the final days of peace.

Wilbert Stratton, an American working for the Pyrene Company in London, made regular trips to the continent, and as tensions rose to boiling point in the summer of 1914, volunteered his services to Nicolai and the ND. His timing was immaculate.

The ND sent Stratton to Petrograd to see what he could unearth. On the long train journey east he encountered many signs of Russian mobilisation and sent coded telegrams to Germany. Several of the telegrams failed to arrive in Berlin, but those that did were enough to give the German military advance warning of Russian activities and they were able to organise their forces accordingly.

Nicolai was delighted with Stratton's efforts and further expeditions to Stockholm and another trip to Russia quickly followed. However, attempts to persuade him to continue with his espionage work in London were unsuccessful.

Stratton's motivation in spying for Germany has never been made clear, but interestingly, the Pyrene Company has been unable to locate any reference to Wilbert Stratton in their employment records. If the story is true and he did exist, Stratton seems to have been expunged from the record books.[8]

The French secret service also enjoyed a measure of success in these last days before war finally erupted. Some time before August 1914 they obtained the full details of the Schlieffen Plan from a German army officer who had agreed to betray his country in an act of vengeance for some imagined sleight.

The Schlieffen Plan was Germany's long prepared battle plan which, their High Command felt, would bring them quick victory over the French. It consisted of a lightning-fast right hook by columns of infantry and Uhlans (lancers) which would take their armies through neutral Belgium and deep into the French countryside.

To some extent the Schlieffen Plan was an obvious tactic, so obvious that none of the French military planners and generals even considered it a worthwhile option. They felt it was outdated, consigned to the history books, and would never be used.

As for the German informant, that was merely the stuff of spy thrillers the world over. When the time came for him to meet his French contact the German officer appeared swathed in bandages, supposedly covering an injury but in reality simply hiding his face from the French agent. The French authorities could not believe that anybody ever really behaved or looked like that.

Perhaps it was because of this theatricality that the French High Command refused to believe that the Germans would attack France through Belgium. They preferred to content themselves with the belief that when Germany attacked it would be on another front altogether. The German traitor, they declared, was simply a plant by the ND.

As it happened, of course, the French secret service had been right all along. The Schlieffen Plan, designed by a long-dead German General, caught everyone – British, French and Belgian –totally by surprise and nearly led to the fall of Paris.

Quite why it should have surprised everyone was strange. As almost every military brain in Europe knew only too well, this was the only plan that the Germans had. Attacking anywhere else made little sense and was one of the reasons why, in the early years of the nineteenth century, Britain had signed a treaty to defend the new and really undefendable country of Belgium. The fact that almost everyone in Britain, from army officers to government ministers, had forgotten the ancient pact, simply summed up the arrogance and ineptitude that infected both the British and French leadership.

So the inevitable happened. In the summer of 1914 the Germans duly launched their attack through Belgium and for several weeks their armies swept everyone and everything before them. The Belgian frontier forts were smashed into oblivion by German artillery and before anyone realised what was happening Brussels had fallen. The German legions marched on.

The British Expeditionary Force fought a delaying action at Mons before starting a 200-mile retreat in blazing sunshine and almost unbearable heat. Meanwhile the French armies fell back to take up defensive positions in front of Paris. It seemed as if the German war machine was unbeatable.

Only a diversion from the original plan, a switch in the direction of the advance to capture the psychologically important French capital city, gave the Allies hope; that and the dogged resistance by the French as they fell back on their capital.

With thousands of French soldiers transported to the front by taxi and bus, the French eventually fought the Germans to a standstill along the banks of the River Marne. It was a brutal and bitterly contested battle that lasted for several days but the French held their lines and finally forced the German advance to halt.

Paris held and did not fall. Defeat in August and September 1914 would have brought the war to a very rapid conclusion. On the other hand, if Joffre and the rest of the French generals had listened to their secret service there would have been no problem to begin with.

The ramifications of German violation of Belgian neutrality enshrined in that long-forgotten treaty of the nineteenth century were immense. Originally formulated with the best interests of Belgium in mind, Britain had moved on to become a colonial power. Now, suddenly, British politicians were reminded of their duty. The British government felt that they had no choice. They issued Germany with an ultimatum – withdraw your troops or we will declare war.

It was blithely and easily done, a decision that was accepted without argument from the British public. At this early stage very few people in the country realised what the demand entailed or where it would lead.

AN ADVANCE INTO WAR

Kaiser Wilhelm had been pushing his luck for too long, people thought; it was time to put him in his place.

By the early days of August, with German troops pouring across the Belgian frontier and no response having been received to the ultimatum, there was no alternative. The British government had to make its threat real.

In what was a clear case of the domino effect, it was not long before almost every country in Europe had become involved in the conflict. Before the war finally ended four years later it had spread to the rest of the world.

The war of 1914-1918, the Great War as it was later described, was the first European conflict for a hundred years. Not since Napoleon had been defeated on the field of Waterloo had soldiers marched in such large numbers across the continent.

There had been wars involving the great nations of the world – notably in the far-off Crimea and in Southern Africa – but Europe had remained untouched. Now the people of France and Belgium, Britain and Russia, Germany and Austro-Hungary suddenly realised what the distant people of faraway lands had endured.

This new war was also the first worldwide conflict involving dozens of nations and spreading its tentacles to almost every part of the globe; something that nobody had expected. Over by Christmas was the refrain from both Britain and Germany.

People like Lord Kitchener, the Minister for War, and Sir Edward Grey, Foreign Secretary, were more realistic and confidently predicted a long and arduous campaign. Grey may or may not have delivered the famous line – 'the lights are going out all over Europe; we shall not see them lit again in our time' – but it remains a suitable epitaph for the brittle peace of Edwardian Britain.

Kitchener, well aware that the British army was undermanned and ill-equipped to take on the military might of Germany, appealed for 100,000 men to come forward as volunteers, and he wanted them by Christmas. He got a million.

Meanwhile the espionage services of all the nations involved immediately cleared for action. They, too, would need volunteers in the months and years ahead.

Chapter Four

Conflict Comes at Last

'To be weak is to invite war; to be strong is to prevent it.'
William Tufnell Le Queux

When, on the night of 4 August 1914, Britain declared war on Germany it was marked by wild celebrations on the streets of London. Crowds sang, danced and cheered as they gathered in front of Buckingham Palace, demanding that King George V and his family appear on the balcony.

Mass hysteria gripped Britain. Thousands of men welcomed the advent of a conflict that would eventually lead to the fall of three long-standing royal dynasties and bring about the deaths of ten million soldiers. At the time nothing could have been further from the minds of the British people. Excitement was the governing emotion, something that was replicated in virtually every other capital in Europe.

None of those who cheered with joy and wild abandon in London, Paris and Berlin, in Vienna and in Munich, had any idea of what awaited them. All they knew was that this sudden acceleration into mass conflict, after years of expectation and anticipation, was an opportunity to gain new experiences, to see new sights and to get away from a humdrum daily existence.

For the British, despite the miniscule size of their army when compared to the vast battalions of France, Russia and Germany, there was a firm belief that they would soon kick the Kaiser's backside. By the time of the British army's introduction to modern warfare at the Battle of Mons it was a view that had disappeared, sunk deeply and terminally into the mud and grime of Flanders Fields.

The British Tommies, mostly army regulars but with the occasional territorial unit mixed in, were shocked by the strength of their German opponents and by the accompanying realisation that this war would probably last a lot longer than anyone had previously imagined.

CONFLICT COMES AT LAST

> When I joined up and signed my name
> They said that I'd be home again
> By Christmas – but they all neglected
> To say which Christmas they'd projected.[1]

Belgium was quickly overrun and France found herself with huge swathes of land under German control. Equally as important, the secret services of all nations suddenly realised that they were no longer engaged in one of Mansfield Cumming's games. They had a considerable task on their hands, one that they were barely equipped to handle.

While Britain's SIS maintained its headquarters in London, the Channel port of Folkestone began to play a pivotal role in its clandestine operations. It was hardly surprising. The German successes in Europe meant that before the war was over more than 180,000 Belgian refugees had passed through the port on their way to safety in Britain. Vernon Kell and his men from MI5 screened them as best as they could but Mansfield Smith-Cumming, more than anyone else, immediately realised that fate had placed a rare opportunity in his hands.

Amongst these refugees Cumming knew that he would find dozens of men and women who were more than happy to go back to their homeland to carry out espionage work on behalf of Britain. There was very little of Belgium that was not occupied, but in those tiny pieces of the country that had escaped German hands Belgian patriotism and the determination not to give in to the invaders was strong. Cumming would exploit this to the full.

Gabrielle Petite, a native of Tournai who had fled the German advance along with thousands of others, was one of many Belgians determined never to roll over and submit. Discovered by Cumming at Folkestone, she duly became one of the first Belgian/Allied spies of the war.

After a brief period of training Gabrielle was turned around and by October 1914 had been sent back to Belgium. There she spied on German troop movements, sending her reports to the Allies written on flimsy cigarette paper. Her rationale was simple. If the Germans intercepted or stopped her she would destroy the information by smoking the incriminating evidence.

The Belgian spy network for which Gabrielle Petite and others worked was known as La Dame Blanche (The White Woman). The name came from an old German legend which declared that the end of the

German Hohenzollern dynasty would be symbolised by the appearance of a woman dressed in white. For the Belgians it was a powerful, almost hypnotic symbol.

Within a relatively short period of time La Dame Blanche grew into a fairly sophisticated organisation. In particular it was noted for its 'tradecraft', particularly inventing code words, the most famous being 'Le Grand Fromage' which was used to describe any big secret that was being transmitted or held. Their skills ranged from the simple effort of counting enemy troop and equipment trains as they steamed through Belgium to women couriers carrying messages wrapped around the whalebone stiffeners of their corsets.

Pigeons, it was quickly discovered, were a perfect means of carrying important messages from agents to their handlers. It was later estimated that over forty per cent of all carrier pigeons used during the war returned to their bases, far more than had ever been anticipated. By the autumn of 1918 over 20,000 of these innocuous looking birds were being used by spies and the German army was giving fourteen days leave to any soldier who managed to shoot and kill one of them.

Messages were also passed in other ingenious ways, hidden inside objects such as potatoes and even false teeth. The numbers on shop invoices, sent by merchants to supposed purchasers, identified the name and location of the sender/spy while prices on the invoices – 26 francs for a shirt and so on – meant that there were twenty-six German guns or aircraft close at hand. It was all very clandestine, very 'Boy's Own' stuff. And yet it was also deadly secret and dangerous.

Gabrielle Petite was eventually betrayed and on 1 April 1916 shot as an enemy agent. Her final words – 'now you will see how a Belgian woman dies' – secured for her a place in Belgian folklore and history.

The leader of La Dame Blanche was a man by the name of Dieudonne Lambrecht. His spy network provided evidence of the coming German attack on Verdun several weeks before it actually took place and enabled the French to make preparations that stalled the German assault. The Battle of Verdun was a bloodbath for both sides, but the forts of Verdun held, thanks in no small degree to the efforts of Lambrecht and La Dame Blanche.

Passing on news of the coming attack on Verdun was a singular success, one of the few occasions in the war when the efforts of the secret services of either side had a direct effect on any of the military engagements. It was a success that was not achieved without cost.

Lambrecht was, like Gabrielle Petite, betrayed and arrested by the Germans soon after he had passed on his news about the Verdun attack. He was found guilty of spying and was duly executed. Without his leadership support for La Dame Blanche declined and by the autumn of 1916 it seemed as if the spy network in Belgium was finished.

La Dame Blanche was saved from ignominious failure by a cousin of Dieudonne Lambrecht, an engineer called Walthère Dewé. On the death of his cousin, and understanding the vital significance of the network, Dewé took over the running of the organisation and handled it successfully until the end of the war.

La Dame Blanche was a successful network of spies, producing valuable evidence and information about a whole range of German military activities and plans. By the end of the war Cumming estimated that seventy per cent of all military intelligence passed to SIS had been supplied by La Dame Blanche, not just in Europe but the world over.

With a total strength of 1,500 active agents operating in Europe alone, Cumming also stated that just under half of these spies were women. It was an important factor in the success of the Belgian spy networks and a testament to the courage of the women who would have been facing certain death, as in the case of Gabrielle Petite, if they were ever captured.

Walthère Dewé, incidentally, revived his organisation and continued espionage work in the Second World War when Belgium was again overrun by German forces. He was shot and killed while escaping from German soldiers after a clandestine operation in 1944.

******

One of the most celebrated Belgian spies was Marthe Mathilde Cnockaert. She was training to be a doctor when the war interrupted her studies, and with her house and village destroyed by the Germans she resolved to do all she could to help the Allied war effort.

She obtained a job in a German field hospital where her medical training and her ability to speak French, German, English and Flemish made her invaluable to the Germans. Marthe was so efficient that she was even awarded the Iron Cross (Second Class) for her work in the German medical service. All the while she was spying for the Allies and passing on vital military information.

Marthe's spying continued when she was transferred to Roulers. For two years she worked in a hospital there and served, in the evenings, as a waitress in her parent's café. She was still spying for the Allies, relaying messages through contacts – a vegetable seller with the wonderful codename of Canteen Ma and a letterbox agent known only as Number 63.

Many of her exploits have been recorded, several of them by Marthe herself during her later career as a novelist when she wrote under her married name of Marthe McKenna. They ranged from the deceptively simple to the highly dangerous.

Destroying a secret telephone line that was being used by a priest who was spying for Germany was one of her simpler tasks, although the operation did effectively put the priest out of the spying business.

As far as the more dangerous exploits were concerned Marthe planned a British air attack on the hospital at Roulers when Kaiser Wilhelm was due to visit. The Kaiser was meant to arrive at the hospital to inspect the facilities and improve the morale of the wounded soldiers. He would attend a matinee performance of an opera in Brussels and then come on to Roulers:

> As I set out to the hospital that Saturday morning the air was fresh and enlivening, the birds sang merrily and the sun shone in the sky. I thought of the "All Highest" sitting silently in his opera box and wondered if today was to be his last. The streets were festooned with gay flags in honour of his coming.[2]

As it happened Marthe and the Belgian resistance were to be disappointed. The Kaiser's visit was cancelled, but it makes interesting speculation to consider what might have happened if the air raid had taken place.

For a while Marthe worked as a double agent when her lodger, a German by the name of Otto, 'persuaded her' that she should lend her support to the Kaiser. For several months she passed on useless information provided by the British and received valuable information in return. After a while the role of double agent became too dangerous, so she simply arranged for Otto to be killed and went back to the hardly less dangerous business of being just a spy for the Allies.

Marthe was eventually caught during a sabotage mission. She lost her watch, which just happened to bear her initials on the back, when she was planting explosives in a disused sewer beneath a German ammunition dump. Inevitably it led the German counterintelligence forces to her door.

In November 1916 Marthe was put on trial and sentenced to death. This was later commuted to life imprisonment because she held the Iron Cross and she spent two years in prison before being released when the Armistice was signed.

When peace returned Marthe Mathilde Cnockaert received many decorations and awards for her spying work, not least the Belgian and French Legion of Honour. She married a British army officer and after the success of her memoirs, which she published in the 1920s, became a novelist.

As a writer Marthe specialised in what she knew best, spying. She produced over a dozen 'pot boilers', all competently written, well received and highly successful. It is more than likely, however, that her books were actually written by her husband; certainly no more were written and produced after he died.

Whether Marthe or her husband wrote her books is immaterial. As a spy and as an agent for the Allies she was hugely successful. That is all that really matters.

******

Perhaps the most famous women from the world of spies, one that has remained in the public consciousness for over a hundred years, is Mata Hari.

The name Mata Hari has become a byword, a catch-all for glamorous, beautiful and exotic female spies – or for anyone in private or public life whose motives might be questionable or unclear. Mata Hari, however, was a stage name adopted by the premier actress and dancer of the early twentieth century, her real name being Margareta Gertruda Zelle.

Born in Leeuwarden, Holland in 1876, Mata Hari had dreams of far-away, exotic places and a life-style to match. She was not conventionally beautiful but she was striking in her looks and personality and soon she married an officer in the army of the Dutch Colonial Service.

From the start it was a troubled and violent relationship, one that was always doomed to fail. But Mata Hari did at least manage to spend half a dozen years in Java where she became fascinated and skilled in the dances of the Far East. Her interpretations of the dances were exactly that, interpretations geared for Western eyes and ears, rather than exact reproductions of Eastern art. They thrilled and captivated those who saw them.

In 1905 Mata Hari decided that it was time to make a change in her life. She went to Paris where she first used her stage name, along with the descriptive phrase 'The Eye of the Morning', and startled the French audiences with her range of titillating dances. Naked or semi-naked she was an instant success, subsequently performing in all the major cities of Europe.

In the years leading up to the First World War Mata Hari was an exotic dancer and high-class prostitute in huge demand, particularly for private soirées and one-to-one meetings with men of wealth and influence. She charged huge fees for her services but men seemed more than willing to pay her price, presumably so that they could claim to have bedded the famous Mata Hari.

She continued with her luxurious lifestyle even though by 1914 she was nearly forty years of age. Her looks and figure had largely disappeared and her dancing had become little more than a combination of pornography and exhibitionism.

When war broke out Mata Hari was in Germany. A British or French woman would have been interned and forced to stay in Berlin. Not Mata Hari. As a neutral she was able to move freely around Europe and she was not going to allow a little thing like a war stop her.

Her regular and seemingly incessant travelling across a war-ravaged continent was something that caused both the Germans and the French to suspect her of spying. There was no proof, however, just her reputation as a courtesan and her friendship with highly placed individuals from all sides of the political divide. And, of course, the fact that for several years she had open access to almost any country she chose to visit.

More significantly, when questioned by British counterintelligence during a trip to London, she freely admitted to having slept with German and French officers, even some French Cabinet ministers. Nationality and patriotism clearly meant nothing to her.

Mata Hari was finally arrested in Paris in 1917 and charged with spying for Germany. She had already admitted to Basil Thomson of Scotland Yard that she had spied – but not for Germany. She had spied for France. This arrest, however, was something totally different. Now she was accused of passing on details of French troops and army movements and a guilty verdict would probably carry with it a sentence of death. Her trial lasted two days, 24-25 June:

> The main evidence against her was a list of payments which Germans, some of whom were in the ND, had made to her in 1916 and 1917. The French authorities had discovered these payments set out in telegrams from the German military attaché in Spain to Berlin, which they had intercepted.[3]

In her defence Mata Hari claimed that the attaché was her lover and that the payments were merely gifts from a man to his mistress. Similar payments – which it soon transpired were actually made by the French – were, she declared, simply more gifts. This time they came from another lover in Holland, Baron von der Capellen. The explanation may have been barely credible but it did add yet another notch in her reputation as one of the most erotic women in Europe.

Mata did admit to receiving a payment of 20,000 francs from the German consul in Amsterdam early in 1916. She declared that this was for supplying information on French troop movements. The information was to be collated and passed on to the consul after her next visit to Paris. In other words, it had not yet happened, so how could she be charged with something that had not occurred, Mata Hari demanded to know. And besides, she had no intention of ever passing any information to the consul.

As for the money, she regarded it simply as compensation for the furs and other clothing she had left in Berlin in 1914. There was no evidence that Mata Hari had ever provided the Germans with information but her defence was, at best, totally naive. Ultimately she fell back on her neutrality, even though she declared that her basic sympathies had always been with France.

Inevitably, considering the 'evidence' and the nature of her defence, Mata Hari was found guilty of spying for Germany. She was executed by firing squad on 15 November 1917, her last performance being one of proud dignity and considerable courage. Whether or not the members of the French firing squad were put off by her bravery and charm, the volley of rifle fire did not kill her and a revolver shot into the ear was needed to finish her off.

Mata Hari may have been a German spy, just as she may also have been a French spy. But if so she was never a very good one. The Germans later admitted that nothing of any value had ever been passed to them by the dancer, but that the publicity surrounding her trial and execution had been more than useful.

The evidence presented at her showcase trial proved that, at worst, Mara Hari was guilty only of naively associating with the enemies of the French nation. An arrest and trial in Germany or Britain would probably have shown exactly the same. Unfortunately for her the final scenes in her life took place in France.

More than anything Mata Hari was a victim of time and place. The French armies, battered and mauled at Verdun, had recently mutinied with many regiments refusing to return to the front lines. The country needed to be shown an example and needed to be warned of the dangers of subverting the structures and the morale of the nation. Mata Hari was destined to be that example.

******

If the case of Mata Hari seems improbable, the downfall of the double agent Colonel Alfred Redl, director of the Austro-Hungarian counterintelligence department, borders on the utterly fantastic. He died in 1913, two years before war broke out, but his activities had a direct and tragic bearing on the opening salvos of the war.

In some respects Redl's story is symbolic of the decadent Austro-Hungarian Empire that he served. By the beginning of the twentieth century the Austrian power block in the centre of Europe was little more than a disjointed conglomeration of nation states with no common purpose other than to act as a reminder of former glory.

Even so, as director of the *Evidenzbureau*, the Austrian counterintelligence department, Alfred Redl was a high ranking official in the Austro-Hungarian military. He had position and status, was the envy of Vienna society. He was also a Russian spy!

On the surface and to begin with Redl seems to have performed well for his country. He introduced advanced technology into the Austrian spy systems, making use of things like cameras, finger printing and early examples of listening and recording devices. Several Russian spies were exposed as a result of Redl's interventions.

CONFLICT COMES AT LAST

His downfall came about as a result one of his own improvements to the counterintelligence service, a case of the biter being well and truly bitten. And this is where the story of Colonel Redl moves away from the norm and becomes more bizarre.

The Black Bureau was a postal interception unit that Redl had established to monitor and check on all incoming and outgoing mail, regardless of the recipients or senders. In March 1913 suspicious officers from the bureau opened two envelopes that were addressed to a post office box in Vienna. They had been posted in Eydtkuhnen on the German border with Russia and that alone apparently made the agents suddenly take greater notice.

There were no letters inside the envelopes, only cash to the tune of over £500. It was a considerable sum of money in 1913 and certainly made the Austrians realise that something irregular was going on. They alerted their superiors. Two bureau agents were quickly assigned to watch the post office to note who arrived to pick up the mail.

By some quirk of fate the officers arrived on the scene just a little too late and missed seeing who came for the envelopes. They did, however, see the man's back as he climbed into a taxi outside the post office. As they stood wondering what to do next, the same taxi reappeared. The agents hailed it and in best spy fiction style demanded to go where the previous occupant had been dropped – a restaurant called The Kaiser. The mysterious man, presumably in an attempt to cover his tracks, had then ordered another taxi to take him to the Hotel Klomser.

While they were in the taxi the agents just happened to find the suede cover to a pocket knife. It had apparently been dropped on the seat without the owner noticing. The hall porter at the Klomser identified the knife cover as belonging to Colonel Redl. The story then becomes even stranger.

Redl left the Klomser Hotel and was followed by the two bureau agents. He spotted them and immediately pulled a sheaf of papers from his pocket. These he ripped to shreds and threw onto the ground, thinking that his pursuers would stop to pick them up. One did exactly that but the other followed him back to the hotel.

When the scraps of paper were pieced together they were seen to be receipts for registered letters sent from Brussels, Lausanne and Warsaw. The addresses showed that they had come from the offices of the Russian and French secret services.

Four bureau officers were immediately sent to the Klomser and found Redl in his room writing farewell letters. He knew the game was up and asked for permission to end things in the honourable way. When this was granted, he blew his brains out with a single revolver shot.

The story resembles William Le Queux at his best – or worst – but there is probably an element of truth in it. Redl certainly had a taste for luxury and owned houses in Vienna and Prague. He also had an estate in the country, an extensive wine cellar and four brand new motor cars. Such luxuries would have been beyond the resources of a mere colonel in the Austrian army, but as it later transpired, he had been receiving over £2,500 a year from the Russian government. That would certainly have fed his expensive appetite.

Redl had betrayed his country, selling out several of the Austrian agents whom he had sent into Russia in the first place. More significantly, he had passed on full details of Plan 111, the Austro-Hungarian plans that had been drawn up for an invasion of Serbia in the event of war. When that invasion did finally happen in the summer of 1914 Serbia clearly knew what was coming and in the opening encounters inflicted heavy losses on the invaders.

Three times the Austro-Hungarians were repelled, only vastly superior numbers finally winning the day for them. Estimates at Austrian casualties put the figure at around half a million – most of them, if not all, attributable to Colonel Alfred Redl.

The reason why he should choose to betray his country has never been discovered. One theory is that the Russians had discovered he was a homosexual and were blackmailing him. He was a confirmed homosexual and exposure would not have done his career any good at all. More likely he just loved money and luxuries and the Russians certainly paid well for his information.

The story of how Redl was unmasked has to be false. Discovery of the pocket knife cover, its identification by the hotel's hall porter, the throwing away of papers – which just happened to implicate him – and the keeping of such incriminating receipts in his pocket are mere fantasy. Such things might happen in the pages of spy and detective novels but surely not in real life.

Redl was known to suffer from severe depression. His suicide note, written in his bedroom at the Hotel Klomser, declared that 'Love and passion have destroyed me.' He might well have ended his life while in the throes of yet another depressive fit.

The fabricated story of his exposure and noble suicide were probably cobbled together, badly it seems, by the Austro-Hungarian secret service in an attempt to explain away the disastrous defeats by Serbia in the opening months of the war.

So, was the Redl story a fabricated invention by the Austro-Hungarian secret service or a perfect example of truth being more bizarre than fiction? We will probably never know. It was, and is, all part of the strange world of spies in the halcyon days of the world's second oldest profession.

******

From the early stages of the war Holland had been established as a major centre of spying, not just for the Allies but for Germany as well. Rotterdam and The Hague were full of foreigners and many of these men and women were spies for one side or another – sometimes for both.

In 1917 Field Marshal Willie Robertson, Chief of the Imperial General Staff, was to comment on the crucial importance of the country to the Allied war effort. If Holland were to be taken out of the picture, he declared: 'The whole of our secret service would break down; as it is through here [Holland] that almost all of our best information is received.'[4]

Rotterdam in particular was a vital centre. Cumming had established the Dutch offices of SIS on a busy quay on the river that divides the city into two and here Richard Bolton Tinsley took up his post as station chief of the Dutch branch of SIS. Known as T – to complement Cumming's C - Tilney became one of the most successful agent runners of the whole war.

Originally a gunner in the Royal Naval Reserve and then a maritime agent for the Cunard Shipping Line, Tilney had spent several years in Holland, and despite a somewhat chequered past which saw him obliged to leave the country for a time, he returned to Rotterdam in 1914 as Cumming's man on the ground.

He found and then worked with Karl Kruger, a former German Naval officer who was able to provide him with valuable information on the construction and deployment of German battleships. Kruger was probably the most successful British spy in Germany, much of his success being down to the support of Richard Tilney.

A diligent and thorough worker, Tilney's good relations with the Dutch police gave him a decided advantage over the enemy. He knew the important contacts in the Dutch police service, and more importantly, knew who to bribe or pay off.

The German ND operated their spy network from the German Imperial Consulate, a building within hailing distance of Tilney's base. From there they infiltrated spies into Britain, slipping them across the North Sea under all manner of disguises. Their efforts, however, were nowhere near as successful as the British, which were also, at best, limited.

Vernon Kell and his teams from MI5 kept a close watch on everyone arriving from Rotterdam and very few of the ND spies were able to get past his watchers. Two of those who did manage to evade MI5 at the border crossings, Willem Roos and Haiche Janssen, were eventually hunted down and caught. They were executed in the Tower of London in 1915.

As a neutral country the position of Holland, close to the warring parties of France and Germany, was both unusual and sometimes perilous. The mixing together of French, British and German soldiers, diplomats and merchants living in or visiting Holland was accepted, provided they did not resort to acts of war that might affect Dutch neutrality. That was, at least, the theory. Richard Tilney made use of this laissez-faire attitude, knowing that as long as he fed the Dutch selected pieces of information on the Germans his activities would be tolerated.

The Germans, however, were not quite as tolerant. Despite the fact that they maintained an accepted presence in Rotterdam, they wanted contact on their own terms. Eventually they decided to close the border between Holland and those parts of Belgium that remained in Allied hands.

Over one million refugees had decamped from Belgium in the first year of the war, some heading for England but most opting to stay in Holland, which was at least close to their homeland. For the Germans it was a security risk, not least because there would be spies and agents contained within this legion of refugees who could easily slip between one country and the next.

CONFLICT COMES AT LAST

Closing the border was achieved by erecting what became known as 'The Wire of Death' along the border between the two countries. It mirrored the barbed wire that was now stretching across Europe but the Wire of Death was considerably more deadly. It was a 130-mile-long stretch of electrified wire between Aix-la-Chapelle and the River Scheldt.

The key word is 'electrified'. Standing between 5 and 10ft in height the 2000-volt wire was in place by the spring of 1915. It meant instant death for anyone who touched it or fell into its coils.

The Wire of Death killed between 2,000 and 3,000 people during the course of the war. They were mainly refugees trying to cross, usually from Belgium into Holland, in order to join their families. Obviously not all of these were spies, though some undoubtedly were.

The Wire was not infallible and many did manage to successfully cross the barrier, using a range of ingenious techniques. One method was using long stepladders that reached above and over the wire. Some escapees tried to tunnel beneath the obstacle, others attempted to climb up and over, using porcelain plates on their shoes and hands to insulate themselves. There were even attempts to pole vault across.

The Wire of Death was, ultimately, counterproductive. Since the end of the Boer War ten years previously, the Dutch people had always had an affinity with Germany and a dislike of Britain. The wire reversed this attitude. The callous nature of the device created a bad feeling that remained for many years.

******

While Mansfield Smith-Cumming and SIS were busy trying hard to infiltrate German organisations and agencies on the continent and in the wider world, Vernon Kell and the members of MI5 were equally as busy back home. Now known by the letter K – to match Cumming's C – Kell's official title, as recorded in *Who's Who*, was Commandant, War Department Constabulary, but he preferred to be known simply as K.

By the swift rounding up the agents of Karl Ernst's spy ring and closing down his post office in the summer of 1914 Kell had effectively cut off the head of German spying activities in Britain before the war really began. If the ND wanted to gather information about British strengths and dispositions they would have to start again, from scratch as it were.

Kell had developed close links with Basil Thomson of Special Branch and now, along with Eric Holt-Wilson, they drafted the Defence of the Realm Act. Such legislation had not been necessary before, but with war raging just a few miles from the British mainland and fear of German agents operating in the country already at fever pitch, some new form of defence was clearly required.

This revolutionary piece of legislation effectively made it an offence for people to communicate with the enemy or help them in any way. In particular publishing information – articles, stories or drawings – that were likely to be of any use to enemy forces was now outlawed by the new Act. It led to many naive and innocent men and women having to spend, at the very least, a night or two in jail.

Almost as soon as Britain entered the war Edward Thomas Davies, a young schoolteacher from Barry in South Wales, fell foul of the Act when he was arrested for making sketches of the coastal area around the artillery fort in the town. The fort lay close to the vitally important and well-guarded coal docks of Penarth, Cardiff and Barry itself.

As it turned out Edward Davies was engaged in nothing more harmful than an exercise for a summer school at the local art college. His sketches were confiscated and he was issued with a stern reprimand. He was lucky. Under the terms of the Defence of the Realm Act he could have been incarcerated for the duration of the war or even shot.[5]

Carl Hans Lody, an officer in the German Naval Reserve, was not so fortunate. He was arrested and put on trial partly because he was caught travelling through Britain on an American passport that clearly did not belong to him. Certainly stupid, but hardly a capital offence.

Unfortunately, Lody had also sent letters and telegrams to a man in Stockholm, allegedly his controller. The letters were chatty, telling the Swede the now famous story of Russian troops travelling through Scotland – with snow on their boots – on their way to the Western Front. The story was ridiculous and well known, having already appeared in several daily papers, and was distinctly old news.

Despite the paucity of real hard evidence Lody was found guilty of passing on confidential information and was shot by firing squad on 6 November 1914. Whether or not he was spying for Germany remains a moot point.

CONFLICT COMES AT LAST

The firing squad was not the automatic end for captured German spies. Only eleven of all the men arrested for spying during the war were actually executed, the most notable among them being Sir Roger Casement.

Casement, a big bluff Irishman, was a former British diplomat who had worked for the British in the Congo. However, by the time war began he had become enthralled by the idea of Irish independence and was one of the main planners for the Dublin Easter Rising of 1916. He had been knighted for work investigating human rights abuses in Peru but by 1916 he was totally opposed to imperialism and had gone to Germany to seek aid and arms for the rising.

Casement soon became sure that the Germans, nothing if not imperialist themselves, were toying with him, promising and not delivering the weapons that he and his colleagues so desperately needed. He saw the terrible danger, knowing that a poorly armed group of partisans would have no chance against the British army. He grew desperate to get back to Ireland to cancel the uprising before it was too late, realising that without German aid it would lead only to death and disaster.

Sick at heart and physically mauled by a reoccurrence of the malaria fever he had picked up in Africa, Casement left Germany on a U-boat. He was put ashore in Tralee Bay just three days before the planned uprising. Hardly able to move, let alone walk, he was captured before he could warn the Irish Volunteers that no help would be coming from Germany.

Despite Casement's efforts the Easter Rising went ahead. As he had suspected it was a disaster. The rebels were besieged and bombarded by artillery in their sanctuary in Dublin's post office and dozens were killed or arrested, including most of the leaders.

The rising was a costly failure although the mismanagement of trials and immediate executions in the wake of the affair led to a huge upswell of support for the rebels. Casement, like so many others, did not survive the purge. He was taken to London and shot by firing squad on 3 August.

Many still believe that Casement's execution had little to do with his politics or with the state of affairs in Ireland. There were other, more unsavoury elements at work.

A renowned homosexual with a decided preference for young boys, Casement had recorded his numerous affairs in what became known as the *Black Diaries*. A strong conservative element amongst Irish

Catholics undermined the huge volume of support he was given during his confinement and trial with the result that a guilty verdict and the death penalty were almost inevitable.

Casement's fate came as a result of the attitudes of the time. The content of the diaries undoubtedly disgusted the conservative faction and contributed to the death of a man who, when captured, was trying to avoid bloodshed rather than encourage it.

Meanwhile the work of MI5 continued. Vernon Kell's greatest contribution to the war effort came in the creation of a huge library of card index files. These listed thousands of possible or potential enemy collaborators: 40,000 of them by 1917.

Clearly by that stage of the conflict the main job of MI5 had shifted in no small degree from the simple 'hands on' practice of arresting enemy spies – the iron hand on the velvet collar – to become instead the collation and analysis of individuals and organisations that might present a danger to the country.

What Kell created was an enormous information bank that would be added to over the years. In 1940 the US State Department estimated that the card index system logging the names and identities of anyone who had ever been remotely suspected of anti-British sentiment or activity stood at over four and a half million.

With the arrival of conscription in 1916 Kell was clear that anyone with links to organisations like the Non-Conscription Fellowship would also now have to be kept under strict surveillance. While his enthusiasm was to be applauded, it has to be noted that most of the 50,000 individuals who now came under his observations were actually innocent of any crime.

There was one other significant success for Kell in the war years. He worked closely with Basil Thomson in monitoring and tracing Indian revolutionaries who were trying to forge links with Germany. There might have been little immediate benefit from his labours, but the information he gathered proved more than useful for the British in the last days of the empire.

Cumming looked on with envious eyes. He was jealous of his colleague's success, firmly believing that Vernon Kell would eventually oust him and take control of both arms of Britain's secret service. In that, at least, Cumming was wrong.

******

If Kell and MI5 had a somewhat better record than SIS during the First World War it was largely due to the level playing field they had created by rounding up Karl Ernst's post office for German agents in August 1914. Cumming, on the other hand, had to go out and find his theatre of operations and then train and develop the spies who would cause him to succeed or fail.

The one enormous success on the Home Front came not from Kell or Cumming but from Admiral Reginald 'Blinker' Hall of naval intelligence and the men who worked out of Room 40 at the Admiralty.

The unsung but undoubtedly brilliant cryptographers managed to break the German naval codes and so gave the Royal Navy and the whole British war machine a considerable advantage that was never lost throughout the war. It was a hugely significant success, and indirectly led to the even greater success of the codebreakers at Bletchley Park during the Second World War.

Much to the chagrin of many more traditional naval officers, Hall employed a wide range of eccentric but highly gifted amateurs to work on deciphering the German codes. From teachers and professors to clerics and crossword specialists, the ability of these men to crack the enemy signals soon became legendary within British secret services.

They were certainly a bizarre lot, many of them straight out of the most fantastic spy novels imaginable. One of them, a classics specialist by the name of Dilly Knox, even enjoyed unravelling coded messages while taking his morning bath. As far as Hall was concerned it did not matter, the end result was all that concerned him.

Room 40 had received a huge boost in the first month of the war when the Russians passed them what became known as the Magdeburg Signal Book. This had been found when the German cruiser *Magdeburg* ran aground during an action off the Estonian coast.

The gift was not total altruism on the part of the Russians. There were in fact three code books; the Russians kept two and gave the third to the British. The difference was that the British actually did something with their copy while the Russian books simply sat in the basement of their Admiralty, cluttering up shelves and serving no useful purpose at all.

Other code books from the sunken German destroyer *S-119* and the German-Australian steamer *Hobart* also found their way into British hands. From these and the Magdeburg Signal Book, 'Blinker' Hall's men were able to decipher almost every coded message the Germans sent by wireless and telegraph. It was an amazing coup that was kept hidden and unknown to most of the fighting forces.

Perhaps the greatest achievement for Hall's team was the deciphering of the Zimmermann Telegram in January 1917. It was a seminal moment for Room 40 and for the whole spying industry, arguably one that was not bettered until the Enigma success of the Second World War.

The clandestine Zimmermann communication from the German Foreign Office to their counterparts in Mexico was a genuine offer that raised the possibility of an alliance between Germany and Mexico. The prize for the Mexicans was to be the recovery of Texas, which they had lost after the Battle of the Alamo nearly one hundred years before. The telegram was promptly shared with the Americans, with the result that the USA entered the war on the side of the Allies.

The rest of Room 40's war did not always have quite such a happy conclusion, however. Over-zealous security measures meant that while much useful information was gathered by the men of Room 40, very little was ever passed on to operational units in the field. Most significant of all was the failure to fully alert Admiral Jellicoe about the movements of the German High Seas Fleet before the Battle of Jutland. Room 40 had intercepted the German radio traffic between Hipper and Von Scheer but the content of the messages was not passed on to Jellicoe. The furious British Admiral never forgave this failure of communication in the intelligence services.

******

It is probably fair to say that while they certainly did not disgrace themselves, none of the secret service agencies from any of the warring nations covered themselves with glory during the First World War.

There may well have been, for the British at least, individual successes. These included La Dame Blanche's early warning of the German attack on Verdun, perhaps the most successful espionage effort of the whole war. There was also the information provided by the talented codebreakers of Britain's Room 40 and the rounding up of the German post office in London on the day war broke out. But in the main the war period was a learning curve – and a pretty steep one at that.

What people mainly remember are the failures, glorious as they might have been. Mata Hari and Alfred Redl are the names people recall, even though they both met brave but ignominious ends and their efficiency as spies or double agents was limited.

Very few of the 280 spies caught in Germany during the war (most of them German and French, only three British) are remembered these days and their achievements, such as they are, have long faded into insignificance: 'The Germans admitted that the number of spies caught and charged represented only a fraction of those at work, but it is hard to believe that SIS under Cumming ever succeeded in getting any worthwhile information out of Germany from British agents.'[6]

German attempts at infiltrating agents into Britain met with even less success, thanks to the efforts of Vernon Kell and his men. In that, at least, there was a degree of success, but Kell's work was counterintelligence: obtaining information from and about the enemy were different matters altogether.

Part of the trouble was getting people to accept and believe the information that spies provided. In that respect the early reactions to the spies were not unlike the hidebound attitude of some British senior officers. When faced by the reconnaissance reports provided by the Royal Flying Corps they responded with the comment that the cavalry could have provided them quicker, and besides, the roar of aircraft engines frightened the officer's horses something shocking.

There is evidence that one of Field Marshal Haig's aides actually suppressed any information that he felt might upset or cause grief to the army commander. News of a probable German counter-attack after British success at the Battle Cambrai, for example, was never passed on to Douglas Haig. It led to British and Canadian forces losing ground they had just gained and losses in the region of 50-60,000 men.

As compassionate as the decision to withhold news of the counter-attack might have been, for Haig at least, for the soldiers under his command it meant blood, death and disaster. With that sort of attitude it is not surprising that the work of spies was held in low regard.

Yet the spies themselves continued their work, labouring away, expecting and getting little in the way of reward and recognition. All sorts of men and women were recruited. Edwin T. Woodhall was a Military Policeman who, after several months serving in the trenches at Ypres, was seconded for intelligence work with SIS. He went on to serve in a variety of locations and held several important positions during the war.

From catching French double agents on the docks at Le Havre to guarding the Prince of Wales on his regular trips up the line, Woodhall was constantly in the thick of the action. He loved it, finding his job a combination of the policing that he knew so well and an adventurous way to serve his country.

He was clear that the French and Belgian locals often unwittingly helped the enemy. Sent to investigate a light that was being displayed on the coast every night, Woodhall discovered that the culprit was not an enemy spy signalling to waiting U-boats but a little old lady who had placed her oil lamp in the same position in the barn almost every night of her adult life:

> When informed that an exposed light on a high eminence looking out to sea might give cause for official perturbation, she innocently replied that it had been her custom for many years and this was the first time any complaint had ever been made [...] There ended an episode which, like many more of a similar nature, turned out to be quite harmless.[7]

Woodhall wrote fully about his wartime exploits and was not above exaggerating his personal involvement and effectiveness in unmasking enemy agents. He took pride in the fact that he had once saved the life of the Prince of Wales, even though in hindsight the claim seems a little tenuous.

Regardless of that, Woodhall was clear that the mistake made by the old woman in placing her light in its usual position was not a one-off event. Many other French and Belgian civilians, he felt, had committed similar offences and some of them had paid most severely for their mistakes. For too many enthusiastic intelligence officers the end result – the capture and exposure of enemy agents – was all that mattered.

If men accepted the glory – to say enjoyed would be too great an exaggeration – women seemed to have a more stoical attitude towards an experience that was new to them and to the whole world. Spies and non-combatants alike, they appear to have retained a more philosophical attitude towards the war: 'One woman, I recollect, stood with her baby in her arms pointing up, and saying "Look at the airyplanes, baby, look at the airyplanes." So I returned and stood in the yard and watched the airyplanes myself.'[8]

Hardly a successful war, then, for the spies. And yet the public still eagerly read stories about brave men and women, on both sides, pitting their wits against impossible odds and fighting their secret war to the bitter end. That fascination continued long after the war ended.

It is not just adult fiction writers who engaged in spy fiction. Children's writer W. E. Johns, the most upright and correct of all specialists in fiction for young people, once had his hero Biggles fall madly in love with a beautiful German spy, a French double agent by the name of Marie.

The romance and glamour of the affair are redolent of the sacrifice of Mata Hari. Before leaving him and going to her death – or maybe not – Marie sends Biggles a final letter:

> Goodbye, my Biggles. You know now. What can I say? Only this – our destinies are not always in our own hands […] I came here tonight to take you away or die with you, but you were not here. We shall meet again, if not in this world then in the next, so I will not say goodbye. Au revoir, Marie.'[9]

Without the example of Mata Hari and her virtual deification it is doubtful that Johns could ever have written that story. Certainly a pattern had been set, one based on sacrifice and failure rather than success. Either way there was glory.

What Mata Hari managed to do was to create an acceptable public image for the spy. Under her posthumous influence spies were seen to inhabit a world filled with glamour and bravery. It was a world full of agents who lived for the moment with their lives always in jeopardy. The image, with a few notable exceptions, has continued to this day. It is quite some legacy for a second-rate spy and for a system that, in 1918, was not yet working to its full potential.

Chapter Five

A Host of Spies – the Interwar Years

'I doubt whether I have known more than a dozen spies in my life, and I am still uncertain about two of them.'

Graham Greene

In the years immediately following the First World War the vast, sprawling empire once ruled over by the now deposed Czar Nicholas II adopted a new persona. Previously an important part of the alliance against the Kaiser's Germany, attitudes changed and Russia began to assume pole position as the number one enemy of the British.

It was a shift that had begun, in a fairly subtle, low key way, when Russia's second revolution in October/ November 1917 took the country out of the war against Germany. Subtle and low key because, even after her defeat, most of Britain's leadership still regarded Germany as their primary European foe.

Germany would rise again, that was the general consensus of opinion, so best keep watch on her. Meanwhile, the power and threat of the new Russia grew like a slow-moving snowball gathering strength and size before finally hurtling down the hill.

Alexander Kerensky and Russia's provisional government, immediate successors to Czar Nicholas and the Romanovs, had felt honour bound to continue supporting their allies in the war against Germany. All British efforts between the fall of the Czar and Lenin's inevitable rise to power – a nine-month period that was really little more than an interregnum – were therefore focussed on supporting Kerensky in his decision to keep Russia fighting the war.

As a consequence of Kerensky's misplaced loyalty to the Allies, Russian soldiers continued to die in their thousands at the battlefront. At home an increasingly hostile and disheartened people carried on suffering the pangs of starvation, all of the time knowing that their sons, husbands and fathers were being sacrificed in an unwinnable struggle against superior forces.

Only Vladimir Lenin and the Bolsheviks seemed able to offer an alternative. The Czar had gone, regretted by only very few, and well-meaning as he might have been, the liberal Kerensky was no match for the promises and propaganda of men like Lenin and Leon Trotsky.

The coming of the Bolsheviks changed everything. Kerensky fell and then fled, the Czar and his family were imprisoned in Siberia, where they were eventually shot, and from that point onwards no amount of effort by outside agencies could keep the Russians fighting.

To the immense chagrin of the Allies, the Treaty of Brest-Litovsk, signed in March 1918, formally ended Russian involvement in the war. It cost the Russians greatly in terms of land and money, but they were finally out of the war and free of the need to sacrifice thousands of Russian lives. After that it was as much a case of a lover scorned as it was hatred of the Bolshevik's political stance that created a new *bête noir* in the minds of British and French security chiefs.

By negotiating a separate peace the Russians had, in one stroke, wiped out the Allies' strongest suit – the alliance that had forced Germany to fight a war on two fronts. The German high command could now throw all of their forces against the British and the French, a prospect that alarmed all Allied politicians and military leaders. Only after that came the fear of communism.

Nobody in Britain or France really understood Bolshevism, Marxism and Communism, but everyone had their preconceptions, usually formed from half-truths, rumours and fears. Bolshevism was, among other things, seen as a malignant force, a German-led plot to bring disaster to its enemies, and a genuine threat to the safety and security of the world.

Whether they understood it or not, for the British ruling classes Bolshevism, like all left-wing political and social movements, was a terrifying spectre that threatened their continued existence. Hundreds of years of built-in conservatism did little to aid acceptance of a different viewpoint from the opposite end of the political spectrum.

It took time but gradually, almost reluctantly, the eyes of Britain's security chiefs began to swing eastwards towards Russia. Arguably they have never yet managed to swing back.

For the SIS the years immediately following the German defeat were marked mainly by the activities of several of their agents whose efforts to dislodge the Bolshevik government were largely ineffectual but which created romantic legends that are still spoken about today. The post-war spies were men who worked under difficult conditions, and for whom financial recompense was often a secondary consideration to the idea of destroying the Bolshevik dream.

They were lucky to be given the opportunity. As far as the British government was concerned the end of the war had left them with a huge degree of uncertainty about their spy networks. There had been no spectacular victories or successes, with the possible exception of the codebreaking carried out in Room 40 at the Admiralty. With the coming of peace there were many who seriously doubted the viability of an independent security service.

Developing or even just maintaining espionage agencies and networks was an expensive business. Britain was virtually bankrupt after the costliest war in history and could hardly afford to splash thousands of pounds on organisations that did not appear to be working: 'Intelligence-gathering is inherently wasteful. I am struck by the number of secret service officers of all nationalities whose only achievement in foreign postings was to stay alive, at hefty cost to their employers.'[1]

Spying in time of war might just be explainable but in peacetime any democratic regime that is obliged to keep its voters happy and content would have to look long and hard at why and what it was providing. In the early 1920s, a period of austerity and compromise, both MI5 and SIS suddenly became vulnerable.

In a total revamp of the secret service organisations control of SIS was passed to the Foreign Office and MI5 to the War Department. Budgets were cut, SIS dropping from £240,000 in 1918 to £125,000 the following year. MI5 was similarly hit, its budget being slashed from a high of £100,000 to a paltry £35,000.

Arguably MI5 suffered worse than SIS. The organisation had finished the war with a staff of 850 agents. However, in 1919 a large portion of its responsibilities were transferred to Special Branch and staffing was reduced to thirty. Vernon Kell found that the duties of his department were now confined to counter-espionage and to combating the growth of communism within the armed forces.

Luckily the secret services, both MI5 and SIS, found an ally in the shape of former Home Secretary and one-time First Lord of the

Admiralty Winston Churchill. He fought fiercely on behalf of SIS when, in 1920, there were proposals to further cut its budget.

Churchill, always a close friend of the underdog, firmly believed that the safety of the country depended on a healthy and active secret service that would keep track of enemy agents and deal with any plots against the security of Britain. He was not going to allow organisations like SIS and MI5 to simply wither away and die.

Churchill's championing of SIS managed to postpone the cuts for twelve months, but it was a short-lived reprieve. By 1921 Cumming's agency was operating on £65,000 a year while Kell's MI5 now received just £25,000. It meant hard times for the secret services and many thought that the end was close at hand. Their demise promised a welcome relief for some, and a dire threat for others like Churchill who believed implicitly in the value of the clandestine organisations.

It was a depressing time for SIS, not made any easier by the sudden death of Mansfield Smith-Cumming in 1923. He had been involved in a bad motor car crash during the war, which had killed his son and further disabled Cumming himself. He was due to retire in a few months but his death forestalled that and gave everyone yet more reason to doubt the survival of SIS.

Cumming was succeeded by another naval officer, Rear Admiral Hugh Francis Paget Sinclair. He had been Director of Naval Intelligence during the war, and in the face of insecurity and compromise was, initially at least, intent on merging MI5 and the SIS. This would, Sinclair felt, make the whole service more efficient and cost effective. It never happened and by 1925 the idea had been dropped.

Sinclair's elevation to the position of security chief in September 1923 was accompanied by several changes. In addition to SIS he now assumed control of the Government Code and Cypher School (GC & CS as it was known), an organisation that eventually morphed into the present-day GCHQ. He then moved SIS and GC &CS into new accommodation at Broadway Buildings near St James's Park, far more palatial and comfortable all round.

Sinclair battled hard for the survival of his command. To begin with it seemed that he was fighting a losing battle. Then, almost unbelievably, there was a total turnabout.

By the closing years of the 1920s the pendulum had suddenly swung the other way as attitudes changed and the SIS budget virtually doubled in size. The reason was simple. The threat had been there since 1917 but only now did the British government finally see and accept it. Almost like an epiphany the danger coming from Soviet Russia was at last acknowledged to be a threat that loomed over Britain and had to be challenged.

The Russians were ahead of them. On 20 December 1917 the Peoples' Commissars had established a counter-revolutionary agency under the command of Felix Dzerzhinsky. It was known by the name Cheka, a gathering together of the initials of its name in Russian, and was the forerunner of the OGPU and the more famous KGB.

Dzerzhinsky was a Pole, able to trace his ancestry back to a family that had significant noble connections, but as a confirmed Marxist he had spent many years in the Czar's prisons. He was a truculent prisoner, being regularly beaten by his jailers, so much so that his jaw and mouth were permanently disfigured. He was known as 'Iron Felix' and feared by comrades and enemies alike.

Lenin – and, later, Stalin as well – regarded Dzerzhinsky as revolutionary hero. The Bolshevik leader personally charged him with creating a secret force that would be capable of combatting internal and external threats to the Soviet state. 'Iron Felix' duly obliged.

Based at Loubianka in Moscow, the vast majority of the Cheka's early agents had previously been members of the Czar's secret police, the Ochrana. Their employment was not through choice. As Dzerzhinsky quickly discovered, there were simply not enough potential agents in Soviet Russia, but the use of Ochrana men did mean the extension of their previous preferred operational mode – penetrate opposition agencies before exterminating them. It was a technique that the Cheka and the KGB were to use for many years.

******

The name Sidney Reilly is synonymous with the activities of British spies in Russia during the early 1920s. He was famously known as Reilly, Ace of Spies, the term being taken from a book by his colleague Bruce Lockhart and a later 1980s television drama, *Reilly, Ace of Spies*, which was based loosely on his life.

Reilly was flamboyant and eccentric, a driven man, propelled and marshalled in his espionage work by a virulent hatred of Bolshevism.

However, despite the plaudits, the books and television series, he was nowhere near as successful a spy as he would have liked to have been. In the words of author and lecturer Christopher Andrew: 'His career was remarkable though largely ineffective.'[2]

Reilly was notoriously cavalier about his past, telling everyone that he was born in the port of Odessa in 1874 to an Irish sailor and a Russian/Jewish mother. It is now accepted that both his parents were Russian Jews who had converted to Catholicism and that his real name was Georgi Rosenblum.

He became Reilly in 1899 when he was living in London and somehow obtained a passport in that name. The passport presumably came from the British government but Reilly never took the name officially or legally. Rumour or legend, call it what you will, says that he had as many as eleven passports, all in different names. It is as Sidney Reilly, however, that he is remembered.

Married three times, Reilly was an inveterate womaniser, using his easy charm to beguile and intrigue the women he encountered. He was always, from an early age, on the fringe of undercover work, having spent time at Port Arthur and Petrograd (when it was still known as St Petersburg) where, amongst other things, he helped in the repatriation of Russian prisoners during the Russo-Japanese War of 1905.

In the days before the First World War Sidney Reilly was in Germany working for a firm of shipbuilders. It was a position that enabled him to copy blueprints of German ship designs and pass them on to Mansfield Smith-Cumming of SIS. When war broke out he returned to London.

After a short period operating out of New York, purchasing arms for the Czar's government, by 1917 he was once more based in Britain. Cumming then sent him back to Germany, his task being to find out how close to defeat the enemy really were. Cumming, along with Winston Churchill, thought highly of Sidney Reilly, but there were others within SIS who viewed him as unscrupulous, conniving and devoid of any real morals.

There is probably a great deal of truth in this judgement. Undoubtedly brave, Reilly was more than capable of operating for two or even three employers at the same time – as long as they paid well. He allegedly spied for four different powers, albeit at different times, but it was as an agent for Britain's Special Branch and SIS that he is best known.

A highly successful businessman in his own rights, Reilly was in Russia during the turbulent days of the Revolution and somehow managed to get himself accepted as a government official by the new Soviet regime. He apparently worked in Trotsky's Foreign Office where he was able to pick up and copy many documents – important or trivial, it hardly mattered to him.

During his time in Russia Reilly developed an intense hatred of Bolshevism and was often quite unhinged in his desire to see Russia's leaders humiliated and ground into the dust. He called the Bolshevik regime 'the arch enemy of the human race' and was beyond reason when it came to any discussion involving Lenin and the others. His beliefs clouded his judgement and were to put him and many of his colleagues in the path of significant danger.

Working undercover, in 1918 Reilly organised the Ambassadors' Plot. The plan called for Latvian soldiers – bodyguards of Lenin and Trotsky – to seize and hold their leaders, thus creating a vacuum and allowing Reilly and other men from the British Embassy to organise a provisional government of anti-Bolshevik activists. They would then run the country until democratic elections could be held.

Reilly's initial idea was that the arrest of the Bolshevik leaders would be a moment of great humiliation for them. Believing that it was far more effective to ridicule than to kill, his plan was simple: 'Reilly's grand plan was to arrest all the Red leaders on 28 August [...] Rather than execute them, Reilly intended to de-bag the Bolshevik hierarchy and with Lenin and Trotsky in front, march them through the streets of Moscow bereft of trousers and underpants.'[3]

The idea of humiliating and ridiculing Lenin and the rest eventually came to nothing. Anti-Bolshevik elements in Reilly's support group preferred a simpler and quicker technique: they would just kill Lenin and Trotsky. In the end it hardly mattered as the plot unravelled before Reilly's eyes.

Nothing was ever totally secret in those days of double, even treble crossing. Felix Dzerzhinsky and the Cheka knew of the plot all along. They had infiltrated Reilly's group and were carefully waiting, watching and monitoring the situation.

Large sums of money had been passed to the anti-Bolshevik groups that were supposed to help in the coup. These sums were quickly diverted into the coffers of the Cheka. Reilly and his helpers were totally deceived, but what followed next was confusing and caused Dzerzhinsky to act before he was quite ready.

On 30 August a young military student forestalled the Ambassador's Plot and murdered Moisei Uritsky, head of the Petrograd Cheka. On the same day the former anarchist Fanya Kaplan, distraught because Lenin had banned her party, the Socialist Revolutionaries, put three shots from a Browning revolver into the body of the Bolshevik leader as he left a factory in Moscow. Kaplan refused to reveal if she had accomplices and was executed by a bullet in the back of her head.

Reilly was furious, guessing rightly that the two assassination attempts had destroyed his plans. The Cheka, he believed, would now be alerted. What he did not know was just how alert the Russian secret service actually was or that they were already on to him.

Lenin had not been killed by Kaplan's shots, but he was gravely wounded. His condition was serious, so much so that it was feared he would die, and rather than wait any longer Dzerzhinsky ordered the plotters to be rounded up. The British Embassy in Petrograd was attacked, the naval attaché, Francis Cromie, was killed in the ensuing gun battle and what has since been known as the Red Terror was immediately instigated.

At Dzerzhinsky's direction the Cheka seized hundreds, possibly even thousands of political opponents and mass executions took place in the Loubianka prison and at other locations across the country. It was a bloody and counter-productive period for the Bolsheviks, and interestingly, when Lenin recovered consciousness, bruised, battered and with permanent disabilities, his first command was to put an end to the Red Terror.

In the confusion Sidney Reilly managed to escape and went into hiding. After paying 60,000 roubles he was eventually smuggled out of Russia on a Dutch freighter. Reilly, along with his accomplice, Bruce Lockhart, was tried in absentia and condemned to death, a sentence that would come back to haunt him in the years ahead. For the moment, however, Reilly was safe in London and not unduly worried by the sentence.

In 1924 he became involved in the scandal of the Zinoviev Letter. Supposedly written by the President of the Communist International, the letter warned British communists to prepare for the coming revolution and the destruction of law and order in Britain. In the meantime they were to further develop links with the Labour Party. A Labour government would, Zinoviev seemed to believe, resume trade and diplomatic relations between Britain and Soviet Russia and this would undoubtedly lead to a British revolution.

The Zinoviev Letter was published in several leading British newspapers just before the October 1924 election and was instrumental in the subsequent defeat of Ramsey MacDonald's Labour Party. The Tories returned to power in triumph. More significantly it led to poor relations between the governments of Britain and Russia, a situation that lasted for many years.

The letter, of course, was a forgery. Reilly was certainly part of the scheme, although the extent of that involvement has never been made clear. But this was the man who had once informed a group of émigrés that if it was proving impossible to get genuine documents from the Russians then they should invent some.

Both Reilly and SIS – conservative, reactionary, Tory through and through – were aware that the letter was a forgery. But as far as they were concerned the most important thing was the end result. In this case the fall of the country's first Labour government and the shelving of any plans – and there were some – to further reduce the power and secret information banks of the SIS and MI5. Embarrassing Soviet Russia was merely an additional bonus.

Reilly's next escapade proved to be his last. He was determined to go back to Russia in order to cause damage to the regime and to help friends who had been 'marooned' there. He had made contact with an anti-Bolshevik organisation called The Trust, working out of Finland to damage the Russian system. Reilly was intent on cooperating with The Trust to create an uprising.

Driven by his fanatical hatred of the Bolsheviks, Reilly was eager to take any opportunity to help in their downfall and he convinced himself that this was a golden opportunity to strike at the heart of their regime. What he did not know was that The Trust was actually a deception unit that had been created by OGPU, the new intelligence agency that had succeeded the Cheka. One of its aims was to lure people like Sidney Reilly into its clutches and then pounce.

True to this secret intent, representatives of The Trust met the unsuspecting Sidney Reilly in Finland. Still believing he was in friendly hands he was taken across the border by a man called Tolero Vaka, a former Finnish Red Guard. Once in Soviet territory he was overpowered and handed over to agents from the OGPU.

He was immediately sent to the Loubianka where he was interrogated and, possibly, tortured. He was certainly subjected to several false executions. In one such incident he was stood against a wall ready to be shot before his guards apparently 'changed their minds'. The aim of such tactics was to break down a suspect's resistance, but whether this worked with Sidney Reilly is not known. His hatred of the Bolsheviks might well have helped him through the ordeal.

During the whole time he was incarcerated Reilly kept a diary, written on cigarette paper and secreted in tiny cracks in the wall of his cell. The diary entries were later found by guards and passed on to higher officials. Reilly, who believed to the last that he would escape or be exchanged for captured Russian agents, was sure that his evidence of the interrogation techniques employed by his captors would be useful to Hugh Sinclair, the new head of SIS.

Reilly had forgotten the basic tenet of the spy world. Captured agents were on their own, deniable to the last. Reilly's usefulness was over and the British government, as might have been expected, made no moves to help him in his hour of need. He had already been condemned to death by the Russians and it was only a matter of time before the sentence was carried out.

For months on end Reilly lay in his cell, enduring the cold and the taunts of his jailers. There could only ever be one conclusion. On 5 November 1925 Sidney Reilly, Ace of Spies, was finally put out of his misery. He was taken to a forest outside Moscow and there he was shot dead.

For years nobody knew what had happened to Reilly; he had simply disappeared. There was no scandal, nothing to prove that he had not been operating as an individual citizen engaged on his own private operation. That was all that mattered to the government.

As Eddie Marsh, Churchill's Private Secretary, wrote in a reply to a letter from Reilly's third and last wife: 'Your husband did not go into Russia at the request of any British official, but he went there on his own private affairs. Mr Churchill very much regrets that he is unable to help you in regard to this matter.'[4]

Friendship, admiration, usefulness – they all meant nothing in the world of spies and secret agents. Sidney Reilly, a man whom many still believe was the model for Fleming's James Bond, was as expendable and as deniable as any other undercover worker, perhaps more so. After all, he knew where many of the bodies were buried.

******

In the world of double agents George Hill was something of a master. A friend and accomplice of Sidney Reilly, even a back-up man in many of his escapades, Hill also conducted his own espionage work on behalf of SIS. In 1917, charged like so many British spies with keeping Russia in the war, he was quite prepared to assist anyone, even the Bolsheviks, who might aid him in his enterprise.

It appears that the new Russian leaders were taken in by this charming and well-educated spy. George Hill worked closely with Leon Trotsky, advising him on how to set up an air force for the new regime, and also became friendly with several of the top Bolshevik brass. Many of these men might not have fully trusted him, but they did nothing to undermine his position.

Perhaps Hill's greatest coup came when he managed to penetrate the German Peace Mission which had been sent to begin negotiations after the Bolsheviks seized power in November 1917. The information he managed to uncover or gain from the members of the Mission was soon passed on to his bosses in London.

Hill also helped the Bolsheviks to establish a counterintelligence unit that would try to eliminate German spies currently working inside Russia. The skills he passed on included deciphering intercepted messages and how to intercept written communications without the enemy realising that his messages were being read. Hill was, of course, still working for SIS and any news or information relating to a possible peace treaty between Russia and Germany was again soon in the hands of Cumming and his men in London.

On his own behalf George Hill created a personal network of agents, including a courier service to take messages to and from London. Much of the work carried out by this network was anti-German, but Hill's informants also collected information on the Bolsheviks. Hill was also proactive in trying to create counter-revolution in Russia. He provided arms and ammunition, false papers and finances for anyone willing to take up arms.

The life of a double agent was invariably dangerous, immensely stressful and usually very short. It was a form of spying where exposure and capture were constant threats, with nobody really knowing who was a friend and who was an enemy.

George Hill lasted longer than most. By the end of the 1920s, however, he was suffering from overwork and stress. Before too long SIS realised he had outlived his usefulness. Hill himself later wrote about his feelings: 'I seldom slept more than three hours in any twenty four. Oh, the agony of wakefulness. It is then that the mind marshals its fears and cares into battalions.'[5]

Recalled to London, Hill left SIS employment, and after a period of rest and recuperation, he worked for several years as a freelance spy, selling his services for cash. Despite the nervous exhaustion which never quite left him, he was not caught and returned to Russia to continue his espionage work during the Second World War.

******

One of the more unusual SIS operatives in Russia was the novelist William Somerset Maugham. He was already a well-published author when war broke out, nine of his novels having appeared in print in just over a dozen years. His first book had sold out within days of publication with the result that he gave up studying medicine to become a full-time writer.

Maugham was eager to do what he could for the war effort. After an initial period working for the Red Cross and then the Ambulance Corps, he served as a military intelligence officer in several different theatres of war. It was good background training for what came next.

In June 1917 he was recruited by Sir William Wiseman and Mansfield Smith-Cumming of SIS for work in Russia, partly because of his previous experience and partly because he spoke Russian. This was after the fall of the Czar but before the rise of Bolshevism and Maugham was happy to do what he could. He was sent to Russia with the initial brief of reporting on conditions amongst the masses, both for SIS and for the American State Department.

There was more than just reporting at stake, however, and Maugham had no illusions about what he was supposed to do. Do what you can to keep the provisional government in control; keep Kerensky in charge;

keep Russia in the war; do not allow the Bolsheviks too close to the seat of power: those were the main thrusts of his instructions.

Maugham had a track record in this type of operation, having spent some of the war working in Switzerland attempting to combat the efforts of the Berlin Committee. Also known as the India Independence Committee this rather strange organisation had been founded in 1914 by Indian activists living and working in Germany.

Its aim was to take advantage of the British preoccupation with fighting the war against the Kaiser, a preoccupation that left the government with little time to concern itself with Indian nationalists. The Berlin Committee was established to promote Indian independence, with propaganda and, if necessary, with violence, and was obviously looked on by the British government with some concern.

Now, with bigger fish to fry, Somerset Maugham travelled to Petrograd by way of Japan, Vladivostok and then the Trans-Siberian Railway. Once established in Russia, he was able to delve into records and interview people in his guise as a writer. He met with Alexander Kerensky and other leaders, but almost from the beginning he could see that the situation was hopeless. He had arrived in the summer of 1917 but his intervention was a clear case of too little, too late.

Maugham sent long and informative reports to SIS in London, detailing the decline of Kerensky's status and position, highlighting the groundswell of support for the Bolsheviks. It was what SIS had feared. The Bolshevik juggernaut was just beginning to gather speed, threatening to sweep Kerensky and his liberal Provisional Government out of office.

The Bolsheviks had suspected that Maugham was a spy from the first moment he set foot in Russia but took no steps against him. This was largely due to the fact that his reports were very accurate, particularly in recording the growth of the Bolshevik faction – something that greatly pleased Lenin, Trotsky and their comrades.

Maugham later commented that he might have been able to achieve something if he had been sent to Russia six months earlier. As it was, the Bolshevik Revolution that October and November ended any hopes he and SIS might have had about keeping Russia in the war.

By the autumn of 1917 Somerset Maugham was seriously ill with TB. He was also depressed, believing that the Bolsheviks had marked him down for retaliation. Forestalling any action by the Bolshevik secret police, he managed to get out of Russia and returned to Britain. His brief time as an SIS spy was well and truly over.

It had not all been a waste, however. Somerset Maugham was able to use his time as an espionage officer, both in Russia and in earlier days against Germany, to good effect. He tapped on those experiences to create the character of Ashenden, one of the more realistic early fictional spies and a character clearly based on his own life and experiences.

In *Ashenden*, the first of his spy stories, when the eponymous hero is first asked to undertake a little espionage work Ashenden takes a stance that is obviously Maugham's. The language might seem a little dated now, clearly of its time, but the writing still smacks of realism: 'Ashenden was acquainted with several European languages and his profession was excellent cover; on the pretext that he was writing a book he could without attracting attention visit any neutral country.'[6]

Somerset Maugham's period as a spy and agent might have been limited and ultimately unsuccessful but it enabled him, when the time came, to write accurately about the world of spying. That was hardly what Cumming and the SIS had wanted or expected, but if the spying fraternity was disappointed the world of literature certainly benefitted.

******

Perhaps the most unscrupulous of all the British spies operating in Soviet Russia at this time was Paul Dukes. He was also one of the most successful.

Dukes, the son of a Congregationalist clergyman from Somerset, was already in Russia when the First World War began, studying music at the conservatoire in St Petersburg. Russia was a different world for him. He loved the atmosphere of St Petersburg, the rugged beauty of the surrounding countryside and the hospitality of the people.

Picking up the language came easily to him and he remained in Russia for the first few years of the conflict, translating the local papers for British consumption, and through the auspices of the Anglo-Russian Commission, helping to organise war supplies for the needy Russian peasants.

In 1917 Dukes returned to Britain, representing the Anglo-Russian Commission at the Foreign Office. It was not the sort of work that he really wanted and when the opportunity came he was happy to revert to a more active occupation.

In the wake of the November Revolution he was approached by the Foreign Office and sent back to what was now Soviet Russia, ostensibly to find out what relief might be required by the people. In fact he was also, in a limited way, commencing his spying career, being charged with reporting back exactly what he had observed in the war-torn country.

He reported faithfully and accurately; so accurately that he was recalled to London after a few months and asked to become a full member of SIS. Mansfield Smith-Cumming himself briefed Dukes, making no bones about the fact that he was being sent on a dangerous, even deadly assignment.

The SIS network of agents inside Russia had been virtually wiped out before, during and after the Bolshevik takeover and Cumming, like so many others, believed that foreigners would soon be prevented from crossing the Russian border altogether. If (or when) this actually occurred, having Dukes already in the country would be an enormous asset for SIS.

Dukes undertook a tortuous journey back to Russia, a trip that involved him travelling alone across rugged country, boarding several trains, and finally a voyage on board a crowded troop ship. In November 1918 he slipped across the Finnish border and moved on to Petrograd. The name of the city might have been changed but it was territory that Dukes knew well and he was pleased to be back in the country that he loved.

His cover name was Joseph Ilitch Afirenko, supposedly a Ukrainian clerk working for the Cheka. It was a bold deception but he had several other false names during his time in Russia, sometimes posing as a soldier in the Red Army and even as a delegate at the Petrograd Soviet.

Paul Dukes was constantly on the run during his time in Russia, rarely spending more than one night at the same address. At each new address he always operated under a new name. A master of disguise he was known as 'The man with a hundred faces' – and he needed all of them. The long arms of the Cheka were never far away, only his wit and cunning keeping him out of their clutches.

There was no support network for Dukes in Russia. Mansfield Cumming had been clear about that from the start. Dukes would be on his own inside a hostile country. It was up to him to create his own network of spies, and, of course, Dukes did that exceptionally well. During his time in Soviet Russia he not only collected considerable amounts of useful information, he also helped many 'White Russians' to escape. This was a costly and dangerous business, which, as far as the British government was concerned, was not always as welcome as might be supposed.

Information came to Dukes from a whole host of sources. These ranged from an off-hand comment by one of his land ladies to stories or 'scoops' from journalists he met in the cafés and bars. Even news that was given to him in confidence by friends was passed on to his handlers back in London. He would exploit every opportunity to collect and pass on vital information, not with the fanaticism of Sidney Reilly but with a cool professionalism that soon came to typify his work.

One of his identities was as a supposed Bolshevik supporter with the result that many Party members confided in him. It meant that, despite their pleas to keep what they told him close to his chest, Cumming and the men of SIS were always well informed of even the closest, most carefully guarded Bolshevik secrets.

It was a hard life for Paul Dukes, constantly expecting the midnight knock on his door, sometimes sleeping out in the open and rarely having enough food to eat. He knew that the Cheka agents were hot on his heels. His skill and ability were all that was keeping him a few steps ahead of them.

Dukes sent his information to London on scraps of thin tissue paper, usually curtesy of some fleeing anti-Bolshevik rebel for whom he had arranged passage. Sometimes he even took the messages himself. On these occasions he would brave the guns of the Kronstadt forts in night-time journeys on fast Royal Navy torpedo boats. Such adventures could have come directly from the pages of Ian Fleming.

He was paid for his efforts, well paid, but for him it was pride in a job well done and the opportunity to view the Bolshevik state at work – from within as it were – that gave him the greatest satisfaction.

By September 1919, with the civil war raging, Dukes knew it was time to leave. Conditions in Russia were chaotic. Food shortages, lack of efficient transport and almost non-existent communication systems had spelled an end to free movement around the country, no matter how effective his disguises or aliases might be. With the Cheka closing in fast he was doubtful if he could achieve much more. Paul Dukes was no fool;

he knew how to balance risk against reality and realised that his days as an SIS spy were over.

He duly wound up his networks and headed north. He slipped past the Red Army lines, through the White Battalions and arrived in Riga from where he took a boat back to Britain. He brought with him several defecting White Russians, almost as a last defiant gesture

Back in London Cumming made sure that Dukes was presented to the king. Prime Minister Lloyd George declined to meet him, preferring to keep his distance from the 'dirty business' of spying – an amazing case of double standards given the little Welshman's track record of deceitfulness, lying and self-serving enterprise.

When he and the king met in 1920 George V told Dukes that, contrary to the opinion of Lloyd George, he regarded spies as the bravest of his soldiers. And he, Paul Dukes, was the bravest of the brave. As a civilian Dukes could not receive the Victoria Cross, a medal that George would have dearly loved to bestow on him, but instead he was awarded a KGB. He remains the only man to be knighted solely for espionage work. How Sidney Reilly would have loved such an accolade.

Paul Dukes spent some time in America and finally turned his hand to writing. The first book, based on his experiences as a spy, came out in 1938. In all he produced ten fast-paced works of high adventure and drama, but all with a lightness of touch and tone that proved very attractive to the reading public.

He moved beyond the world of spies and secret agents and even wrote one book about the benefits of yoga. He had something of a track record in the subject, being one of the first enthusiasts to introduce the practice of yoga to Britain.

It is, however, as a spy – and indeed as a spy writer – that Paul Dukes will always be remembered:

> Kronstadt loomed dimly on the horizon, the dark line of woods lay behind me and all was still as death [...] Slowly and imperceptibly I rose, first on all fours, then kneeling, finally standing upright. The horsemen and the sleigh were gone, I was alone. Only the stars twinkled, as much as to say "It's all over – 'twas a narrow squeak, wasn't it? – but a miss is as good as a mile."[7]

The writing, like the personality of Paul Dukes himself, remains light and accessible. But there is a hard and dangerous edge not far beneath the surface. This is, you feel, an accurate impression of how the man lived and worked, the dangers and the hardships that he faced reduced to just minor hazards. Small wonder that Cumming and the King thought so highly of him.

A brief excursion back into the spy world at the beginning of the Second World War, helping to rescue a Czech businessman who had fallen foul of the invading Nazis, was his last adventure. He died in South Africa in 1967.

******

In 1922 the Cheka was replaced, merged with the People's Commissariat for Internal Affairs into a new counterintelligence agency – the Joint State Political Directorate, better known as the OGPU. The new department was meant to operate with more restraint than the Cheka, but in time its ruthlessness, power and reputation grew to outstrip everything that the leaders of the Cheka had ever dreamed about.

The rise of the OGPU is irrevocably linked to the rise of Joseph Stalin. A tool with which to bend the public to his way of thinking was inevitable given Comrade Stalin's clear desire and intention to create a police state where he felt safe and secure, though not necessarily the other members of the Party or his regime.

In January 1924, after a number of strokes that could and perhaps should have killed him, Vladimir Lenin, worn out and in constant pain, finally died. He had been a virtual invalid since 1922, spending more and more time at his house in Gorki than at the Kremlin.

Lenin's absence from the seat of government and from all involvement in foreign affairs had allowed Stalin to increase his power base with the result that he was able to bypass Leon Trotsky and slip cleverly into the role of Lenin's successor. In Stalin's paranoid hands the OGPU quickly became a major instrument of control, even of terror.

It was Stalin's public decree that any or all opposition views within the Soviet Union must be considered dangerous that effectively gave the OGPU control and all the power it needed to seek out and destroy hostile elements within the country. As a consequence there were dozens of show trials during the first and second of Stalin's Five Year Plans that first saw the light of day in 1928.

The Great Purge was to come ten years later, between 1936 and 1938, but the activities of the OGPU laid the ground for the greater, more brutal exterminations of the future. The OGPU officers were 'Yes Men' but more than that they were unrepentant and dedicated killers who saw that the only way they could keep themselves safe was to do exactly what Comrade Stalin desired.

In particular the OGPU was instrumental in the development of the Gulag system of internal exile, building on the foundations of the old Czarist prison camps in the east. It was also renowned for its persecution of the Russian Orthodox Church and a wide variety of Catholic organisations. Christian worship effectively died in the OGPU's reign of terror.

Above all, during its relatively short life the OGPU became the main agency for the arrest and liquidation of anarchists and other dissident elements within, and sometimes outside, the country. Its officers perfected the terrifying midnight knock on the door so that when the NKVD, and later the KGB, succeeded the OGPU there was nothing new in their tactics. The Russian people were well used to the intimidation.

The OGPU was one of the main players in the policy of collectivisation, a system that created a devastating famine in the Ukraine. The concept of collectivisation began in 1929 with peasant farmers forced to give up their land and join collective farms. There they were not paid for their produce, as they had been since time immemorial, but received wages based on a ration system. This was awarded according to each individual's productivity.

From the beginning Stalin was clear that the Ukrainian peasants would not reach the required level of productivity. He had always wanted the fertile Ukraine to become the 'bread basket' of the Soviet Union, feeding the Party supporters but taking no notice whatsoever of the needs of the Ukrainian peasants.

The eviction of the kulaks (the wealthier land-owning peasants) merely added to the disaster which reached endemic proportions between 1931 and 1934. Émigré Ukrainian papers and journals coined a name for what was going on. It was, they declared, a Holodomor, the term taken from the two Ukrainian words for hunger and extermination.

Above: Kim's Gun, also known as the Zamzama Gun, outside the museum in Lahore. Kipling's spy novel *Kim* opens with the young hero sat astride the barrel of the cannon.

Right: Donald MacLean, a significant member of the Cambridge Five and one of the most successful spies of the Cold War.

Above left: Arthur Ransome, renowned for his *Swallows and Amazon* stories, also served as a spy in Communist Russia during the Russian Civil War.

Above right: Mansfield Smith-Cumming, the eccentric and bizarre first director of SIS, later MI6. Known throughout the service as C, he famously traversed the corridors of his headquarters on a child's scooter and wrote all of his memos and letters in green ink.

Below left: Gabrielle Petite, one of C's first agents, was a member of the Belgian resistance group La Dame Blanche during the First World War. She was caught and executed in April 1916.

Below right: Ian Fleming, the best-known spy writer in the world – if not always the most accurate. Unlike many similar writers he did at least have a background in the espionage business.

Above left: Admiral Wilhelm Canaris, head of the German *Abwehr* from 1935. Always lukewarm towards the Nazis, he became involved in the July Plot of 1944 to assassinate Hitler and was thrown into a concentration camp where he was executed a few weeks before the end of the war.

Above right: Felix Dzerzhinsky, the iron-hearted chief of Stalin's *Cheka*.

Below: Patricia (left) and Arthur Owens (right), one a Hollywood film star, the other a Welsh spy.

Above left: Melita Norwood, Russian spy, unmasked 13 years after she retired.

Above right: Mata Hari, perhaps the most famour spy of all time but also one of the most inefficient.

Left: Alan Turing, code breaker supreme. The photo shows him at the age of sixteen.

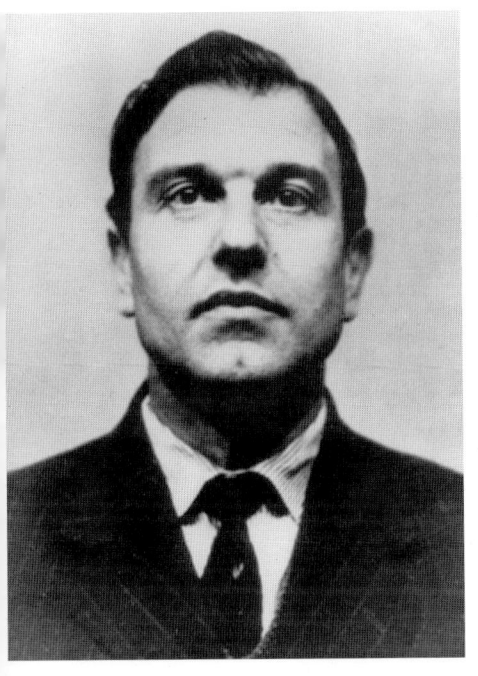

Above left: George Blake, Russian spy and escaper from British prison.

Above right: Buster Crabbe, the frogman who disappeared while investigating the hull of a Russian cruiser in 1956.

Right: Admiral Reginald "Blinker" Hall, the man who ran Room 40 during the First World War.

Above left: Alfred Redl, head of the Austro-Hungarian spy agency - and a double agent for Russia.

Above right: Richard Sorge, arguably the greatest spy ever, the man who warned Stalin of the impending German attack in 1941.

Below: Guy Burgess, one of the Cambridge Five, seen here with politician Tom Driberg.

Good time girl or spy, philanderer or indescreet politician: Christine Keeler and John Profumo who shocked the world with their antics in 1963.

Columbus, the codebreaking machine at Bletchley Park.

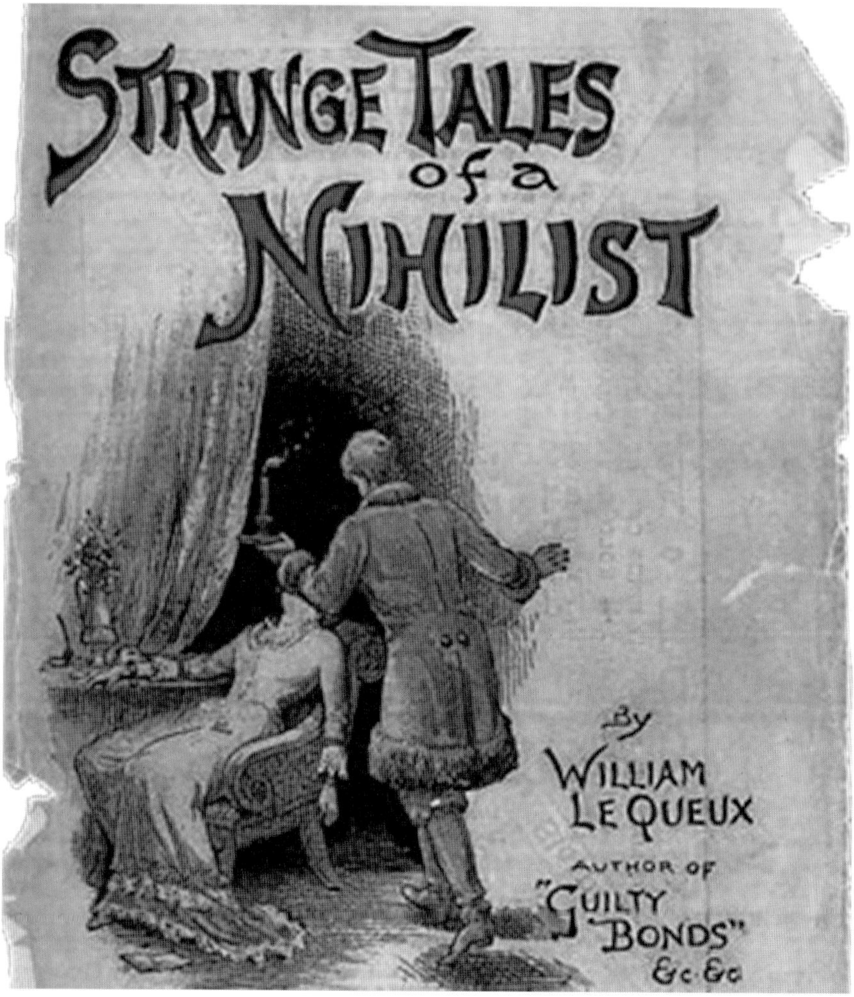

Above: The cover of one of William Le Queux's best-selling novels.

Left: Dick White, the only man to head up both MI5 and MI6.

Dilly's Fillies as they were known, the young women who worked the decoding machines for codebreaker Dilly Knox.

Early spy writer and Irish patriot Erskine Childers, seen here whilst serving in a Yeomanry Regiment during the Boer War.

Left: The atom spies Julius and Ethel Rosenberg.

Below: Spying goes back a long way. This artist's impression shows the capture of a French spy during the Franco-Prussian War of 1870.

Rear Admiral Hugh Sinclair, future head of MI6, circa 1916.

Above left: Oleg Penkovsky, the most important double agent of the Cold War. Thanks to his information the CIA was able to locate and identify Soviet missile sites on Cuba.

Above right: John Buchan, one of the best spy novelists of the Twentieth Century, famous for *The 39 Steps* and *Greenmantle*.

Kim Philby, the man whose spying exploits in the 1950s summed up the Cold War espionage business.

Above left: Klaus Fuchs, one of the most important scientists employed on the US Manhattan Project to develop the atom bomb - and a Russian spy!

Above right: Dilly Knox, decoder par excellence.

Right: Laurenti Beria, probably the most dangerous and deadly Soviet counter espionage officer. He was eventually executed by his own people after Stalin's death.

Below: A painting depicting the attempt on Lenin's life. Three shots to the body failed to kill him but probably helped to shorten his life.

Another view of the exotic Mata Hari.

Above left: Rudyard Kipling, one of the early spy novelists – a portrait by Burne-Jones.

Above right: Vernon Kell, Director of MI5, with his family.

The Wire of Death, a 200-mile electrified fence that divided Holland and Germany during the First World War. Nearly 3,000 people died attempting to cross the barrier.

Modern technology – a U2 spy plane. American CIA pilot Gary Powers was shot down when flying one over Russia in 1960, but U2 photographs later provided the Americans with the first real proof of nuclear weapons on Cuba.

Above: Wild Bill Donovan, Director of OSS during the Second World War.

Left: William Le Queux, the man whose dramatic page-turning novels started the whole spying business for Britain.

Nearly 10 million people died in the famine, a man-made disaster that went almost unnoticed by people in the West. Unnoticed, that is, until a young British journalist exposed the scandal.

Gareth Jones came from Barry in South Wales and was educated at Aberystwyth and Cambridge Universities. He worked for a while as Research Advisor in Foreign Affairs to former Prime Minister David Lloyd George before becoming a freelance news reporter. He was in Germany when Hitler rose to power and even travelled in the same aeroplane as the German dictator and his henchman, Dr Joseph Goebbels. If that plane had crashed, Gareth Jones later declared, the history of the twentieth century would have been very different indeed.

Jones was never a spy but when he went to the Ukraine and discovered the extent of the disaster he was appalled. Despite being 'warned off' by the Soviet authorities and by the British Embassy he packed his rucksack with bread and cheese and travelled by train and on foot through the Ukraine. He wrote reports on what he saw for *The Western Mail*, *The Manchester Guardian* and *The New York Evening Post*, exposing the rotten core of Stalin's regime. He was not afraid to use personal testimony to illustrate his points:

> I walked through the country, visiting villages and investigating twelve collective farms. Everywhere I heard the cry "There is no bread. We are dying." [...] Most officials deny that any famine exists but a few minutes after one such denial in a train I chanced to throw away a stale piece of my bread. Like a shot a peasant dived to the floor, grabbed the crust and devoured it.[8]

Jones later dropped an orange peel into a spittoon and the same Ukrainian again dived for the remains. And still the communists refused to accept, or would not admit, that there was a famine in the country.

A few years later Gareth Jones was kidnapped, then shot and killed while reporting on events in China. Rumour – and it has never been anything more than rumour – states that his death was an assassination by the NKVD, the successor to the OGPU, a revenge killing for his articles exposing the famine in the Ukraine.

The NKVD, the Peoples Commissariat for Internal Affairs as it was formally known, had been in existence as a regular police organisation since 1917. As well as policing the streets the NKVD also had control of prisons and labour camps. However, in 1930 it had been disbanded, its duties spread out across several other agencies. Surprisingly, it was brought back into existence in July 1934 with the OGPU being merged or transferred into its remit.

Clearly Stalin already had his Great Purge in mind and the combination of the OGPU and NKVD gave him the means to carry this out. Leaders of the new organisation included Genrikh Yogada, Nicolai Yezhov and the diminutive but lethal Lowentiy Beria.

Perhaps the greatest success of the OGPU was the Trust Operation. Capturing and then killing Sidney Reilly was just one aspect of this plan. The tentacles of the OGPU reached far wider and were considerably more deadly than that.

OGPU officers contacted dozens of émigré Russians in the West, telling them about the organisation and informing them that The Trust was there for one purpose only – the destruction of the communist regime in Russia. And the émigrés fell for it, convinced, as Sidney Reilly had been convinced, by the sincerity of the message.

Many émigrés were lured back to Russia, among them the terrorist and anti-Bolshevist fighter Boris Savinkov. He returned in 1924 and was immediately arrested and shot. There is a school of thought that says Sidney Reilly knew The Trust was a counterfeit organisation run by the OGPU and only went back to Russia to avenge Savinkov. There is no evidence for this and it seems far more likely that Reilly had his own agenda or reason for returning; it had nothing to do with Boris Savinkov or revenge.

The exiled Russians, as requested by The Trust, sent large sums of money and supplies from the West into Soviet Russia. It was useful cash for the Bolshevik regime and the possibility of people like Sidney Reilly and Boris Savinkov falling into the clutches of the OGPU was always there. Their capture, like the arrest of many more anti-Bolshevik individuals, was a huge bonus.

******

If Sidney Reilly was hated by the Bolsheviks then Robert Bruce Lockhart was both hated and feared. He was a Scotsman who, like Somerset Maugham and Paul Dukes, had spent several years in Russia before the war. A fluent Russian speaker he became acting Consul General in Moscow until the November Revolution of 1917. Then, as was customary at the time, he took up a post as an agent, something of a compromise position, part diplomatic and part information gatherer, and was acknowledged as such by the Bolsheviks.

As a young diplomat Lockhart had been an accepted member of Russian society for several years, even playing football for a local team and helping them to win the Moscow League Championship of 1912. He was not a great player, unlike his brother who was a Scottish rugby international, but his enthusiasm and popularity carried him through.

When the Bolsheviks assumed power in 1917 Bruce Lockhart, who had witnessed the deprivation endured by the Russian people, had a degree of sympathy for their position. At the same time he held a very poor opinion of the SIS agents operating in Russia.

He was particularly opposed to men like Sidney Reilly who had convinced the British government that all it needed to overthrow communist rule in Russia was a lot of money and a handful of British soldiers. Lockhart knew it would take a great deal more than money to achieve that and said so, more than volubly.

His voice was ignored, however. No one in SIS had any better ideas than to throw money at the problem and after a short period back in Britain Lockhart returned to Russia, now in the pay of SIS and with nearly £700 worth of diamonds in his luggage. The jewels were to be used to create a network of spies. It was against Lockhart's better judgement but nevertheless he obeyed his orders.

Under the cover of his diplomatic position Lockhart became friendly with Trotsky and Lenin and even shook hands with Stalin. All the while he was reporting back to SIS and doing what he could to help his country. He arranged for Trotsky's secretary, Eugenia Shelepina, to escape from Russia – she later married the writer Arthur Ransome – and tried his best to curb the more outlandish plots and ideas of men like Sidney Reilly.

It was once again against all his basic instincts that Lockhart became involved in the Ambassadors' Plot, Reilly's plan to use Latvian guards to capture and imprison Lenin and Trotsky. Never one to keep his opinions to himself, Lockhart told Reilly that the plan – the Lockhart Conspiracy as the Russians dubbed it – was both dangerous and unlikely to succeed. It was a view that caused Reilly to withdraw sulkily, never to see Lockhart again. It is not totally clear but it seems that despite this disagreement Lockhart gave his reluctant approval to the scheme.

As already noted, Felix Dzerzhinsky had managed to infiltrate Reilly's group and the plot failed dismally. It led, not to the fall of the Bolshevik regime, but to the Red Terror and the death of thousands. While Reilly went into hiding, Bruce Lockhart was arrested and imprisoned in the Kremlin where for several weeks he feared for his life.

Every turn of the key in the lock, every footstep in the corridor outside his cell, Lockhart's life and his nerves hung in the balance. He was fortunate. He was eventually freed in an exchange of agents and returned to London. Like Sidney Reilly, he was then tried in absentia by the Bolsheviks and sentenced to death. It seems a strange turn of events but presumably, as far as the new Russian leaders were concerned, death in absentia was more politically correct and less damaging to foreign relations than a dead body on the courtyard of the Kremlin.

The disaster ended Lockhart's involvement in espionage work. He went to Prague as Commercial Secretary of the British Legation but found the work unstimulating. It was hardly surprising considering his previous activities in the field of spying and counter-espionage.

Bruce Lockhart then turned his hand to writing. He produced twenty volumes of spy-centred fiction and autobiography, but none of them had the success of his initial effort, *Memoirs of a British Agent*, which became an instant best-seller. His books sold well enough, however, for him to make a living as a writer. He died in 1970.

The number of British spies who became writers when they retired from their initial employment is legion. Sometimes already well-published writers were drawn into the world of spying. Somerset Maugham, of course, was one, but a more unlikely writer-cum-spy was Arthur Ransome, the creator of the *Swallows and Amazons* series of children's novels.

Ransome went to Russia in 1913 to study the folklore of the country and to write about the subject. He was already a successful author who specialised in children's books and the fantasy world, and had a vague idea about incorporating Russian fables into a book.

When war was declared he became the foreign correspondent for *The Daily News*, a radical left-wing paper, and grew quite close to many of the Bolshevik leaders.

On the face of it he had something of an affinity for the Bolshevik point of view and at one stage was actually accused by Reginald Leeper from the Foreign Office of holding disloyal opinions. He was told that any articles he wrote in the future must be submitted for editing and, if necessary, vetoing.

Ransome was indignant. Unknown to Leeper he was working for SIS where he had been given the code or designation of S 76. Everything that he wrote about the Russian situation was produced with the direct aim of buttressing his relationship with and access to the Bolshevik leadership.

A perpetual champion of the underdog, one of Arthur Ransome's greatest triumphs as an agent was carrying secret armistice proposals from the Estonians who were then fighting for their independence from Russia.

The Baltic provinces of Latvia, Lithuania and Estonia had long maintained a deep affection for the Romanovs, more romantic than realistic, and their fight for freedom from the new Russia was ultimately doomed. Thousands died and the Estonians were forced to sue for peace, hence Ransome's dangerous journey.

Ransome's odyssey was on foot across several battlefields and was fraught with danger, filled with anxiety. He got through the lines, however, and delivered the verbal armistice request to Maxim Litvinov in Moscow. The terms were duly accepted.

By that time the civil war between the Bolshevik Reds and the Whites, the last supporters of the Czar, was raging. Trotsky's Red Army was more than holding its own against the American- and British-backed Whites, but the conflict, like all civil wars, was bloody and brutal.

The defeat of the Baltic provinces and victory in the civil war meant that by 1922 Russia had found a degree of breathing space. As a consequence Lenin and his government found time to look to the future. Despite the crippling illnesses and injuries that would soon kill him, Lenin managed to turn Bolshevik Russia into the Union of Soviet Socialist Republics (the USSR).

As Lenin envisaged it – and as Stalin later developed it – the USSR was to be a one-party state with a strong central government and economy. The aim was to protect the revolution and increase the standards of living for the people. That had been impossible to achieve when a civil war was raging but now that the uneasy peace had come Lenin knew that it was time to unite a totally disunited people.

The USSR, or Soviet Union as it soon became known, covered an enormous land mass – over 6,000 miles east to west, 4,500 north to south – and taking in areas like the previous Russian, Transcaucasian, Ukrainian and Belorussian republics. In all the USSR covered eleven time zones and five different climate zones.

******

After his success as a peace bringer Arthur Ransome retired as a spy and began to concentrate more fully on his career as a writer. The *Swallows and Amazon* series, which first appeared in 1930, became a huge success and is still read today by children and adults alike.

It is sometimes difficult to fit Arthur Ransome into the role of spy. Men like Rudyard Kipling and Somerset Maugham, fellow writers as they might be, seem to have been well fitted for the task. They, like their characters, were rugged and hard edged. They were men more than capable of suffering setbacks and pain.

But Arthur Ransome did not appear, at least at first glance, to have either the physical qualities or the emotional inclination to dabble in spying. That is probably stereotyping but it shows how wrong first opinions can be. The least likely agent or spy is invariably one of the best.

It is, therefore, interesting to wonder if the thousands of young people who avidly follow the adventures of the two competing bands of children on the lakes of Cumbria ever realise that the creator of John, Susan, Nancy and the others once had a career as a spy.

More than that, he was man who braved the bullets of a battlefield in an attempt to bring peace to a troubled land. You have to wonder if Ransome's children's books were actually an attempt to expunge the horrors he had witnessed in Russia. It is at least possible.

Arthur Ransome was not just an ordinary collector of facts and figures, a dabbler in the hidden arts, but a red-blooded warrior for freedom, someone who had put his life at risk for the sake of British intelligence. The answer to the hypothetical question of the previous paragraph is probably not – which, surely, is exactly how Arthur Ransome and the shadowy men of SIS would have wanted it.

Chapter Six

A Gathering Storm

'There's an east wind coming, such a wind as never blew on England yet. It will be cold and bitter, Watson, and a good many of us may wither before its blast.'
Arthur Conan Doyle *His Last Bow*

If the 1930s saw great changes in the organisations that ran the spies and agents of the world, it also saw yet more adjustments in the targets at which they were aimed.

Regardless of the rapid growth of Nazi Germany, the burgeoning 'Red Threat' of the Soviet Union never quite went away, and when the Second World War broke out there were many in the government and the espionage world who felt that Britain was fighting the wrong enemy. However, from 1933, with the Nazi Party firmly ensconced in power, it was inevitable that the eyes of the spy masters should, at the very least, sneak a glance or two at what Hitler was doing in Germany.

As the decade unravelled – 'This low dishonest decade,' as the poet WH Auden called it – and as Hitler began to claim back those parts of the country that had been taken away by the Treaty of Versailles, Germany began to receive more and more attention from Europe's spies. That was inevitable, but it did mean that the Soviet Union was left very much to its own devices. The results, as we shall see, were predictable.

The situation was made even more problematic because SIS was battling against itself for the majority of those ten years. It was an internal conflict that had to be won if Britain's spy agencies were to operate efficiently and effectively, but for a long while it seemed as if the uneven contest had already been decided.

The 1930s were perhaps the least productive of all decades for the SIS. There were many reasons for this failure. It was partly due to the ineptitude of staff and managers, but it was also partly down to underfunding and an inadequate number of staff allocated to the job. It resulted in a refusal by most government departments to accept what little information they were being given with the result that SIS found itself sidelined, almost without function or purpose.

The attitude of the Air Ministry, for example, was so anti-SIS that it almost automatically dismissed anything that the country's premier intelligence gathering agency managed to put its way. It was a strange attitude. The Air Ministry was the newest of all the government ministries and should, on the face of it, have been a little more open to new ideas. It was not to be.

Despite the bombing of Guernica and other tragedies of the Spanish Civil War nobody in the Air Ministry ever seriously thought that Germany would have the capabilities to build an aerial fleet able to cause great harm to Britain. The warnings of SIS were simply cast aside.

Part of the trouble was the residue of 'Empire-thinking'. At all costs keep out the left-wing intelligentsia and activists, that was the implicit message: we know how to run things, always have, and always will. It was a form of snobbery and elitism that haunted British politics in the 1930s. Not only that, it was also rife within SIS itself.

In a decade when the Labour Party was gathering strength and Communism was beginning to become a force in British politics, SIS restricted its recruitment almost exclusively to men and women of the old school. Elitism, prejudice, call it what you will, there was a distinct preference, both within and without SIS, to maintain the status quo by employing or using only men and women who knew the rules, who knew how to behave and knew their place in the world.

Such an attitude cut out many of the more able and intellectually gifted men and women of the age. The universities were full of erudite and interested left wingers, people who would challenge the old perceptions and values. They were rarely approached and recruitment continued to come mainly from upper-class elements of society who might well know how to behave at a cocktail party but had little awareness of information gathering. The recruits were pleasant enough but had little understanding of the espionage world, and as all managers realise, a below par staff group will only ever produce a below par performance.

GC & CS had long been the most efficient department of Sinclair's SIS. They had been successfully intercepting and deciphering Russian messages for some time, but in the 1920s the Soviet government changed its codes. Suddenly, despite their abilities, the decoders seemed powerless to unlock the new systems.

That was just the beginning of significant problems. With the codebreakers unable to hack into Russian messages SIS was desperate for intelligence from 'the other side'. When they were approached by a contact in Tallinn who claimed to have access to a large number of communications to and from Moscow, SIS leapt at the offer.

The man from Tallinn produced over 200 messages and SIS eagerly paid the asking price before gathering them in. Amongst these messages was what appeared to be evidence that the Soviet government was helping to fund the Sinn Fein Party in Ireland.

A similar Soviet project on the borders of India was also discovered in the batch of messages. From the early Victorian age any threat to India had always been treated seriously and now this joint threat to the empire resulted in strong diplomatic protests from Britain. It might well have been a toothless response but there was little more that the government could do.

The Soviet Union pleaded ignorance. In reality they barely had the funds to operate any form of secret service, let alone mount numerous covert operations. It meant that the Russians could not have been aiding Sinn Fein or helping disaffected groups on the Indian frontier and the protests did little more than sour relations between Britain and Russia for many years.

Just as British officials were beginning to think that they had managed to quash the Russian efforts in Ireland and on the Indian borders, a bombshell exploded in the midst of their Whitehall retreats. Much to the chagrin of SIS and the government, it was discovered that the messages and the information with which they had accused the Soviets were false. The SIS had been duped and sold a very distinct pup.

If SIS information had been questionable before, now the organisation was virtually shunned. No one, least of all government ministers who were still smarting from the embarrassment of having to eat humble pie in front of the Soviets, could retain even the faintest glimmerings of faith in any of its dealings. The inevitable result was that even when first-class and accurate information was passed to government it was either rejected or ignored.

There was distant light at the end of the tunnel, however. Following the disaster of the Tallinn affair a thorough investigation into the

SIS procedure for collecting information was immediately ordered and undertaken. Without being unduly critical, the report declared that SIS was, at best, somewhat naive in its collation, assessment and eventual distribution of its material.

As a result a grading system to ensure the viability of information received was implemented. To receive an A1 grade the information had to have come from a known and exceptionally viable source. Copies of documents were no longer good enough; the originals now had to be physically held by SIS officers.

More importantly, the grading concept finally put an end to actions taken solely on the word of people like Sidney Reilly. The Ace of Spies was only one of many agents who had promised that the collapse of the Soviet regime was an event just waiting to happen, provided it was given a quick push in the right direction. The failure of so many SIS schemes in the dark days since the Russian Revolution was proof positive of the fallacy and ineptitude of Reilly's opinions.

The idea of grading did not solve all the SIS problems at one sweep. There continued to be significant failures, like the inability of SIS to give advance warning about the Anschluss of 1938 or any hint about the discussions leading to the Russo-German pact of the following year. But it was a start of a long road back.

******

If there is one characteristic that can be used to sum up Soviet espionage work during the inter-war period it has to be patience. Kim Philby, their arch mole in British intelligence, was recruited as early as 1933 when he was still a young and idealistic communist supporter.

Philby had no connection with any of the British espionage agencies when he was recruited by Moscow. He spent thirty years building his persona – his cover – and was encouraged by his handlers to think only of his duty when he finally joined SIS. Living and breathing his cover was the essential part of his treachery. Benefits to the Soviet Union could and undoubtedly would come later.

Nazi Germany, on the other hand, had neither the time nor the inclination to sit back and wait for schemes to mature. In a self-centred, draconian regime where everyone from the lowest recruits to the men at the top of the tree was jostling for power and position it was essential to hit first and hit fast. Rivalry between people like Göring and Himmler was commonplace, a situation that was acknowledged and possibly even encouraged by Adolf Hitler.

There were so many espionage units or intelligence departments within Germany at this time that it is sometimes difficult to keep track. The army intelligence section, the *Abwehr*, was perhaps the most powerful of these and was certainly the best funded and equipped.

The early days of Hitler's time as Chancellor of Germany were dangerous and fuelled by violence. Ernst Rohm and his SA thugs still roamed the streets, dishing out their own particular brand of justice, and Hitler knew that if the Nazi Party was to remain in power there would have to be some sort of reckoning with the rowdier elements of the regime.

The SA had always been the strong arm of the Party, being comprised of the rabble-rousers and street corner thugs who had helped to bully Hitler into power. That was now immaterial to the Führer. The SA was the past, Hitler was concerned with the future.

The reckoning came in the summer of 1934 when Rohm and many SA leaders were executed in the brutal cull that soon became known as The Night of the Long Knives. But it was not just Rohm and the SA who were sacrificed. This mass killing was also an opportunity to take out those individuals – some records say as many as 1,000 men and women - who did not quite see the future in the same way as Hitler and the other party leaders.

One of the leading victims was the *Abwehr* chief, Ferdinand von Bredow. Admiral Wilhelm Canaris, a naval hero from the First World War, was appointed to replace him, taking up his post on 1 January 1935. Never a Nazi, Canaris trod a delicate path between support for Hitler and a barely concealed but innately human desire to do what was right. It was a path that the Admiral walked for nearly ten years before fate and the long arm of the Nazi leadership finally caught up with him.

When Reinhard Heydrich formed the SD (the *Sicherheitsdienst*) in 1931 it was with the direct intention of providing Heinrich Himmler, himself and the SS with an espionage agency and a loyal group of secret policemen. The SD was efficient, vicious and ruthless, operating as a direct rival to Admiral Canaris's *Abwehr*.

The most dangerous of their many attributes, however, was their ambition. Heydrich and his state-sanctioned killers wanted to take over all of the espionage work of the Third Reich. It was an attitude fully in keeping with Himmler's desire to create a state within a state.

The research department of the Reich Air Ministry was established solely to intercept and decode foreign messages. It was run by Herman Göring, head of the *Luftwaffe*, but it actually had little to do with flying or with the rapid growth of German air power. It was there to break codes and obtain information, both internally and across wider Europe, and the knowledge it unearthed made Göring one of the most powerful men in the Nazi party.

Even Joachim von Ribbentrop, the inept, effete and snobbish Reich Foreign Minister, had his own spy network. This was the *Informationsstelle III*, which was linked to German diplomatic missions and embassies in foreign countries. It regularly provided Ribbentrop with the delicious tit-bits and pieces of gossip that he and Hitler so relished.

Joseph Goebbels, the Reich propaganda minister, was not to be left out. He created a spy network that operated within the genuine and quite legal German Press Agency. Part news gathering, part clandestine spy organisation, the *Deutsche Nachrichtenburo* was one of the most successful Nazi espionage units of the inter-war years. It was an organisation that helped create for Goebbels the myth that he was the man who heard and knew everything.

Rudolph Hess, Hitler's long-standing friend and comrade from the early days of street brawls and beer hall gatherings, also created his own private espionage agency. It was an unofficial group that was tolerated by the party, and not only gave him news from abroad but also kept an active watch on his political rivals within the Reich.

The German espionage system might seem, at first glance, to have been an effective and efficient network of interlocking agencies. And yet, from the beginning, the very nature of the Nazi regime worked against it. As the Third Reich developed its power base the conflicting interests of each individual part soon began to clash with the others. It began with antagonism but soon developed into bitter hatred and rivalry: 'The German intelligence system had a fatal flaw – it was hydra-headed and each head was reluctant to abdicate its power because, as with all intelligence agencies, possession of intelligence titbits gave access to the leader.'[1]

It did not stop there. Individual efforts made by men and women not assigned to any of the German espionage agencies but determined to do their damndest for their country were also a significant factor. These 'extra-curricular' spies included men like Hermann Goertz, a former army intelligence officer, whose spying activities seem to have had just one significant aim – to push his own self-importance. Goertz could only survive by persuading the *Luftwaffe* that the information he provided was inherently valuable. Once that was agreed, according to his plan, Göring would appoint him to the position of intelligence officer within the new air force.

All his amateur efforts eventually got for him was arrest and a four-year jail sentence for espionage. He was lucky. A few years later with Britain and Germany at war he would undoubtedly have been shot.

Goertz, like so many other spies in the pay of the *Abwehr* at this time, was hardly the most efficient of agents. MI5 raided his bungalow at Broadstairs and found the place littered with incriminating evidence: maps of the South-East counties of England with RAF stations drawn onto them, a detailed letter of application to join the *Luftwaffe* and the full 1935 RAF list.

There were other spies, men like Donald Adams who sent his reports in longhand directly to a known *Abwehr* address in Germany. Adams was kept on a long leash, not because he might lead to the apprehending of more spies but because the information he was passing was little more than public knowledge and could have been gleaned from any national or local newspaper.

Adams and Goertz were typical of the amateur, second-rate agents at work in Britain during the inter-war years. Small wonder that Vernon Kell and the men of MI5 were able to pick up these German spies almost at will. And yet the *Abwehr* continued to send them to Britain.

The senior officers of the *Abwehr* felt that Wales was an area that was particularly ripe for plucking. It was an opinion largely based on the traditional antagonism between the Welsh and the English. No one could deny that dissent but what the *Abwehr* failed to notice was that apart from a few fanatical zealots, it tended to reside in the public houses of the Welsh valleys and on the terraces of Cardiff Arms Park and was reserved mainly for Saturday afternoons and evenings.

As the *Abwehr* saw it Plaid Cymru, the Welsh Nationalist Party, was growing in strength. That offered a groundswell of anti-English opinion, but beyond that there was a far more extreme group of nationalists, men who were driven by a virulent hatred of England, the empire and all it stood for. The men of the Abwehr insisted that Wales was an oppressed nation with an enormous propensity for rebellion and revolt against their overlords:

> In Berlin it was believed at that time that the more fanatical Welsh nationalists – not the Welsh Nationalist Party – might provide useful recruits for certain work in the event of war with England, and there was competition among different German groups for the Welshmen's services.[2]

A large number of German spies were therefore despatched to Wales in the years before war broke out. They were a varied and all-encompassing group.

To all intents and purposes Hans Heinrich Kuenemann was just the director of a German engineering firm in Cardiff but in reality he was also a spy for Reinhard Heydrich. He provided information on British industrial plants and fled his home in Marlborough Road in Cardiff just twenty-four hours before Britain and Germany went to war.

Other Welsh spies included Professor Friedrich Schoberth, a visiting lecturer at Cardiff University, and Franz Richter who, in 1933, took up a position as manager of an enamel factory in Barry. Both of them were warned of the approaching war and managed to leave the country before hostilities began. A nurse who operated out of Pembrokeshire – later found dead near Wantage in 1943 – and Dr Walter Reinhard, German consul in Liverpool, who concentrated his efforts on Welsh extremists in North Wales, were among the most notable of these agents.[3]

Perhaps the most famous, or infamous. of them all, however, was Arthur Owen or, as the *Abwehr* knew him, Johnny O'Brien. Born in the Swansea Valley of South Wales, he had spent several years in Canada and hated the English with a degree of vitriol that surprised even Nikolaos Riter who was Owen's handler for most of his time as a spy.

Arthur Owen actually began his spying career working for the Russians. He was on business in Kiel, centre of German shipbuilding, when he was approached by a Soviet agent. Despite his natural right-wing views he was soon reporting to his agent on the progress of German shipbuilding in Kiel and other ports. He saw no harm in passing on this information, which could have little impact on Britain, but even as he developed his espionage skills he knew that his real target was Germany.

Owen's motivation was simple – money. He sold his services to the *Abwehr*, just as he had sold them to the Soviets, for a handsome return. Provided with a radio transmitter, stored in the left luggage department of Victoria Station, Owen operated as the chief *Abwehr* agent in Britain up to and including the early days of the war. Operating under the codename Snow, he seemingly had no qualms about betraying his country, at least not to begin with.

There is a degree of confusion over what happened next. In some accounts Owen simply had second thoughts, and with war now raging spying for Germany was, at best, a perilous occupation. And so he turned himself in to MI5. He also handed over his secret codebooks and radio transmitter.

The other story is that he was eventually reported to MI5 by his wife. An inveterate philanderer, Arthur Owen had transgressed once too often. A woman scorned knows no boundaries and, if this version is correct, Mrs Owen took great pleasure in 'shopping' her errant husband.

Either way, with the war against Germany having barely begun he wound up in Wandsworth Prison. There MI5 managed to turn him – not a particularly difficult task, needing only the promise of money and a few dire threats – and Owen began a career as a double agent. He even broadcast messages to his German handler from his lonely cell in Wandsworth Prison, using his secret transmitter which had been returned to him.

By the end of 1940, now released from Wandsworth, Arthur Owen had become one of the initial contacts for German spies who had been parachuted into Britain. He waited for messages from Germany telling him who was about to arrive, where and when. He collected the spies from their drop zones, fed them, made them feel secure and safe, and then turned them in to the British. The *Abwehr* and other German spy agencies did not suspect foul play, putting the capture of their agents down to good policing by MI5.

Even so, Owen was never really trusted by either side. Like all double agents his motives were unclear and the nagging thought that he could be betraying both Britain and Germany was always there. Nevertheless, he was certainly well used by both sides in the conflict.

When he and another turncoat, a cashiered squadron Leader by the name of Walter Dicketts, somehow managed to get to Lisbon, both the British and the German secret services sat up and took notice. Travelling to a neutral country in wartime was never easy but Owen and Dicketts – the latter working under the name of Brown – smuggled themselves on board separate ships in a convoy and simply dropped off in Lisbon. The journey had not been pleasant and Owen, in particular, suffered badly from sea sickness.

In Lisbon the two agents met Owen's contact who appeared very interested in what Dicketts had to say and sell. As a former RAF technical advisor and officer he had vast reams of information that was of interest to the Germans. Owen, the *Abwehr* decided, had provided the man and was now best employed in his previous role of double agent.

Dicketts was duly sent on to Germany but Owen was returned to Britain. Arthur Owen was not best pleased – he had envisaged a new life in Berlin, away from the pressures of being a spy. He might even become a new Lord Haw-Haw, he thought, receiving all of the luxuries he had been given on his trips to Hamburg before the war. It was not to be. Back to Britain he was sent.

There MI5 was waiting, alarmed that despite his value as a double agent, this time he had played the game a little too close to the bone and had actually helped a rogue scientist to escape the country. He was arrested and spent the rest of the war in Dartmoor.[4]

After 1945 Arthur Owen led a varied life. He spent time in Ireland where he established contact with Sinn Fein and remained staunchly anti-British to the end. His daughter, Patricia, went to Hollywood and made a successful career in the film industry. Owen kept his distance from her but was sufficiently attracted to the movie industry to allow a big budget film to be made about his life. That film was 'Triple Cross' starring Christopher Plummer.

Arthur Owen died in 1957, successful and relatively wealthy. He had survived the war, playing one of the most dangerous games any man could imagine. That was considerably more than could be said about the German espionage agencies that operated the spies.

The greatest German success of the spy war came from Turkey where Cicero, real name Elyesa Bazna, was employed as the valet for Sir Hughe Knatchbull-Hugessen, the British ambassador in Ankara. Apparently he would, on a regular basis, open the ambassador's safe while his chief was asleep, photograph the documents and replace everything before Sir Hughe awoke. Cicero would then sell his photos to the German intelligence units.

A GATHERING STORM

Yet much of Cicero's material was suspect. The *Abwehr* and SD felt that it was all too perfect, too pat to be true, and refused to believe what they were reading unless the material was corroborated by third party sources.

Cicero knew it was time to run when, thanks to the codebreakers at Bletchley Park, MI5 intercepted messages from Ankara to Berlin quoting leaked information that could only have come from him. The enemy was beginning to get too close, Cicero felt, and promptly disappeared from view. He took to his heels with German-provided money – £200,000 to be exact – in his pocket.

Where the *Abwehr* did manage to score a significant degree of success was the USA. Long before Canaris took over, the industrial giants of Farben and Krupp had instructed their American representatives to be on the lookout for any military developments or changes in the country. Canaris merely extended this task, receiving much valuable information about oil production, aircraft engines and so on.

Admiral Canaris was helped by a huge degree of naivety from the Americans who were, at that stage, desperate to stand apart from the posturing and manoeuvring of European states but still wanting to make as much money as they possibly could out of the situation.

The *Abwehr*'s greatest moment of success came in 1938 when its agents managed to lay their hands on the plans for the new American Norden bombsight. This new aid to bombing was indeed revolutionary, but in the event the *Luftwaffe* simply did not have the time to install it in German bombers before war broke out. It would have been invaluable during the Battle of Britain but it was never produced in sufficient quantities. After 1940 Germany did not have the opportunity to launch another significant bombing campaign.

******

As early as 1936 it became apparent that many parts of SIS had been compromised and were leaking like a badly made sieve. Hugh Sinclair knew that if his organisation was to survive then something fairly drastic would have to be done.

His response to the crisis was to create two new departments, each to be a part of SIS but to work entirely independently. They were both distinctly 'hush-hush' – in theory at least – and were supposed to rebuild the reputation of their parent organisation.

The first was known as the Z Organisation and was run by Claude Dansey, a former soldier and a member of MI5. Dansey had since joined SIS but then had a falling out with his chief. After a few months, Sinclair could stand Dansey no longer, and keen to get him out of his hair, made him head of the Z Organisation, which operated out of Bush House on the Strand.

Dansey may not have been a charlatan but there is no doubt that he came perilously close. His hatred of the Americans was renowned, and when the USA finally entered the fray, his attitude hindered any significant cooperation between the two nations. There was no reasoning with Dansey when it came to the 'American cousins'.

His agents operated under the cover of journalistic or commercial enterprise, something in peacetime that gave them free licence to roam across Europe. However, over half of the agents he claimed to be running were actually figments of his imagination and those that were genuine, like the infamous Captain Sigismund Best, were just no good.

As for the Z Organisation being a secret arm of SIS, the men and women who turned up for work at the office each day were indistinguishable from other employees of the main organisation. The rolled umbrella, the pinstriped suits of the men and the pearls and twin sets of the women, declared to everyone that these were employees of the government.

The second new organisation set up by Hugh Sinclair was Section D, which was established in 1938. It was run by Colonel Laurence Grand and had a very particular and important function. Its purpose was quite simple: '[It was] to plan, prepare and when necessary carry out sabotage and other clandestine operations, as opposed to the gathering of intelligence.'[5]

Grand was industrious in his planning. Schemes were laid out for the destruction of German telephone communications and their electricity industry. There were also plans to ruin German agriculture, food supplies and railways. At the same time Colonel Grand mapped out means and methods to protect Britain's own power stations and communication networks from any type of German attack.

Possibly the most significant development in the final years of peace came in July 1938 with the purchase of Bletchley Park in Buckinghamshire. When he was told that there was no money for such an acquisition, Sinclair, following in the tradition of Cumming and Kell, simply produced his chequebook and wrote out a personal cheque for the purchase price of £6000.

During the Munich Crisis Sinclair moved both SIS and GC & CS to Bletchley. The SIS soon returned to London but the decoders stayed on in their country house. Section D also established its base at Bletchley Park, where there was enough space to develop their stock-in-trade weapons such as incendiary devices and plastic explosives.

One of the successes of SIS intelligence work at this time was the production of a massive dossier on the personality and character of Adolf Hitler. It was meticulous research, highlighting the German dictator's tenacity, but contrasting it with a clear steak of madness and fanaticism. Sadly, the SIS dossier did not fit in with the theme of appeasement which then dominated government thinking and the report was duly filed.

During the final years of the 1930s Hugh Sinclair was seriously ill with cancer. He underwent a painful operation in a vain attempt to save his life but died on 4 November 1939.

Sinclair had inherited an under-functioning organisation that had been battling for years to achieve adequate funding and support. Unfortunately for him, it was a time of appeasement, when the idea of peace at all costs governed most government thinking. Intelligence funding and development were far from the minds of most politicians.

Sinclair had toiled long and hard to bring SIS back to an acceptable standard and the efforts he made undoubtedly had a detrimental effect on his health. He, like Mansfield Cumming, was unflinching in his support for SIS, digging deep into his own pockets on several occasions.

Sinclair was succeeded by his deputy, Colonel Stewart Menzies. When he took up his post the war had barely begun and he had only 42 officers and 55 secretaries with which to challenge the might of Nazi Germany. It was not just Germany as Soviet Russia, although claiming neutrality was now effectively an enemy, thanks to the Ribbentrop-Molotov Pact that had unexpectedly brought Germany and Russia together.

The war saw a dramatic expansion in the empire of Stewart Menzies. By the summer of 1944, when the Allied invasion forces went ashore on the Normandy beaches, over 830 agents, officers and secretaries were working for SIS. It was a work force that Hugh Sinclair would never have dreamed possible.

******

The USSR had spent the final years of peace embroiled in the last of Stalin's purges. It was a self-destructive period in Soviet history but it was still a time when the secret police and the espionage agencies established firm roots in the political running of the country. Perhaps more importantly, this was the decade when the Soviets first began to stretch out their hands and gather in the disaffected youth of the world.

MI5 and SIS may not have been willing to enlist the help of the left-wing students at Oxford, Cambridge and other great universities, but the NKVD and later the KGB certainly were. They did so with aplomb and a skill that was remarkable.

The group that later became known as The Cambridge Five – the Magnificent Five as the KGB called them – were all recruited in the 1930s, either while they were studying at Cambridge University or just after. They were all dedicated left-wing supporters, but none of them, in these early stages of their spying lives, were actively involved in politics. When they became NKVD/KGB moles they were told, clearly and definitively, no politics for you; lie low and bury yourselves in the system, we will call you when we need you.

The Cambridge spies were a fascinating bunch of individuals, each with their own strengths and weaknesses. Only Harold 'Kim' Philby was an actual member of SIS but the others were all well placed in the diplomatic service. One of them, Anthony Blunt, was even Surveyor of the King's Pictures while at the same time working for MI5.

Donald MacLean began passing information to the Soviet Union in 1934, while Guy Burgess was operational from 1936. Kim Philby, who was actually recruited earlier, in 1933, was kept under wraps for some time. The other two, Anthony Blunt and John Cairncross, became active soviet spies in the final few years before war.

Philby's first operation for the Soviets came in 1937 when he was ordered to travel out to Spain under the cover of his role as a journalist. His real purpose was to assess and report back on the capabilities of the fascists involved in the Spanish Civil War: Nazi Germany, Mussolini's Italy and Franco's Falange. When he ran out of money the Soviets simply sent him more.

Kim Philby had been writing as a freelance reporter but on his return from Spain he managed to secure a job on *The Times*. The paper had long been a traditional recruiting agency for SIS and Philby was no exception. He was duly enrolled, given the standard basic training, and, as the NKVD had instructed, began to play his role as a British intelligence agent.

However, as a fully ordained member of the British espionage organisation he also began his real career – spying for Russia. Philby, like the rest of the Cambridge Five, firmly believed that the Marxist-Leninist model of communism, as shown in Soviet Russia, was immeasurably preferable and superior to any other form of government. It was, in particular, markedly better than the insipid, lukewarm democratic beliefs of Britain and the USA.

From the 1930s until well into the 1950s the Cambridge Five passed on thousands, possibly even hundreds of thousands, of secret messages and papers to the Russians. Kim Philby alone gave his Soviet handlers over 900 documents. In fact the KGB, which became the premier Soviet intelligence agency from 1954 onwards, was receiving such an enormous quantity of top-class information that at one stage they even suspected a double cross.

Planting moles – agents who buried deep into Western culture and government agencies – was only one aspect of the NKVD and KGB's work. They also trained and sent out spies of their own. Perhaps the most successful of these was their 'super spy' Richard Sorge.

Sorge was born in Germany and even fought for the Kaiser during the First World War. Seriously wounded, he spent a considerable time in hospital and there began reading and studying the work and ideology of Karl Marx. He embraced communism, went to live in Russia and eventually became an agent for Soviet intelligence.

Studying came easily to Richard Sorge. He soon gained a doctorate in political sciences and seemed to be heading for a career in writing. It was a useful cover. Posing as a journalist, Sorge served in Germany, where he infiltrated and joined the Nazi party, but he spent periods in China and in the UK. His most lasting work, however, came in the early 1930s during his time in Japan.

Between 1933 and 1934 Sorge created a hugely efficient network of agents and informants that totally exposed Japanese plans for the future. Significant amongst his agents was Ozaki Hotsumi, a member of the ruling elite of Japan who had become a Marxist and a great opponent of militarism of all sorts. Sorge's greatest coup came in 1941 when he discovered and relayed to Moscow news of the German intention to attack Russia in June.

A few weeks later he followed up that information with the reassuring message that Japan had no intention of attacking the Soviet Union in 1941. Rather than direct an attack northwards to Moscow, as Hitler had hoped, the Japanese would concentrate their efforts by driving south to the Philippines and into British-held territory in the Far East.

The news allowed Stalin to move eighteen divisions and thousands of tanks and aircraft from the east and use them in the defence of Moscow. Those extra resources were crucial in the battle for the Russian capital and for the survival of Stalin's regime.

Later reports that the Soviet codebreakers had already discovered the Japanese intentions may or may not have been true. Even if it was correct, the story did not damage Sorge's reputation in any way. If nothing else his reports were confirmation of the Japanese war plans.

Richard Sorge was undoubtedly dedicated to his job. He once had to give up alcohol – being a very heavy drinker – in case his tongue should be loosened during one of his regular drunken binges. As he later declared: 'That was the bravest thing I ever did. Never will I be able to drink enough to make up for that time.'[6]

He knew, like all spies working under deep cover, that his time was limited. And yet he stuck to his task. By the summer of 1941 the Japanese were already closing in on his network, and just one month after delivering the news of Japan's decision not to invade Russia, on 14 October 1941, Sorge was arrested.

Sorge was taken to the Sugamo Prison where he was interrogated and tortured. The Japanese believed him to be an *Abwehr* agent, but eventually he admitted to being a spy for the Soviet Union. The Japanese tried on three separate occasions to exchange him for some of their own agents, but Soviet Russia, in the tradition of all spy-runners, declined to cooperate.

Richard Sorge was eventually hanged at 10.20am on the morning of 7 November 1944. It apparently took him twenty minutes to die. Many believe him to have been the finest spy and agent of all time, but like all tributes it eventually comes down to personal views and preferences.

One thing is certain – Richard Sorge was one of the few men to hold bravery awards from two warring countries, perhaps not at the same time but certainly within striking distance of each other. He had been awarded Germany's Iron Cross during the First World War and in 1964, after many years of denial, Russia finally declared him a Hero of the Soviet Union. Not a bad tribute to a man who, far more than Sidney Reilly, surely deserves the epigram and accolade Ace of Spies.

******

Sorge was one of several spies operating in Japanese colours, albeit hidden, in the years leading up to America's entry into the Second World War. At least two of them were British.

Frederick Rutland – 'Rutland of Jutland' as he was known in the Royal Navy – was a hero of that great battle between Britain and Germany in the summer of 1916. He flew the float plane that first located the German battlecruiser fleet for Admiral Beatty and then rescued a drowning sailor who fell into the water as he was being evacuated from the cruiser *Warrior*. For his bravery Rutland was awarded the DSC.

After the war Rutland, totally disenchanted with a lack of promotion prospects and the way he saw the Royal Navy being run, resigned his commission. He received an offer to go to Japan to advise the Imperial Japanese Navy, particularly with regard to the use of aircraft on seagoing vessels.

Japan had been Britain's ally in the war and no one sensed any type of problem, at least to begin with. The Japanese military machine, however, had designs on control of the Pacific, and while they may have assisted Britain in the first great war of the twentieth century they had no intention of repeating that service in the second.

Rutland remained in Japan until 1932 when he moved, along with his family, to Santa Monica in the USA. There he opened his own company, the Japan Aircraft Company as it was called, ostensibly building aeroplanes but in reality providing Japanese naval officers with exactly the sort of cover they needed to analyse American preparedness for war. According to some sources, the Japanese paid for Rutland's move and financed the setting up of his new business.

The FBI had already opened a dossier on Rutland, however. He was carefully watched, and in June 1941 Hoover's men arrested one of his agents, a naval officer who was trying to gain information about the US Pacific Fleet. The link with Rutland was quickly and easily made.

As a decorated war hero it would have been too embarrassing to see Frederick Rutland arrested and charged with espionage and so, in

October 1941, just a few weeks before the Pearl Harbour attack, he was sent back to Britain, leaving his business and his family behind him in America.

Once back in the UK Rutland thought he was safe. However, almost before he had settled into life in the old country war was declared on Japan. Rutland was interned as a collaborator and imprisoned on the Isle of Man under the Defence of the Realm Regulations.

Along with most of the internees, Rutland was released and sent home from the Isle of Man in 1943. He was free now to pick up the strings of his previous life, but made no attempt to rejoin his wife and children whom he had left stranded in the USA. He grew steadily more depressed and committed suicide by gassing himself in January 1949.

The other British traitor/spy was William Francis Forbes-Sempill, the 19th Lord Sempill. A pioneer in flying in general and naval aviation in particular, he began passing secrets to the Japanese in the 1920s. His motives were never clear.

He was uncovered as an agent but for some reason was allowed to retain his commission in the navy, possibly because Japan had been an ally in the war and the main and obvious target in the 1930s was Nazi Germany.

Sempill continued to pass on official secrets to the Japanese throughout his naval career. When, just a few weeks before the Pearl Harbour attack, his perfidy was once again exposed, Lord Sempill was finally forced to resign his commission – something that should have happened many years before.

Takeo Yoshikawa was Japan's top agent in Hawaii at the time of the Pearl Harbour attack. A former naval flyer, he was then serving as a diplomat under the cover name of Tadashi Morimura, living in an apartment overlooking the US fleet anchorage and sending regular reports back to Tokyo.

Takeo had continued to fly and during his time in Hawaii regularly piloted his small seaplane over American naval installations. He even went diving in the harbour where the US ships were moored, using a hollow reed as a breathing tube.

He was a hugely successful agent. Adolf Hitler once sent Takeo a personal letter of thanks after information he provided allowed German U-boats to sink a large portion of a British convoy *en route* from South Africa.

His greatest coup, however, was providing the Japanese Navy with a detailed map of the US anchorage in Pearl Harbour, dividing it up into five zones or segments. It was the most accurate plan of the harbour ever received and Admiral Yamamoto used these segments as the basis for his 7 December attack.

Although picked up by the FBI on the day of Yamamoto's attack, Takeo had already destroyed all incriminating documents and there was simply no evidence against him. He was sent back to Japan under a diplomat prisoner exchange in August 1942. His adventures, however, were far from finished.

Afraid that they had finally realised the truth of his activities on Hawaii, Takeo had to disguise himself as a Buddhist monk when American forces occupied Japan. It was an unfounded fear. The war was over and the American government had considerably more to think about than one out-of-date spy. After a short period Takeo dropped his disguise and came out of hiding.

He was later to experience considerable hostility from the Japanese people, however. They apparently blamed him for starting the war and for the horror of the two atom bombs. It was a level of hatred Takeo Yoshikawa, patriot to the end, never understood.

Chapter Seven

War!

'No leader wants to go down in history as the ass who destroyed his country in an afternoon.'

John Le Carre

The Second World War began on 1 September 1939. Given the problems they had been battling against in the 1930s it was perhaps inevitable that at the beginning things did not go at all well for the British espionage agencies.

On 9 November 1939 two British agents from SIS, Captain Sigismund Best and Major Richard Stevens, were taken prisoner at gunpoint in Venlo in Holland. The tiny village sat only a dozen yards away from the German border.

The two British agents were not there by accident, so dangerously close to German territory. They had been informed about an underground German opposition group that was willing to work with them to overthrow Hitler and the Nazis.

There was nothing unusual in that. It was a theory that obsessed many SIS and Foreign Office representatives in the early war years. A meeting with the supposed general in charge of the opposition group was arranged to take place in a small café in Venlo.

But SIS had yet again fallen into a trap. Franz Fischer, the man who had set up the meeting, was a Gestapo double agent who was working for both Germany and Britain. The eagerness of SIS to play a dynamic and influential part in the conflict had turned the heads of the two officers and checks on Fischer were at best cursory, and in reality non-existent.

Captain Best and Major Stevens were accompanied on their trip to Venlo by Lieutenant Dirk Klop, a Dutch intelligence officer who was armed and suspicious. He was correct in his judgement. Almost as soon as the SIS men arrived at the rendezvous a German car, full of black-coated machine gun-toting guards, smashed through the border barriers and hurtled towards them.

Drawing his pistol Klop immediately charged at the Germans but was shot down before he had gone a dozen yards. He later died from his wounds. The wounded Klop and the two British officers were bundled into the Gestapo car and driven quickly back across the border. The captives were taken to Düsseldorf where they were interrogated. For the Gestapo it was a triumph; for Britain and the men of SIS an unmitigated disaster.

To make matters even worse Best and Stevens later admitted giving information to the Gestapo. They survived the war, being eventually found lying low in a small village in the German Tyrol. SIS and the British government, in a moment of clemency, decided not to prosecute as the publicity and embarrassment would have been too great. And, of course, the information given to the Gestapo had been procured under torture.

As if that failure wasn't enough, the death of Hugh Sinclair was another huge blow for SIS, coming as it did within a few months of war breaking out. He had been in charge for nearly sixteen years, since the demise of Mansfield Smith-Cumming, and had led SIS through some of its most difficult moments. Given the economic conditions of the time, he had done the best that he was able.

Vernon Kell of MI5 did not last much longer. He had been due to retire in 1938 but with war looming he had been asked to stay on and provide a degree of continuity within the organisation. Kell was happy to agree.

By June 1940, however, Vernon Kell had clearly passed his sell by date. He had served for over thirty years at the head of MI5, most of that time without either the resources or the personnel to do the job properly, and now he was clearly struggling.

Winston Churchill, the new prime minister, was never afraid of making a tough decision and on 10 June he sacked Kell from his position as head of the organisation. Day-to-day running of MI5 was eventually taken up by Sir David Petrie while political control passed to Lord Swinton, formerly the air minister. Swinton began an immediate reformation of MI5 and appeared to be considering a similar reorganisation with SIS.

Swinton had clearly upset Churchill, however, and he was quickly moved on to become resident minister in West Africa, a position where he could do little or no damage to the prime minister's plans and ideas. Overall political control of Britain's espionage agencies went to Duff Cooper but the espionage agencies were low down on his agenda and he showed no inclination to do anything that might help to reform SIS.

The British and French disasters in the first year of war were significant. Both nations had shown an inability to stop the German assault on Poland or to prevent the fall of Norway. The rapid German advance through France and the Low Countries took everyone by surprise. As far as SIS was concerned it literally wiped out their networks in Europe.

While hardly welcome news, this was probably not the great blow that it appeared to be at the time. The writer and historian Hugh Trevor Roper, himself an SIS operative, later claimed that if SIS had somehow managed to retain contact with its sources in Europe it would have been doing little more than gathering information from some very dubious individuals.

The SIS leaders, being of what Trevor Roper called 'remarkable stupidity,' would have accepted this information as hard fact and passed it on to the relevant government departments. It would have led to disastrous consequences for Britain and the war effort.[1]

******

As far as the German secret services were concerned the opening salvos of the conflict were something of a technical masterpiece, so much so that the SD, the *Abwehr* and the SS can be rightly judged to have fired the shots that began the Second World War.

The Polish Corridor, that wide strip of land between the western part of Germany and the east, had been created by the Treaty of Versailles in 1919. The Corridor, along with the city of Danzig, was taken from Germany without discussion or agreement, and apart from the punitive nature of the decision, was intended to give Poland access to the sea. More significantly, it cut Germany into two and was a major cause of bitterness and dissent in the German people. When trouble came it would, almost inevitably, involve the Polish Corridor.

The ploy to reclaim the Corridor and ultimately wipe Poland from the map was codenamed Operation Himmler. However, what went on was soon to acquire the name by which it has always been known, the Gleiwitz Incident. It was a bold plan and from the beginning everything went like clockwork. With hindsight it is easy to look back and decide that the SD and *Abwehr* deceptions should have fooled no one, but at the time the scheme, carefully plotted and planned by Reinhard Heydrich, took in virtually everyone.

Heydrich, the evil genius behind many of the early depredations of the Third Reich, and Heinrich Muller, the shadowy operational head of the Gestapo, had organised it down to the last detail. They plotted and schemed, drew up the orders, but the actual running or playing out of the incident was down to the *Abwehr*.

On 31 August 1939, seemingly without due cause, Polish soldiers suddenly attacked a German radio station alongside the Polish Corridor and killed a large number of the defenders. Except that they didn't.

Franciszek Honiok, a local farmer and activist known to be sympathetic to the Poles, had been chosen by Heydrich to be the 'fall guy' in the operation. On the evening of 30 August Honiok was arrested, drugged and taken to the Gleiwitz Radio Station. There he was shot in the head and killed, thus becoming the first unwitting casualty of the war.

Along with a small group of prisoners from Dachau Concentration Camp, Honiok was then dressed in a Polish army uniform. The bodies of Honiok and the concentration camp prisoners were dropped casually onto the steps of the radio station. To all intents and purposes they were Polish soldiers who had been shot down during an attempt to storm the German base.

A few of the dead prisoners were dressed in German uniforms and their bodies scattered around the perimeter of the station: gallant martyrs defending the Nazi cause as propaganda minister Joseph Goebbels later called them. Major Alfred Naujocks, who was in command of the killing unit at Gleiwitz, was to describe Honiok and the concentration camp victims in a rather more prosaic but perhaps more accurate phrase as 'canned goods'.

A gun battle between the German forces and the Poles was then rigged. To anyone who did not know the Nazi propensity for trickery it seemed as if the whole incident was deliberate provocation by the Polish armed forces.

Nobody stopped to question why the Polish army should suddenly act in this fashion, launching an assault that was bound to create a reaction in Germany. Even so, this fabrication was the excuse that Hitler needed and he immediately ordered his forces to attack Poland. Within days the German tanks were rolling across the Polish border and the Second World War had begun.

With Poland quickly conquered, the so-called Phoney War settled across Europe. It lasted for a number of months, but while the armies of both sides sat and twiddled their thumbs the German espionage agencies were hard at work. It resulted in a highly effective and efficient network of spies so that when hostilities did finally commence the Germans clearly had a head start on the Allies.

The British spy networks in Holland were compromised during the early stages of the war. The *Abwehr* controller in Holland, Major Herman Giskes, was so effective in his work that many agents were caught almost as soon as they parachuted into Europe. Once in captivity the agents were interrogated and the vast majority yielded to torture. Whether they talked or did not was something that barely mattered to the Germans, the SS and SD in particular: 'The broad truth about spies of all nationalities who fell into enemy hands was that they were kept alive as long as they could serve a purpose, and shot when their usefulness expired.'[2]

Giskes' success began with just one agent who was captured and, under torture, forced to broadcast to Britain. The fact that the agent deliberately omitted the pre-arranged security check from this initial broadcast should have alerted the British. It did not and the ineptitude of SIS operators contributed greatly, if not wholly, to the disaster of what was to follow.

The effectiveness of Herman Gilkes's counterintelligence work resulted in him operating no fewer than fourteen captured radio sets over the next two years (some accounts say he was using as many as seventeen sets). The British refused to believe their networks had been compromised and continued to send spies and agents into what was, literally, a killing field.

By continuing to believe that the messages coming out of Holland were genuine, SIS condemned to death nearly one hundred men and women from British secret service agencies. Not only that, copious amounts of equipment intended for the Dutch and French Resistance were parachuted or flown directly into German hands. Small wonder that one outside observer later remarked of senior officers in the British secret services that they could only be described as nutcases.

WAR!

Employing British radio sets was only one aspect of German trickery. Despite the nation being fed on a diet of books and movies about brave and honourable British soldiers fighting to their last breath, instances of British traitors were not as rare as might be imagined.

One of these traitors was a man calling himself Captain Harold Cole. He claimed to have been left behind after the Dunkirk evacuation with the aim of going underground and working to set up French resistance networks. Instead of assisting the resistance workers Cole became friendly with, and useful to, the German occupation forces. As a 'friend' he was allowed considerable freedom of movement around Occupied Europe.

Cole had never been asked to work undercover. He was not actually a commissioned officer at all; he was Sergeant Harold Cole, who had deserted from his unit before the fall of France, complete with the Mess funds, and been adrift ever since. He made such a nuisance of himself, providing nothing in return for his freedom, that the *Abwehr* eventually ordered he should be shot on sight. Despite this death sentence, Cole managed to survive. He was arrested by Vichy France police and sentenced to a long term of imprisonment.

The *Abwehr* had been 'running' Cole as an agent, a particularly ineffective agent it must be noted, for some time, but like so many spies, once the end of the war was in sight it was clear that he had outlived his usefulness. He was killed in 1945 in a shoot-out with police. MI9, the escapers' branch of the War Office, reckoned that Cole was responsible for the deaths of over fifty British escapees and their French helpers.

Harold Cole was just one of several traitors. Men like ex-army officer Norman Baillie-Stewart and William Joyce, Lord Haw-Haw as he was known, were considerably more active than Sergeant Cole, regularly broadcasting to Britain in a misguided attempt to destroy morale.

Unluckily for William Joyce and for Germany the ludicrous nature of his broadcasts was so bizarre and unbelievable that they quickly became a source of entertainment rather than German propaganda. Inevitably preceded by his plummy introduction – 'Jairmany calling, Jairmany calling' – Joyce's broadcasts were a source of irritation for the government and people were actually forbidden to listen to him. But listen they did: 'Many did find him humorous, although others regarded him as omniscient, as when he was alleged to have stated that Darlington Town Hall clock was two minutes slow – it was.'[3]

Perhaps understandably, the activities of the traitors were, at the time, played down but no matter how ineffective British intelligence was in these early days of the war, it was clear that the Germans were better – better prepared, better equipped and, frankly, better at their job.

******

It was perhaps inevitable that the early success of the *Abwehr* and the other German spy organisations was destined not to last. They began the war in a commanding position but yard by yard SIS and MI5 managed to catch and eventually overhaul them. The success of MI5, a hare and the tortoise situation if ever there was one, was something that was particularly galling for the German spy organisations.

Despite his rather inept final years, the departure of Vernon Kell left MI5 in something of a crisis. His immediate successor, a brigadier by the name of Jasper Harper, was so inefficient that he was downgraded to serve as deputy to the new controller, Sir David Petrie. It took time and effort but by the end of 1942 Petrie had totally turned around the fortunes of MI5.

The Double Cross System was probably the highlight of MI5's war. Feeding disinformation to the *Abwehr* through agents who, realising that betrayal of Germany was infinitely preferable to the firing squad, was not a uniquely British skill. But MI5 got it down to a fine art.

The turning of German agents began slowly and tentatively enough with just one candidate, Arthur Owens, the Welsh engineer. However, by the end of 1945 nearly 120 German agents had been turned and used very effectively indeed against their handlers.

The day to day operation was overseen by a small group of officers led by J. C. Masterman. The group was known as the Twenty Committee, so called because the Roman numerals XX represented a double cross. It was an ingenious piece of nomenclature or labelling that was rivalled only by the intricacies of the operation itself. Masterman ran a tight ship, aided by the codebreakers at Bletchley Park. He was later to accurately claim: 'We actively ran and controlled the German espionage system in this country.'[4]

He was probably right. The effectiveness of the Twenty Committee meant that by 1942-43 there were very few, if any, German agents operating independently in Britain. The *Abwehr* had been totally stymied and Admiral Canaris, already suspected of lukewarm feelings about the Nazi Party, found himself under increasing pressure from the SD and the Gestapo. He was eventually incriminated in the 1944 Plot against Hitler, dismissed and sent to a concentration camp where he was executed a few weeks before the end of the war.

MI5 also targeted groups of individuals in Britain who might, in the event of a German invasion, be inclined to help the Nazi Party. This fifth column operation was overseen by Victor Rothschild and involved MI5 officer Eric Roberts masquerading as a Gestapo agent in London.

Roberts encouraged Nazi sympathisers, many of whom were former members of the British Fascist Party, to join him and then 'turned them in'. It was a controversial operation, regarded by some as entrapment. So it was, but this was wartime and there was little time for niceties. Eventually over 500 Nazi sympathisers were identified and locked away for the duration. Not all of them were prosecuted but they were all listed on MI5's index of potential traitors.

MI5 also ran the London Reception Centre where all foreigners looking for asylum or a welcome in Britain were sent. There they were examined and questioned and a decision made about their future: should they be released to start a new life in Britain or should they be locked away in Camp 020, Latchmere House, for further interrogation.

David Petrie and his men fought a useful and varied war. They had to change base several times, once even transferring to Wormwood Scrubs prison – a German bombing raid soon ended that particular enterprise – before finishing up at Blenheim Palace near Oxford. Wherever they were based, one thing was clear: between 1942 and 1946 MI5 contributed greatly to the safety and security of the nation.

******

By the spring and summer of 1940 Stewart Menzies was beginning to understand the intricacies of his role as head of SIS. Not only that, he was beginning to see exactly what sort of poisoned chalice he had inherited.

Hardly the most popular of choices for the post and not really a 'secret service man' at all, Menzies did at least have the crucial ability to wheel and deal with the Whitehall warriors, leaving the day-to-day running of his agency in the hands of his deputies. In the months following the fall of France, Stewart Menzies would need all of his skills to keep SIS alive.

Since 1936 the newly created Joint Intelligence Committee, in addition to overseeing and coordinating the activities of the three main British intelligence agencies – SIS, MI5 and the Foreign Office - had been assessing the roles and results of the organisations. None of them had performed particularly well but SIS in particular appeared to be lacking in purpose and direction.

The JIC burrowed deeper and deeper as war approached and things did not change much after September 1939. Faced by this intensive and intrusive style of management from above, Stewart Menzies quickly found that there was little loyalty or love lost between the three agencies. They were all spending more time looking over their shoulders than they were dealing with the job in hand.

As a consequence he found that SIS was virtually always under attack from MI5 and the Foreign Office. It was cleverly done by the two rival agencies. After all, there was no better way of deflecting criticism of their own performance than to push blame and criticism onto the weakest member of the group.

As the war progressed and the significantly improved performance of MI5 under Sir David Petrie became common knowledge within the espionage world, Menzies might have been excused for thinking of packing it all in. The MI5 successes served only to highlight the poor record of SIS and resentment grew.

Menzies tried to stop the deteriorating relationship between the two agencies by appointing an SIS liaison officer to work within MI5. It was not well received. Most people interpreted the post simply as a way of establishing a mole within a friendly, or perhaps not so friendly, camp.

The continued poor performance of SIS did little to help Menzies fight his corner, and for a long while his powder seemed inordinately damp. Like the commanders of the British Expeditionary Force, SIS had been caught out by the rapid German attack through France. That resulted in staff having to drop everything and flee to London.

There had not been enough time to set up networks that would continue to operate in the conquered countries with the result that for some time defence forces in Britain had little or no knowledge of what was going on in Europe. With a potential German invasion expected any moment, that vacuum was like a yawning chasm, one that threatened to grow deeper and wider every day.

Even in the neutral countries things were not easy. The Portuguese capital, Lisbon, soon became a centre for spies but there were as many Axis agents as there were Allied ones and the material that was gathered was often common knowledge between both sides.

In Spain the British Ambassador, Samuel Hoare, had been an arch appeaser in the 1930s and even now he remained a man who would do nothing to upset General Franco. As a consequence, he opposed almost every plan the Spanish section of SIS ever came up with, even blocking a scheme to debrief escaped Allied prisoners of war who had made it to Spain.

Menzies knew the importance of the information these men carried, and reluctantly agreed with MI9 to move the debriefing operation to Portugal. It was a farcical situation, one that would have been laughable had it not been so downright tragic. What it all meant was that almost from the beginning of the war SIS officers in Franco's fascist state found themselves emasculated and utterly helpless.

It has to be admitted that on many occasions SIS did not exactly help itself. Its officers had a marked tendency, like those in power at Whitehall, to ignore what good sense and even the most basic understanding of the espionage systems should have told them were little nuggets of gold.

The Alliance organisation in France, for example, passed them news of the departure of the battlecruisers *Scharnhorst* and *Gneisenau* from Brest in 1942. SIS ignored the warnings with the result that the race of the two capital warships up the Channel was one of the greatest German naval successes of the war.

The so-called Oslo Report, a small package that contained incredible details about German technical advances, was another piece of information that got itself lost in SIS files, mainly because operatives believed it was a Gestapo trick, part of a double cross deception. There were several other missed opportunities, bungled chances that could and should have been taken. Fear of being made to look like fools – again – was ever present in the SIS ranks.

Lack of success meant that for a while there was a distinct possibility SIS would be disbanded and that its functions would be split between the army, navy and RAF. In the end it was the success of the codebreakers of GC & CS rather than any daring escapade or mission that saved Menzies' bacon. Even in the early days of the war, these unsung heroes were beavering away in their remote Buckinghamshire hideout, unacknowledged and virtually unknown by almost anyone outside SIS and MI5. Their day would come.

******

The success of the codebreakers lay in the future. In 1940 Menzies had another problem on his hands, one that had been created by Prime Minister Winston Churchill. In July that year the Special Operations Executive (SOE), at the PM's behest, was created. SOE was Churchill's way of continuing the war after the Allied armies had been run out of France and had one purpose – 'to set Europe ablaze,' as the prime minister so dramatically described it.

SOE was the very antithesis of everything the secret services of Britain had been trying to achieve for years. SIS and MI5 needed quiet and secrecy to achieve their ends; SOE depended on making as much noise and causing as much chaos as possible to unhinge and frighten the enemy. They employed hit-and-run tactics, destroying oil tanks, sinking enemy shipping and through their sabotage escapades making a thorough nuisance of themselves.

The SOE operatives were buccaneers, guerrilla fighters, men who had found little satisfaction in the regular military services. SOE welcomed them with open arms. Stewart Menzies, on the other hand, was far less accepting. He vented his spleen to his former comrade Bruce Lockhart, by then a retired agent, a full-time writer and Director of the Political Warfare Executive: '"Could nothing be done about this show, which was bogus through and through,"' C demanded. They never achieved anything, they compromised all his agents, and they were amateurs in political matters.'[5]

Despite Menzies' expressed desire to see SOE wound up, the organisation continued to exist and operate for most of the war. SOE operatives were particularly active in the hills of Yugoslavia and in rural France, aiding the resistance groups and doing just as Churchill wanted, causing confusion and panic in German ranks.

At home, however, there was little love lost between the two organisations. Things were not made any easier when, on Churchill's orders, SIS's Section D, the department that was meant to specialise in sabotage and damage, was amalgamated with SOE. It was done without consultation and was a loss of face for Stewart Menzies, a slight he bitterly resented.

Whatever feelings they may have had about each other, the men of SIS and SOE still had to work together. As part of that joint enterprise, between 1941 and 1944 the Royal Air Force flew 320 sorties into France, carrying over 1,000 SOE and SIS personnel into and out from the occupied country.

The Lysander aircraft of the RAF, ideal for dropping down into short and narrow spaces, proved to be a valued lifeline for British agents. Getting them in was one thing, lifting them out was something else entirely. So many agents were betrayed and captured by the Nazis that the life of a spy behind enemy lines could be measured in days rather than weeks.

The SOE employed a wide variety of weapons in its work: these ranged from Sten guns and hand grenades to itching powder and home-made bombs. The most bizarre of these were the exploding rats. Explosives were inserted into the bodies of dead rats. They would then be primed and left in ditches, sewers and guttering. It was a ploy later used to spectacular effect by David Niven in the film *The Guns of Navarone*.

Regardless of the novelty of the exploding rats, the favourite weapon of most SOE men was the Sten gun. This was perhaps a little unfortunate as Sten guns had a propensity to jam at crucial moments – as we shall see.

One of the most famous of all SOE's many sorties was the assassination of Reinhard Heydrich who had been appointed as *Reichpratektor* of Moravia and Bohemia with his base in the Czech capital of Prague. Specific assassinations were not within the usual remit of SOE, but this attempt was planned and put into operation at the request of Edvard Benes, head of the Czech government-in-exile. Soldiers from the remnants of the Czech army, then stationed in Britain, were brought into SOE where they were trained and equipped to carry out the actual killing.

The two chosen assassins, Jan Kubis and Jozef Gabcik, were dropped by parachute, landing close to Pilsen, fifty miles from Prague. It was 28 December 1941. They were accompanied by seven other agents who, although engaged on totally separate missions, would give them assistance if it should be required.

Kubis and Gabcik spent five months hiding in Prague, planning the assassination. They discarded their original intention of killing Heydrich with a rocket grenade while he was travelling by train as they could not be sure exactly where he would be sitting. Eventually they decided on ambushing him as he journeyed from his home in Panenske Brezany to his desk at Prague Castle. The attempt was scheduled for the morning of 27 May 1942.

As Heydrich's open-topped Mercedes slowed for a corner close to Bulovka Hospital, Gabcik stepped into the roadway and prepared to open fire with his Sten. It promptly jammed. As Heydrich leapt to his feet to fire at the would-be assassin, Jan Kubis threw a modified anti-tank grenade at the car. It bounced off the bodywork, rolled under the vehicle and exploded. Reinhard Heydrich was grievously wounded, not by the explosion but by pieces of the car seat and his clothing which were hurled upwards into his body.

The two assassins made their escape, pursued and shot at by Heydrich's driver. Heydrich was taken to hospital where, after seeming to make a recovery, he lapsed into a coma and later died from sepsis. Kubis and Gabcik escaped from the scene of the attack and hid out during the intensive search organised by the SS and SD. The atmosphere in Prague was tense and nobody dared step out of line. Arrests were made nearly every day but for a long while even the substantial reward of 500,000 Reichsmarks offered by the Nazis failed to bring results.

Kubis and Gabcik were eventually betrayed, for money and a new identity, by Karel Curda, one of the other Czech agents who had originally parachuted into Czechoslovakia with them several months before. Curda survived the war but was arrested by the restored Czech government, tried for his treason and executed.

With five members of the other SOE teams in Czechoslovakia, Kubis and Gabcik were finally tracked to the Church of Saints Cyril and Methodius where they were besieged by over 700 German soldiers armed with machine guns, artillery and grenades. The SOE men were armed only with pistols. After a dramatic defence all of the Czech agents died, Kubis from German bullets, Gabcik by putting one of his last bullets into his brain.

Reprisals, which the Czechs had expected and dreaded, were quick. Over 5,000 Czech citizens were murdered and the village of Lidice – which supposedly had links to the assassins – was razed to the ground. Nearly 200 men from the village were shot, and 195 women sent to Ravensbrück concentration camp. Of the ninety-five children taken prisoner eighty-one later died. Eight were adopted by German families.

Opinions have varied ever since 1942 as to whether or not the assassination of Reinhard Heydrich, politically important as it appeared at the time, was worth even one of those dreadful deaths. It still remains a debatable point. Benes and the Czech government-in-exile had been warned of the possible consequences of the operation but insisted that it should go ahead.

Operatives of the SOE and even Winston Churchill would probably have backed Benes. There was one man in particular who clearly would not – Stewart Menzies of SIS.

******

From the early days of the conflict many people had taken to calling SIS by the name MI6. It was never an official decision and technically the term SIS still applies to the organisation: 'The origins of the use of MI6 are to be found at the start of the Second World War when the abbreviation was adopted as a flag of convenience for SIS. It was used extensively throughout the war.'[6]

Whatever the organisation called itself, it still had a job to do and from fairly ignominious beginnings Menzies and his staff set about doing that job. The Special Operations Executive would go about its set task of causing confusion behind enemy lines, but SIS/MI6 was more intent on gathering information. With its original networks blown or destroyed after the fall of France, the most important task now was to create new and efficient sources that would be able to provide the information that would win the war.

Service Clarence was probably the most effective of all the MI6 networks in Occupied Europe. Based in Belgium and run by Hector Demarque and Walther Dewe, both of whom had already had experience of running clandestine operations with La Dame Blanche in the First World War, Service Clarence operated from 1940 until the end of the conflict. It provided MI6 with a wide range of vital information on German military activity, everything from coastal defences to the effects of Allied bombing raids and German troop movements.

The Alliance Network in France was run by Marie-Madeleine Fourcade, an elegant and glamorous woman known to everyone who ever encountered her as the typical, copybook female spy. She was incredibly beautiful, a modern-day Mata Hari but considerably more efficient. By August 1942 the Alliance Network had 145 operational agents, all providing information for MI6 and sometimes carrying out sabotage operations.

In 1944 Olaf Reed Olsen was parachuted into Norway with the brief that he should set up a secret radio station close to the Kristiansand Fiord. This became known in MI6 circles as the Makir Wireless Station which for over six months broadcast approximately ten messages a day to MI6 headquarters in London.

Olsen cleverly disguised and camouflaged his radio station so that the Germans could not find it. He reported daily on German troop movements, enemy morale – essential information in the closing stages of the war – and the comings and goings of German destroyers along the fiords and out into the North Sea.

Also in 1944 MI6 was instrumental, along with the American Office of Strategic Services and the Free French forces, in setting up a specific operation with the innocuous codename of Project Sussex. Pairs of spies were dropped behind German lines within a few days of the Allied landings in Normandy. The idea was to uncover and then provide accurate frontline intelligence that would help local commanders with the deployment of their forces.

By August, just two months after D-Day, there were thirty 'Sussex teams' operating in France. The information they gathered and radioed back to MI6 was vital in enabling army units to switch the direction of their attacks and to hit the enemy where he was weakest. It was intelligence work of the highest order and showed exactly how far MI6/SIS had come since the dispiriting and depressing early days of the war.

If MI6 managed to improve its performance the same could not always be said of SOE. Of course, Churchill's 'secret army' had its successes, particularly in those enterprises that needed flair and dash. The destruction of the German heavy water plant at Vemork in 1943 was probably the most remarkable high point as it almost certainly prevented the Nazis from creating an atom bomb, but there were other successes as well.

WAR!

The numerous SOE interventions in Yugoslavia certainly helped Marshal Tito to establish a regime that, while communist in ideology, was strong enough to stand up to Stalin in the years after 1945. When Churchill, always strongly anti-Communist, was warned of this possibility his response was that he did not have to live there so let the Yugoslavs do as they wished.

Turning pro-Japanese security men to the Allied side in Burma was another major achievement for SOE, one that is now almost forgotten. Winning the jungle war was a slow and dangerous process that involved Allied soldiers relearning their trade. SOE was there to help.

And yet the failures or disasters tend to outweigh SOE's successes. The assassination of Heydrich resulted in the deaths of many thousands and has always been a controversial episode. It may have been successful in killing its target, but the consequences point to a different conclusion.

In March 1945, just a few weeks before the end of the war, the Special Ops Executive launched an aerial attack on a Gestapo prison in Copenhagen. The attack, at such a late stage of the war, was not only totally unnecessary but killed a large number of Danish children and teachers in the school next door to the prison.

Other failures were of a more subliminal nature. Throughout their operational existence SOE blithely dropped arms and ammunition all over Europe. More than that, its operatives trained willing volunteers in occupied countries how to use guerrilla tactics. Inevitably, many of the men and women who queued up for SOE combat training were communists. They were not the type of fighters who would want to restore the old regimes and the old way of life once the Nazis were beaten. They were hell-bent on creating new worlds and new ways of life for ordinary people.

From Palestine to Greece, from Egypt to Cyprus, the weapons were stored and hidden while the revolutionaries practiced their new-found skills. In time both weapons and fighting techniques would be used against British troops by freedom fighters from the various countries. It was hardly what SOE or the British government had expected.

In the summer of 1943, in an attempt to improve the performance of its agents, SOE began a specialised training programme. Previously SOE operatives – apart from rare exceptions like Operation Anthropoid, the assassination of Heydrich – had been left to their own devices. Now, however, with Commander Kenneth Cohen appointed as Chief Staff

Officer (Training) an altogether more professional approach was applied. Training manuals and textbooks were virtually unknown quantities to most SOE men; now they became a necessary evil for the agents.

One of the least known aspects of SOE's work was the detention centre it ran for failed or reluctant volunteers. Working to the principle that 'once in, always in' its purpose was simple – to keep failed agents or those who, after training, decided that SOE was not for them, out of public view. They had been given information that would certainly be of use to the enemy. Now they had to stay out of circulation until the end of the war.

The detention centre was created at Inverlair Lodge in the Northeast of Scotland. Guarded by units of the Cameron Highlanders, failed SOE volunteers, along with some MI6 operatives of the same ilk, were detained until well beyond May 1945. It was a fairly luxurious existence but it was still captivity. The men received no visitors and mail was heavily censored and rare.

In time, Inverlair Lodge became the idea behind the successful cult television series *The Prisoner*. Even though the show was filmed at the Italianate village of Portmeirion in North Wales, its origins and inspiration came from the SOE Detention Centre.

The Special Ops Executive had always had plenty of would-be agents, men and women who wanted or needed a little adventure in their lives. It had been set up for exactly these types of people. At its height, operating out of offices in Baker Street, SOE employed almost 10,000 men and 3,000 women. It was an enormous army of romantics and ruffians, almost all of them imagining themselves a cross between Richard Hannay and Bulldog Drummond: 'They took it for granted that one Englishman was worth five Germans, ten Italians and an incalculable number of lesser breeds [...] Practically every officer in SOE imagined himself to be Richard Hannay, or Hannay's friend, Sandy Arbuthnot.'[7]

SOE was eventually disbanded on 30 June 1946. For a brief period it had been thought that, along with America's Office of Strategic Services, SOE might be useful in any forthcoming war with Soviet Russia. Open conflict never occurred and the world settled into that bizarre existence known as the Cold War. There was no place for SOE within such a restrictive situation. MI6/SIS had managed to outlive its most insidious and deadly enemy.

******

WAR!

The greatest British intelligence success of the whole war undoubtedly came from the codebreakers at Bletchley Park. It was a phenomenal success that deserved to be lauded by the whole country, but even knowledge of its existence was classified information and the work that went on there was kept completely secret until well into the 1970s.

Britain's track record at decoding was impressive. The success of Admiral 'Blinker' Hall and Room 40 during the First World War was renowned within the espionage circles, but at the beginning of the second great conflict of the twentieth century there were grave doubts – given the recent failure of GC & CS to break Soviet codes – that such a feat could be repeated.

The cynics were soon silenced when the codebreakers at Bletchley Park began producing Ultra intelligence. This was the codename given to intelligence obtained after breaking high level German communications and was reckoned to have shortened the war by at least two years. Many writers and researchers believe that without the intelligence gathering from Bletchley the whole outcome of the war might have been very different. They have a point. If nothing else the Ultra information from Bletchley effectively ended the German U-boat threat.

When the Battle of the Atlantic was at its height, Britain was on the cusp of defeat and starvation. As Churchill said, the only thing that ever frightened him during the war was the thought of losing the Battle of the Atlantic. The Ultra information from Bletchley Park made sure that Britain won that particular fight.

There were many successful aspects of the work at Bletchley Park, not least the cracking of the two most important German codes, Enigma and Lorenz. The development of Colossus, the world's first programmable digital electronic computer, was another huge breakthrough.

The Enigma machine used to encipher messages had been invented by an engineer from Berlin in the years after the First World War. It was patented, as a commercial proposition, under the name Enigma and was an ingenious device in that the keyboard operator did not control the letters chosen to represent the coded words. It was pure random choice on the part of the machine.

Initially unsuccessful, the German Navy adopted the coding machine in 1926, the army two years later. Both services were delighted with the Enigma, knowing that their secret messages were now exactly that, secret. That is until the codebreakers entered the fray.

At the time, their names were unknown, but now men like Alan Turing, Hugh Alexander, Stuart Milner-Barry and Gordon Welchman have finally acquired the respect and recognition they deserve. At the risk of falling into cliché, they fought an unheroic war but one that was crucial to Allied success. And it was not just those four.

Brilliant men and women of 'the professor type', as Alastair Dennison – leader of Bletchley Park until 1942 – requested should be sent to him were soon arriving in droves. Civilians and service men and women alike, it hardly mattered to Dennison as long as that single word 'brilliant' could always be applied to the new recruits.

There were mathematicians from Oxford and Cambridge, chess champions from London and the regions; ordinary men and women who had proved they could think laterally. So wide-ranging was the catchment group that the GC & CS unit soon acquired the nickname within Secret Service circles as the 'Golf, Cheese and Chess Society'.

Dennison got his recruits from wherever he could. At one stage *The Daily Telegraph* was asked to run a cryptic crossword competition. The puzzle was devilishly difficult and the winners were then discretely approached by MI6 officers to see if they would be prepared to work at Bletchley Park. Very few refused.

Cryptanalysts like Dilly Knox, who had served his country so well in the First World War, were hauled out of retirement and put to immediate use at Bletchley. The women who worked in his hut, most of them young Wrens barely out of their teens, were promptly christened 'Dilly's Fillies'.

At its height there were approximately 10,000 people working at Bletchley, at its listening posts in areas like Norfolk and Leicestershire and at its various outstations. Three-quarters of the people employed in this vital task were women. Most of them were used as typists, machine operators and clerks, but one, Joan Clarke, rose to become Deputy Head of Hut 8. She was one of the very few women employed at Bletchley as a cryptanalyst.

The war was not very old when Bletchley Park began to produce high-quality results. Churchill, his War Cabinet and the senior officers of the armed forces were all astounded at the success which, from the beginning, was kept ultra-ultra-secret. Alan Brook, then Chief of the Imperial General Staff, wrote in his diary: 'Took lunch in the car and went to see the organisation for breaking down ciphers – a wonderful set of professors and genii. I marvel at the work they succeed in doing.'[8]

WAR!

The results were undoubtedly spectacular, particularly when the Enigma Code of the German Navy was broken and the Battle of the Atlantic finally began to swing Britain's way. In fact, the code had been broken by Polish cryptanalysts as early as 1932 by the simple but logical move of buying a commercially available machine and studying it in conjunction with drawings of the German military machines which their secret service had managed to obtain.

However, by 1939 the Germans had adapted their machines, making them increasingly complex and confusing. The Poles lost the basic skills and information required for breaking Enigma and passed on their Enigma machines to the British and the French. Stewart Menzies seized his machine with alacrity, passed it on to Bletchley Park and the rest, as they say, is history.

It would be wrong to say that the task was easy, but for skilled and highly intelligent operators breaking the code was simply a technical problem that needed to be solved. Given time and the correct material the cryptanalysts were sure that it could be done.

Alan Turing and the others knew that it needed persistence to keep trying various combinations of twenty or so plain word characters (like the date of Hitler's birth or the first day of the war) which might or might not reveal the entrance to the puzzle. That and possession of German naval codebooks would bring the problem to a successful conclusion. Turing and his colleagues were able to offer the necessary skill and perseverance; the capture of codebooks from the disabled and sinking U559 and U110 provided the rest.

One of the most important breakthroughs came with the invention of the Bombe, a machine devised by Alan Turing and Gordon Welchman which was used to discover the daily settings of the German Enigma machines. In theory the Enigma code should have been unbreakable but there were flaws in the German procedures and this, combined with human error from the operators, helped Turing with his work.

If breaking the Enigma Code was the highlight of Bletchley Park's war, the other major success was cracking the Lorenz Code. This was a code used for communications between the German High Command and field units. Breaking the code resulted in huge amounts of information being passed to American and British commanders so that prior to the D-Day landings the Allies knew the location of all but two of Germany's fifty-eight divisions along the Western Front.

General Bernard Montgomery, Britain's most successful land commander of the war, had a picture of his arch enemy Erwin Rommel pinned to the wall of his mobile HQ, the caravan that went everywhere with him. He liked to say he was reading Rommel's mind. In fact, thanks to Bletchley Park and the cracking of the Lorenz Code, he was reading Rommel's electronic communications.

Hard work was the key to Bletchley's success. Most of the women employed there had little or no idea about what was going on or why they were doing it. They knew it was important, after all they had signed the Official Secrets Act, but what it was all about was reserved for the cryptanalysts and senior staff. The actual work was tedious and boring and many of them resented being kept in the dark about the purpose of Bletchley Park.

People working there had little time off and as one of them, Kathleen Norris from Neath in South Wales, later commented, any time they had a day or two free they would just head home. Anything was better than the cold comforts of the Bletchley Park huts. The old mansion house was reserved for meetings and the senior officers. The only time Kathleen Norris went there was to collect her wages from the front office.

Most of the staff, the Wrens and WAAF in particular, were billeted in lodgings around the town. For those who were housed some way from Bletchley there was a limited degree of transport available. Mostly people just walked to and from work: 'I was lucky because I was actually billeted in Bletchley itself, but a lot were billeted in outlying villages. When we were coming off duty at twelve, or going in at twelve, there was transport. Otherwise we were within walking distance.'[9]

Kathleen Norris worked mainly in Hut D with twenty-five other girls, all beavering away at their machines. Unlike most of the temporary accommodation at Bletchley, which were terrapin buildings, Hut D was made from concrete blocks and was both cold and noisy:

> There were these big machines. We were given special drums, depending what was on that particular day. And then just sheets or strips of Morse code which were coming in from the listening stations. I typed away and ticker-tape came out, in blocks of five letters. We didn't know any more than that. We were either on the machines or we were "sticker-ups!" You had to stick all these letters onto card; where they went and what happened to them we never knew.[10]

Leisure time was limited. A trip to the pictures in Bletchley or a cup of tea in one of the cafés or the Mess Hall and that was about it. The stories about all of the dances and plays supposedly put on for the staff Kathleen regards as just that – stories: 'All those things that went on at Bletchley I knew nothing about. I never saw skating on the lake, I never saw tennis matches, never saw amateur dramatics, plays or societies, or anything like that.'[11]

She also never saw people like Alan Turing or Dilly Knox. They kept themselves to themselves in what was really quite a structured and class-conscious environment. It hardly mattered. Kathleen, like so many other Wrens, WAAFs and civilians, was there to help win the war and that was exactly what she did.

The story of the Bletchley Park codebreakers during the Second World War was not all success. In November 1942 the ever-suspicious German Navy began to use a four-rotor Enigma machine, which meant that Bletchley could no longer read German signals to and from their U-boats. It was nearly ten months before the code was broken again. Dozens of convoys were attacked during the year of silence, hundreds of merchant ships sunk or damaged, but the cryptologists stuck to their task and eventually managed to get back into the code once more.

The complex was bombed on the night of 20-21 November 1940 – by accident. The German aircraft were probably aiming to hit nearby Bletchley railway station or the railway works at Wolverton. Hut 4 was blown off its foundations but was winched back into place and the work inside carried on throughout the entire operation.

More worryingly, although not known until after the war, John Cairncross, one of the Cambridge spy ring, managed to infiltrate the operation and leaked a considerable amount of Ultra material to the Soviet Union. As the British government had never told Moscow about the existence of Bletchley Park it was a damaging and embarrassing episode.

Churchill had personally forbidden GC & CS to monitor Russian broadcasts or messages when Germany attacked the Soviet Union in 1941. Previously the monitoring of Soviet radio traffic had been a regular occurrence for the codebreakers.

The USSR was now an ally and to begin with at least Churchill was willing to give them the benefit of the doubt. He did not trust Stalin but Britain needed the Russians to keep Hitler fighting in the east. Therefore, as far as Churchill was concerned, they would stop monitoring their radio traffic but keep sending convoys with supplies that the Soviets really did not need.

Interestingly, in late 1944 a small cypher and decoding section of GC & CS was established in Sloane Square with the deliberate intention of monitoring Soviet messages. Churchill, knowing the end of Hitler's war was within sight, was already assessing the West's enemies in the coming Cold War.

When the war ended GC & CS transferred its operations to Eastcote. That was in 1946, but soon afterwards the coding unit, now known as GCHQ, relocated to Cheltenham. Bletchley Park remained in rural isolation, used by the Post Office for a time, until the creation of the nearby New Town of Milton Keynes eventually began to disturb its tranquillity. Its vital role in defeating the German war machine remained secret for many years.

******

Protecting Enigma and the Ultra information had been essential throughout the war years. The Bletchley complex was heavily but discreetly guarded and security remained tight. However, denial was always the best form of defence. By keeping the place secret and not disclosing its function MI6 was continuing with the long-held traditions of the espionage service.

The Americans, as Britain's most important ally, were kept in the loop and their cryptographers took over Hut 7 and worked alongside their British counterparts. Eventually over 100 American service men and women were working at Bletchley Park. They may not always have been happy about the way that the intelligence gathered by Turing's Bombe machines was used but they were aware of the significance of Bletchley and freely admitted to learning much from Alan Turing, Gordon Welchman and the other British codebreakers.

The USA had been made aware of the British success some months before the two countries became allies. In February 1941, nine months before the Pearl Harbour attack catapulted the USA into the war, the Sinkov Mission, named after the American leader of the group, brought four US code experts to Bletchley. It was a seminal moment.

WAR!

As a result of the clandestine meeting a long-standing relationship between the secret intelligence agencies of Britain and the USA was established. Tense and taut at times, that relationship has remained in place until the present day. The USA had broken the Japanese codes and now, as part of the Sinkov Mission, shared their secret with Dennison at Bletchley. He reciprocated with the story and the facts of Enigma.

American codebreakers were just as skilled as their British counterparts. They had cracked the Japanese codes just before the Battle of Midway in 1942, using the information to inflict a catastrophic defeat on their enemy. Equally as important, they soon discovered that Admiral Yamamoto, the brains behind the Pearl Harbour attack, was about to visit Japanese bases in the Pacific. The Americans laid an ambush, shot down and killed Yamamoto and deprived the Japanese Navy of its most important and skilled leader.

After the success of the Sinkov Mission, America and Britain formed a pact and made an agreement to share intelligence. They also agreed to divide up the interception duties across the world. After the war Canada, Australia and New Zealand were added to the pact, thus creating what was referred to as 'The Five Eyes'. Tested at times, but never broken, the agreement still stands.

The secretive nature of what was going on at Bletchley Park inevitably led to dozens of myths about the place. Like any closed society, the very nature of the organisation precluded easy entry with the result that stories and legends about what went on inside the charmed circle were soon taken as fact. There were so many tales about the GC & CS operation in deepest, darkest Buckinghamshire that they have now become almost an accepted part of the Bletchley story. Their veracity and validity, however, remain questionable.

The story that Winston Churchill deliberately sacrificed some convoys so as not to alert the German Navy that their codes had been broken is probably no more than an urban myth – in much the same way as the story of him deliberately not warning Coventry of an impending German air attack is fantasy. Churchill, like Bletchley Park, was an easy target for the myth makers.

Winston Churchill would certainly have been ruthless enough to do such a thing, had it been essential for winning the war, but there is no evidence about him ever making such a decision, either for the convoys or for Coventry. It is true that MI6 did learn of an impending attack on

Coventry but only two hours before it was launched, by which time it was too late to do anything.

What was done, however, was to run a very clever and successful deception ploy. MI6 invented a master spy by the name of Boniface and then made sure that the *Abwehr* and the SD knew all about the entirely fictional network that he supposedly ran.

He or she, it was said, controlled this network of spies based in Germany, France and other parts of Occupied Europe. Ultra intelligence results were credited to Boniface rather than the reality of a broken Enigma code. It was a wonderful piece of deception work.

Like the streams of Ultra intelligence information pouring from Bletchley Park, for many years the creation of Boniface remained a little-known success story for MI6. The efficiency of the Boniface deception, and the fact that it remained secret throughout the war years and for some time afterwards, is proof of how efficient MI6 had now become.

By the end of the war both Stewart Menzies's MI6 and David Petrie's MI5 were amazingly adept at the art of using double agents. It was a hard-learned lesson for both of them, but once gained it was a skill both organisations put to good use.

Perhaps the most successful of these double agents was Juan Pujol Garcia, a Spanish spy who operated under the codename Garbo. Having developed a fanatical hatred of Fascism during the Spanish Civil War, he offered his services to Britain and duped the Germans into believing that, like the non-existent Boniface, he was running a large network of spies. The network was pure fabrication but the Germans, who knew him as Alaric, were completely taken in.

Garbo's most important contribution to the war effort was helping to convince the German army and the *Abwehr* that the Allied landings, when they came, would be in the Pas de Calais area rather than any other part of Europe.

It was a clever ruse as the twenty-one miles of water between England and Calais seemed to be the easiest and most logical invasion route. Once the notion had been planted in the combined minds of the German High Command they seemed almost to convince themselves that there was no other option. From that moment on it was just a matter of continuing to reinforce the notion and that was where Garbo came in.

Garbo did not achieve that deception on his own. Dummy tanks, General Patton's posting to the Kent area and 'leaked' radio traffic all combined to add to the deception, but Garbo's involvement – the trusted, ever-so reliable Garbo – was undoubtedly one of the main factors in the success.

Regardless of who orchestrated it, the deception resulted in large numbers of German troops and tanks being stationed many miles away from the actual Normandy landing beaches. There, in the quiet confines of Calais and Boulogne, they sat idly, guns trained on empty beaches, ready to oppose the mythical landings that the Germans *knew* would be in the Calais area.

Even when news of the Normandy invasion reached the German High Command, they refused to believe that this was the main assault. These were just initial landings, surely, or a diversionary attack. They would be followed up by further landings in the Pas de Calais; they had to be, after all Garbo had said that they would.

Several writers have questioned the accuracy of this story and the Garbo legend, quoting the RAF's intense bombing of the area between Normandy and Paris as giving away the true location of the landings. A spy in SOE had also, it is claimed, revealed to the Germans directions sent to the French Resistance asking them to assemble in the Normandy area ready for an invasion.

It is all hypothetical. A case could just as easily be made for an anti-Hitler group within the *Abwehr* – and such a thing did exist – convincing the German High Command that Garbo's intelligence was correct. The answer is probably a combination of all these factors.

Ultimately, it was seen as a superb coup for Garbo, the only man in the Second World War to be awarded military decorations from both sides, the MBE from Britain and the much-coveted Iron Cross from Germany.

The Second World War had been a costly experience for the men and women of MI6/SIS and MI5. They had made mistakes, often quite grievous mistakes, but the war years provided important grounding for the challenges that lay ahead for Britain's secret intelligence services.

It was unfortunate that MI6, and to a lesser extent MI5, had already been infiltrated by the moles and spies of the Soviet Union. In the years ahead it was to cause major problems and discomfort at all levels of British society.

Chapter Eight

A Cold, Cold Comfort

'The Iceman Cometh.'
Eugene O'Neill

The surrender of Germany and Japan in May and September 1945 did not provide the easy ending of world conflicts that so many had envisaged. Rather, it marked the beginning of a very different type of war.

Use of the atom bomb, many thought, would be the ultimate guarantee of peace. With America now installed as the world's policeman, brandishing the most brutal and terrible weapon mankind had ever imagined, there would be no country, no power on earth, willing to risk incurring her wrath or stepping out of line.

It was not just the advent of weapons of mass destruction, the diplomats and politicians of the world smugly told themselves. The increasingly sophisticated and structured efficiency of traditional forces – the ships, aircraft and armies of the great nations – had made the wars of the past virtually obsolete. Now resorting to the battlefield as a first option in any dispute was not going to be the best reaction. World harmony was guaranteed.

It was, of course, a delusion. The first few years of 'peace' saw the advent of a more bitter and insidious type of conflict than anyone had imagined as strong powers immediately began pressurising other nations, big and small alike, into making decisions they would not otherwise have made. It was the start of the Cold War.

Churchill's Iron Curtain quickly came down across Europe as the Soviet Union withdrew into a self-imposed exile. Joseph Stalin, who had spent the previous five years feeling left out and marginalised by Britain and the USA, was also greatly aggrieved. His people had sacrificed more, had suffered more and had been abused far more at the hands of the Nazis than any of the other members of the Allied alliance. And yet their efforts were not appreciated. The simple fact that the USA was now keeping the secret of the atom bomb from Soviet scientists was proof positive of the duplicity and the deviousness of the capitalist West.

Stalin's concept of communist ideology may not have been exactly what Marx or even Lenin had in mind, but when all was said and done it was ruthlessly efficient. In order to cement the position of his regime Stalin had implemented the great purges of the 1930s. In order to maintain the status quo within the Soviet Union he had implemented a police state. Now he needed to implement even more draconian measures to ensure its continuation.

The espionage and secret police agencies of the Soviet Union had, from the 1930s until the creation of the KGB – and arguably even beyond – been given a bewildering variety of names. However, they all did basically the same job, with minor additions or alterations to fit the requirements of the moment and the time.

The infamous SMERSH, so beloved by Ian Fleming and all James Bond enthusiasts, was formally acknowledged and announced in the spring of 1943 although it may well have come into existence a year or eighteen months earlier.

An umbrella organisation for three independent counterintelligence agencies in the Red Army, SMERSH was intended to subvert German attempts to infiltrate Soviet armed forces and was run by Viktor Abakumov. With its terrifying name and motto of 'Death to Spies', it seemed in the immediate post-war years to exemplify the dictatorial nature of Stalin's regime:

> A great deal of killing has to be done in the USSR, not because the average Russian is a cruel man [...] but as an instrument of policy. People who act against the State are enemies of the State, and the State has no room for enemies.[1]

SMERSH, the name being a shortening of its official title *Smiert Spionam*, was very much the brainchild of the increasingly paranoid and violent Joseph Stalin. He coined the name, he listed the tasks he required the organisation to carry out and he gave his approval to the individuals SMERSH was to employ in order to carry out those tasks.

The first two aims were fairly clear – counterintelligence and counter terrorism. Then there were the two major tasks of limiting foreign knowledge of the Red Army and protecting the front lines from penetration by enemy spies, wherever those front lines might be.

SMERSH was also charged with investigating traitors and deserters, and, in fact, taking control of anyone or anything that was likely to cause harm to the army. Part of this last charge was the investigation of any personnel returning from capitalist countries. In other words ensuring that no one in the organisation had been turned by the West.

Clearly SMERSH was more than just a spy agency. It was intended to collect information and intelligence, but equally as significant, it was to operate as a proactive arm of the Russian state. It was not there just to wipe out threats to the Soviet regime but it was also to act in an aggressive fashion, initiating projects that were likely to cause harm to the Western democracies.

The concept, to any foreign observers who had the insight to look beyond their own immediate needs and desires, was terrifying. With such an organisation operating from behind the Iron Curtain the future seemed very dark indeed.

In fact SMERSH had only a very short lifespan as an independent espionage agency. It existed only until May 1946 when it fell victim to Stalin's incessant desire for security and protection and was subsumed as an independent, self-standing agency by the Third Directorate of the MGB.

This time, however, it was not just Stalin's paranoia that was leading the charge. There was a degree of logic to the amalgamation. It soon became clear that MGB's Third Directorate and SMERSH were pretty much the same thing, ruthless killing machines. It was both expensive and inefficient to have two agencies or units carrying out the same job. One had to go.

The MGB (the Ministry for State Security) had been founded in 1941, replacing the NKVD and inheriting most of its functions. In addition to those, after the end of the Second World War one of its most important tasks was to bring the newly acquired Eastern Bloc states – Poland, East Germany, Czechoslovakia and the rest – under effective Soviet control.

It was a feat that was managed quite brilliantly, if more than a little brutally. Wherever possible the MGB employed 'local labour' to carry out the more draconian policies of the Soviet Union.

The East German State Security Service, the Stasi as it became known, was the stick used by the MGB and KGB to beat citizens of the German Democratic Republic. This terrifying secret police and intelligence organisation came into existence in February 1950, lasting for forty years until the unification of East and West Germany. Together with MI6, the CIA and the KGB, it was probably the most active secret espionage agency of the Cold War.

The Stasi's main purpose was to spy on the people of East Germany. As such it arrested more than 250,000 suspects in its forty-year existence. Most of that time it was run by Erich Mielke with Markus Wolf as Head of the Main Directorate for Reconnaissance, the section that dealt with espionage and covert operations in foreign countries.

The MGB itself had a number of different sections, or directorates as they were known. The First Directorate dealt with foreign affairs, the Second with domestic and internal matters. The Third Directorate which subsumed SMERSH was a military counterintelligence unit.

There were other, minor directorates which meshed together to form a cohesive whole, protecting the Soviet ideals and causing damage to as many Western ideologies as possible. As an independent force SMERSH may have gone but as an essential piece of Soviet espionage aggression it was still there and still just as effective.

Both during and after the Second World War the approach of the USSR to gathering intelligence was virtually a microcosm of the whole Soviet state. It was an enormous centralised process where people like Laventi Beria sat at the centre of a huge spider's web, gleefully gathering the scraps of intelligence that had been sent to him by the KGB and MGB, by trading missions and so on.

There was so much information coming across his desk that the diminutive but vicious Beria was almost swamped by the volume. Nevertheless, he would still dutifully pass on that information, all of it, to Stalin who sat at the centre of an infinitely bigger and more dangerous web than Beria's own.

Stalin knew, as Marx had written, that knowledge was power. But it was inevitable that the arch mover and fixer would eventually find the sheer volume of intelligence too great to give it anything like reasonable attention. Even to a confirmed paranoid like him it gradually became clear that he would have to let go of some of the reins.

The answer was F. I. Golikov, chief of the General Staff Administration. In many respects a typical faceless bureaucrat, Golikov became an enormously powerful sieve, taking the intelligence that was gathered, assessing it and then passing on only the most important bits to Stalin.

Where the system failed was in the stubbornness of Joseph Stalin's personality and his rigid opinions about the Western world. Golikov, ever conscious of his own place and position, made sure that his lord and master received only intelligence matters that were in keeping with Stalin's own ideals. As a consequence, Stalin, and therefore the whole Soviet system, simply ignored intelligence material that was not liked or with which 'the boss' did not agree.

Warnings from the West that the German forces would round on their Soviet allies in 1941 were, for example, ignored by Stalin. Such messages were regarded simply as devious attempts to influence and manipulate the USSR. Far from alerting the Soviets, the warnings helped to create an attitude within the Soviet Union that lasted throughout the war years and well into the Cold War period.

Stalin's beliefs and suspicions about the West were reinforced by the briefest of glances at the war situation. Nobody in their right mind, he thought, not even Adolf Hitler, would ever contemplate fighting a war on two fronts. Therefore the British warnings were little more than a plot to lure him into making a pre-emptive strike against Germany.

If that was ever to happen Stalin and members of the Presidium were convinced that Britain and Germany would conclude a quick peace and then, together, would round on the Soviet Union. Why else had Rudolf Hess made that strange flight to Scotland on 15 May 1941? Hitler might protest and deny as much as he liked but the mission of his long-time friend and colleague could only be proof that Churchill and he were hatching a conspiracy.

If ever there was a case of someone being over-informed or making the wrong deductions about enemy motives from genuinely accurate information it has to be this. Stalin's inability to read the situation correctly in the months leading up to the launch of Operation Barbarossa on 22 June 1941 was perhaps his biggest mistake.

The exact date of the attack had been fed to Stalin by the Lucy Spy Ring, the Soviet Union's most efficient spy network in enemy territory. Stalin chose to ignore it and thereby condemned millions of Russians to death.

******

The sources for Soviet information or intelligence gathering were many and varied. They included one of the most successful spy networks ever created, the so-called Lucy Spy Ring which operated out of Switzerland and was quite probably fed valuable pieces of information by the Swiss Secret Service – on the condition, of course, that the Soviets would respond in kind. Many claim that the intelligence provided by the Lucy Ring was all that Stalin needed to fight his war against Germany.

Richard Sorge and his Japanese confederate Ozaki Hotsumi were, without doubt, equally as effective. Sorge was never totally trusted by the Soviets and did indeed pass information to the Nazi regime from time to time. The duplicity was needed to continue his double identity role, but at heart Sorge was always a communist and always an agent for the USSR.

One of the most potent of all the Russian intelligence sources, however, had to be the disaffected left-wing sympathisers in Britain. These 'angry young men' began their activities in the years before the Second World War and continued with their most effective work into the 1950s and, arguably, even into the early 1960s.

Products of the social and intellectual climate of post-Great War Britain, this small group of university educated individuals managed to turn MI5 and MI6 inside out and in so doing create one of the great myths of the espionage world. It is relatively easy, in hindsight, to see why this should occur in Britain.

It might, at first glance, appear naive or even downright stupid but the character of the British people in the nineteenth and twentieth centuries was largely one of blind trust and acceptance. Of course there was discontent throughout the nineteenth century, as events like the Peterloo Massacre, the Rebecca Riots and the Luddite Dissent show only too clearly. These, however, were working-class upheavals. In the main, the British secret services found their recruits in the middle or upper classes.

The reaction of the espionage services is easy to imagine. Security checks? Unheard of! Not needed, old chap! The school tie and a quick rendition of *Jerusalem,* sung in perfect tune, of course, or perhaps a verse or two of *Gaudeamus Igitur* – don't worry what it means – will offer all the assurances that the service needs: 'The Foreign Office, in particular, was like a club – "entry to it automatically meant that you were assumed to be totally loyal and the most important virtue was keeping the club together."'[2]

To enquire into someone's private thoughts or beliefs, apart from the obvious ideal of sustaining the empire and the solid standing of an

Englishman (certainly not a Welshman, or a Scot or an Irishman) was just not done. Inevitably there would be bounders for whom the values of the upright middle classes meant very little, but these could be dealt with by schoolboy punishments like sending them to Coventry or, as a final resort, expulsion from the club.

It could not last. In 1939 the arrest and conviction for spying of a clerk in the Foreign Office led to the managers of all three security agencies throwing their hands into the air in horror and the creation of an early system of security checks.

It was a momentary panic. A system might be in place, but for the moment at least, nobody took it seriously or even gave it much of a second thought. A security officer (unpaid) was appointed but he was given no staff until the end of the war. It hardly mattered; the top brass had done their job and created the system. Now get on with the real work.

Part of the trouble lay in the ingrained attitudes of the managers of MI6 and the other arms of the service. Threats, if they came, would be from outside the organisation, from SMERSH or the MGB but never from within. What nobody expected or even dreamed of as a possibility was that the threats were already there, already embedded in the British security services.

And so the security apparatus of Britain rolled easily along, content in its own self-importance and buoyed by its occasional successes. When things went wrong, as they inevitably did in the dangerous and dimly lit world of espionage, there was always the strength and quality of the Enigma solutions on which to fall back.

When, in the wake of Germany's defeat, the potential new enemy was quickly revealed as the Soviet Union there were many members of MI5 and MI6 who breathed a sigh of relief. Now they could at last fight the war they had wanted for so long.

Others, men and women from inside the security services, nodded knowingly and smiled to themselves: they had been waiting for what seemed like an eternity. Now it was time to act.

******

The Russian moles, buried deeply into British society and embedded into the British secret service system, came of age during the dark days of the Second World War. They matured into full adulthood during the early stages of the Cold War.

Between them the moles must have betrayed their country thousands of times. It is estimated that in 1943 alone Guy Burgess passed on 389 top secret messages or pieces of vital intelligence to his handlers in the Soviet Union. After the war the deceptions of the various moles continued, Burgess handing over a further 168 documents in December 1949.[3]

The Cambridge Five – Kim Philby, Guy Burgess, Donald Maclean, Anthony Blunt and John Cairncross – might have been the tip of the iceberg but there was no doubt about their efficiency and effectiveness. So much so that their personalities and the name by which they became known have come to be regarded as the epitome of the espionage world, as instantly recognisable as Mata Hari and Sidney Reilly, Ace of Spies.

The exact dates of their engagement in Soviet espionage work are not totally clear. Perceived wisdom says that it was while they were all studying at Cambridge, but Anthony Blunt, slightly older than the rest and someone used as a talent spotter for the Russians, was clear that their recruitment came after they had left university. Whenever it occurred, the timing of their exposure is precise.

It began with Burgess and Maclean. The pair had met in the early 1930s and gone on to work as diplomats in the Foreign Office. Both had developed a hatred for capitalist democracy and their slide towards the communist ideals of Soviet Russia was as inevitable as the world's gradual decline into war against Germany.

Burgess and Maclean were known as 'the hopeless drunks' by Soviet espionage officers as both of them were heavy and committed drinkers. Both were totally indiscreet when 'in their cups'. Guy Burgess, while in the middle of a long and heavy session in the pub, apparently once dropped a secret file that he had illegally removed from the Foreign Office. He often shouted out in his drunken fury that MI5 should keep a more careful watch on him; he was the British Alger Hiss.

No one took notice of his outbursts. Perhaps they should have done. Alger Hiss was an American government official accused in 1948 of spying for the Soviet Union. The statutes of limitations had expired for espionage but Hiss was convicted on two counts of perjury and sentenced to two consecutive five-year terms in prison.

Maclean, it is said, told his brother and several friends about his spying activities. Again, nobody took him seriously and simply put the claims down to bravado and his excessive drinking. It was inevitable, however, that before long the pair would be unmasked.

During time spent serving as a diplomat in Egypt and the Middle East Donald Maclean was particularly dissolute. He was often drunk and violent, even smashing up the house and furniture of an American diplomat while in one of his alcohol-fuelled rages. His wife was apparently having an affair at the time and that, combined with the pressure of spying for the Soviets and the fear of exposure was beginning to tell. He was eventually recalled, patched things up with his wife and managed to sober up – within reason. Like Burgess he remained a heavy drinker.

Despite both being suspect at certain times in their careers, Burgess and Maclean rose to high positions in the Foreign Office. Being a suspected Soviet spy did not, it seems, hinder promotion prospects.

Donald Maclean spent time as Head of Chancery in Cairo when the Middle East was a crucial element in American and British foreign policy. Between 1944 and 1948 he was First Secretary at the British Embassy in Washington and went on to become Head of the American Department at the Foreign Office, all the while with suspicion and doubt hovering above his head.

Guy Burgess, despite having been a member of the British Communist Party, was once Confidential Secretary to Ernest Bevin, then British Foreign Secretary. That gave him unrestricted access to virtually all aspects of British foreign policy during the immediate post-war years. In 1950 he went on to become Second Secretary at the British Embassy in Washington.

Maclean was unmasked as a result of the American-led Venona Project, a counterintelligence system which operated throughout the Cold War. Venona was intended to decrypt coded signals from the various Soviet intelligence agencies and in the thirty-seven years of its existence it successfully decoded over 3,000 messages, thanks to the Russian mistake of reusing old cypher pages in order to keep up with demand.

There are those who now question the veracity of the accepted version, but it appears that in 1950 codebreakers for Venona uncovered a number of messages between Washington, New York and Moscow. The messages had been sent by a spy known only as Homer, but Kim Philby, then serving in the USA, recognised the codename as belonging to Donald Maclean.

Philby immediately contacted Guy Burgess and told him that Maclean was bound to be arrested. He, Burgess, must get back to London to warn him. Philby knew that it would mean the end of both Burgess and Maclean as double agents but he also knew that his own safety depended on how quickly Guy Burgess moved.

Together they cooked up a record of 'bad behaviour', including alcohol misuse and three speeding offences in one day. The office took the bait and Burgess was sent home in disgrace. Once back in England, as planned, Burgess told his colleague of the danger and on 25 May 1951, the day of his thirty-eighth birthday, Donald Maclean made his move. He disappeared.

As Philby had imagined, and believed inevitable, Guy Burgess went with him, even though he was not suspected of any involvement with Maclean at that time. After a late supper at Maclean's house in Kent the pair drove to Southampton and caught the night boat to France, leaving their car unlocked on the quayside. From that moment they disappeared from view.

For several years the two missing men stayed under cover. There was no sight or sound of them until, in 1956, Nikita Khrushchev and the two long-vanished agents appeared at a press conference in Moscow. The truth, long suspected, was finally out in the public domain.

Guy Burgess never really adapted to the Russian way of life. He lived a solitary, lonely existence, drinking heavily and learning to speak only a few words of Russian. Donald Maclean, on the other hand, carved out a career for himself as a specialist advisor in British foreign policy. Burgess, his health in rapid decline, died in 1963. Maclean lasted longer, finally dying on 6 March 1983.

The exact value of the intelligence passed on by Burgess and Maclean has never been made clear. The Soviet and British governments have remained tight-lipped about exactly what information they managed to obtain and leak to the KGB. Even without confirmation, in spying careers that lasted for over twenty years it must have been considerable.

Perhaps their greatest value lay in the damage their treachery managed to inflict on the Anglo-American relationship at the time. In the wake of their defection, the Americans were naturally furious and did not trust British espionage services again for a number of years.

******

Harold 'Kim' Philby was the doyen of the Cambridge Five. He was introduced into MI6 in 1940, soon after the fall of Dunkirk, by Guy Burgess and began his secret service life working for Section D at Bletchley. When Section D became part of the SOE he went to work as a lecturer in political propaganda at Beaulieu, the SOE training school in Hampshire.

Philby had been a committed communist and an agent for the KGB since 1934. He had been a well-regarded journalist but never a British spy, at least not until now. In his cover role as a full-time agent of SSIS/MI6 he turned his hand to discovering the stance that the British government was likely to take on post-war Europe. What he found out and relayed back to Moscow had a profound effect on Soviet thinking and planning during the final years of the Second World War and for the early part of the Cold War.

Despite their support for communist resistance fighters in combat zones like France and Yugoslavia, Kim Philby – through meetings with prominent politicians like Hugh Gaitskell and Hugh Dalton who accepted him at face value – quickly discovered that Britain had no desire to see communism take hold on the Continent. As far as the British were concerned the end of the war would signal a return to the pre-war situation, preferably even a pre-Hitler one.

A move to the counter espionage section of MI6 enabled Philby to compile a list of all MI6 agents working on the Continent, and in particular within Russia. The list was, naturally and gleefully, forwarded to Moscow.

Periods as night duty officer at the MI6 head office in London gave Philby open access to communications from government and military stations all over the world. This included discussions about military assistance for Russia, the decision to restrict the amount of Ultra intelligence to be shared with the Soviet Union, and many more top-secret documents. Thanks to Philby they became common knowledge in Moscow almost before they were read in British government circles.

By the end of the war Kim Philby was a top MI6 man. He had become Head of Section 1X, the anti-Soviet hunters within MI6, and was a confidante of most senior officers, drinking and dining with them on a regular basis. Then he was made head of British intelligence in Turkey, his public persona being that of First Secretary in the Embassy.

In his capacity as an MI6 operative he organised several raids and spy drops into places like Georgia, Armenia and Albania. It was like sending lambs to the slaughter. Most of the incursions ended in disaster with the agents blown and shot almost as soon as they crossed the border from Turkey. As Philby later said about just one of these episodes: 'The agents we sent into Albania were armed men intent on murder, sabotage and assassination. They knew the risks they were running [...] To the extent that I helped to defeat them, even if it caused their deaths, I have no regrets.'[4]

By 1949 Philby had moved on to become chief British intelligence officer in Washington. It was never intended to be more than a temporary stop on his rise to the top. Highly regarded by his managers, he was already being groomed for the leadership. A Soviet double agent as head of MI6 – it remains a fascinating thought.

The following year came the moment that all spies dread, the denouement of his closest comrades. It forced him into action, but by warning Burgess and Maclean of their imminent unmasking he had also brought his own situation under scrutiny. It was inevitable that Philby should fall under suspicion of being a Russian spy, at least as far as the Americans were concerned. There was no evidence but the rumours in the corridors of power were rife.

Philby had played the affair too close for comfort, but with his own safety in mind, knew that he had had no other option. He managed to ignore the rumours, deny the accusations and survive until the autumn of 1955 when he was finally named in the press as the so-called 'Third Man' in the Burgess/Maclean affair. After reports in the American papers, an article in the British *Sunday News* was followed up by questions in the House of Commons. Philby was clearly teetering on the edge of a very deep chasm.

By now he was back in Britain again. It was the era of Senator McCarthy and American witch hunts designed to root out communist sympathisers in the USA. The arch anti-communist and the man behind much of the anti-Philby sentiment was none other than FBI Director J. Edgar Hoover, but while his motives may have been correct he had badly misjudged the moment. People in Britain viewed the attempts to blacken Philby's name as mere persecution – how dare the Americans, until so very recently the country's allies, attack a British citizen.

Philby was again saved, this time by Foreign Secretary and future prime minister Harold Macmillan who appeared in front of Parliament to clear his name. Macmillan had little time for the espionage world and even less for Philby. Nevertheless, defending this possible Soviet spy was a political step that he and the Tory government felt they had to take.

Following Macmillan's face-saving address in Parliament, Philby called a relaxed, almost laconic press conference to further advance his innocence. He had never spied for the Soviet Union, he declared, and had never been a communist.

Unfortunately the affair had made Kim Philby a public figure, not exactly the ideal situation for a spy from either side. He resigned from MI6 and took up a post as foreign correspondent for *The Economist* and *The Observer* in the Middle East.

At some stage in the next few years Kim Philby began working again for MI6, and presumably for the KGB as well, sending them reports on conditions in Syria, Egypt and other Middle Eastern countries. He was now 'unofficial', a freelancer picking up information wherever he could. To some extent the position and style of operation suited Philby.

The net was closing, however. He had run his course and there was little more that he could do. He was drinking more and more and had become quite promiscuous in his relationships with women. Once again there were rumours, even stories in the press.

Sir Richard 'Dick' White had been given the position of chief of MI6 in 1956, transferring across from his post as Director General of MI5. The move had been made at the direct request of Prime Minister Anthony Eden following the debacle of the Burgess and Maclean affair and was an attempt to mollify the growing American criticism of the British secret services.

The move meant that White became the only individual ever to head up both British espionage agencies. He brought a fresh approach to MI6 and by the late 1950s the new boy had grown more than a little suspicious of the ubiquitous Kim Philby.

Dick White had a long history of working in the espionage field, and to him Philby seemed too close to disaster and scandal for comfort. His all-seeing eyes were now firmly fixed on this plausible member of his own organisation, wondering when and if to strike.

In 1961 the matter was taken out of his hands when the Soviet defector Anatoliy Golitsyn named White's chief suspect as a KGB mole. Philby, now living in Beirut with Eleanor Brewer, his third wife, immediately subsided into a drunken stupor and deep depression. He was suddenly afraid that he might be 'lifted' by the FBI and taken to America for interrogation.

A COLD, COLD COMFORT

Dick White sent an agent, Philby's friend Nicholas Elliot, to interview him. Elliot and Philby had always been close but the matter of Philby's treachery had remained hidden. Now, however, he apparently confessed to Elliot everything he had done on behalf of the Soviets.

If that is true and if we believe Elliot's account of the interview, Philby's old friend must have been devastated. Elliot knew that Philby, like all agents, played things close to the wire at times, but this was outright betrayal and deception.

According to Nicholas Elliott, his friend turned up at his hotel with half a dozen sheets of closely typed paper, detailing all his misdemeanours. Before Elliott could pass them on to MI6, Kim Philby fled Beirut on a Soviet steamer, leaving port so hurriedly that half its cargo lay strewn about the dockside for days afterwards.

Hoover, Director of America's FBI and the man responsible for leaking the original story about Philby to the press in 1955, was told the news of Philby's defection and flight. As might be expected he was furious and in light of the defection of Burgess, Maclean and now Kim Philby he was moved to remark: 'Tell 'em, Jesus Christ had twelve [disciples] and only one of them was a double agent.'[5]

When he arrived in Moscow, Philby found that he was not, as he had been led to believe, a colonel in the KGB. In fact, it was a further ten years before he was even able to visit the KGB headquarters. He was not exactly a non-person but it was a very close call.

He lived under virtual house arrest, the Soviets for some reason being frightened that he might take it into his head to disappear and escape back to the West. It was a strange fear that may have been connected to Philby's easy duplicity and long service for the Soviet Union – over fifty years and the presentation of thousands of top-secret documents. It was, however, a misjudgement.

Nobody in the West, not even a rapacious and virulent press corps, furious at what most scandal sheets saw as betrayal of their standing and position, would have welcomed Kim Philby back into their midst. The very act of defection had made him *persona non grata* in their eyes. And so he sat in Moscow without a job, without purpose and without prospects of any sort.

With nothing to do and no one to see – he did not even meet up with his old friend Guy Burgess as might have been expected – Philby became depressed and resorted more and more to alcohol. He once tried to kill himself by slashing his wrists.

He married again, this time to the Russian Rufina Pukhova, and had a brief affair with Donald Maclean's wife, Melinda. She eventually returned to Maclean, leaving Philby more depressed than ever. His OBE was annulled and his book on his career as a spy found a publisher in the West but not in the Soviet Union.

At the time of his defection Philby was certainly 'hot news' but the depth of his treachery did not really resonate with a people still gloating over their victory in the recent war with Germany. And yet the extent of his treachery was vast:

> The scale of Philby's betrayal is barely imaginable to anyone who has not been in the business. In Eastern Europe alone, dozens and perhaps hundreds of British agents were imprisoned, tortured and shot. Those who had not been betrayed by Philby were betrayed by George Blake, another MI6 double agent.[6]

Philby betrayed without regret and without compunction. It is only now, in hindsight, that the enormity of his treachery has been accepted. For too many years after his defection he remained 'Good old Kim', occupying a peculiar, almost unexplainable place in people's affections. It is difficult to reconcile the personality of the man with the enormity of his actions.

There is no doubt that Philby was ideologically motivated. He had steadfastly waited to be called to the colours, long after he had signed up for Stalin's shilling. Nobody but a committed idealist would have been prepared to sit on his hands and wait like that.

But Philby was also vain enough to want titles like a colonel-ship in the KGB and medals from the Soviet Union. Money also exchanged hands so it was not all altruism on behalf of the USSR's master spy. And yet the only time he displayed any real emotion was on those occasions when his own exposure as a double agent appeared to be a distinct possibility.

Like Guy Burgess, Philby lived out the lonely, sad life of most used-up agents and spies, his purpose gone and his mission consigned to history. There were many in the West who would have said it was no more than he deserved. He died in Moscow from heart failure in 1988.

Chapter Nine

The Yanks are Coming

'And we won't come back till it's over, over there.'
Popular US song, circa 1917

Before the entry of the USA into the Second World War the Americans had no official, centralised secret service. That did not mean, however, that they had no vehicles or mechanisms for intelligence gathering. There were several such organisations.

The US Office of Naval Intelligence had been created as early as 1882, the Military Intelligence Department just three years later. And, of course, the Federal Bureau of Investigation, the famous FBI, had been operating since 1910. All three agencies had the men and the structure to offer an efficient service to the US central administration.

Yet they were all independent agencies with little or no inclination to cooperate either with each other or with the federal government. Indeed, the attitude of Hoover's FBI rather summed up the situation in US intelligence gathering – parochial, insular and almost mindlessly intent on doing what it wanted to do, regardless of the wider issues.

The wartime president, Franklin Delano Roosevelt, was a man who had an immense interest in espionage. He had been involved, peripherally, in spying as part of his role as Assistant Secretary of the US Navy during the First World War. Since then the USA had taken a backward step in spying and counter-espionage but Roosevelt's interest did not wane.

Partly because of that FDR actually established his own personal intelligence service. It was entirely unofficial and operated in much the same way as the famous Roughriders of his distant relative and former president Theodore Roosevelt. Teddy had created his Roughriders, 'leasing' them to the government for the war in Cuba and FDR was prepared to do the same with his agents.

His spy agency had begun with a rich, influential but entirely unofficial group of 'spy enthusiasts', men like Vincent Astor and Nelson Doubleday. Known as The Room, they engaged in off-the-record enterprises like surveying the Japanese bases in the Pacific and, under orders from Roosevelt, tightening border controls with Mexico.

Apart from The Room and organisations like the FBI or the Office of Naval Intelligence there were several other unofficial American agencies operating during the early stages of the Second World War. One of the most notable was the Pyrene Company of London, the same organisation that supposedly employed Wilbert Stratton in the days before the First World War.

The idea of a centralised, civilian but official espionage agency ran in direct contrast to all American belief systems and was alien to the culture of the American people. After all, in the eighteenth century they had fought a war to rid themselves of exactly that style of centralised authority. To attempt the creation of such an organisation in peacetime would have been political suicide for any president. FDR was well aware of the danger and respected it, hence the creation of his private espionage service.

However, viewing from a distance, what did emerge in the early 1940s was a bizarre and totally inaccurate view of the British secret services. MI5 and MI6, along with the Foreign Office, the Americans believed, offered a prime example of first-class espionage systems. The British were experienced in the field and their renowned practices should be emulated.

The belief was wildly misjudged and totally erroneous. And yet this early example of the 'Special Relationship' between the two countries did throw the USA and Britain even closer together and ensured that when the US intelligence agency did finally emerge it would be based along the lines of the British espionage system.

At this point there entered into the debate the two most influential men in the creation of America's future spy network. First there was Colonel Bill Stephenson, Head of MI6 in New York and the main MI6 man in America. Then came soldier-turned-lawyer William 'Wild Bill' Donovan. Their contribution should never be underplayed for without them it is highly likely that nothing would have been done for many years.

Donovan, despite his Irish descent and decidedly Fenian leanings, had been identified by Bill Stephenson as a useful ally early on in the game. At Stephenson's behest Donovan was courted and fêted by the British secret service, taken to England and treated as something of a conquering hero. He was enamoured by what he saw, enchanted by the country and enthralled by the determination of the people. America, he decided, must help a beleaguered Britain before she was ground under the heel of Nazi Germany. Convincing Wild Bill of their integrity was surely one of the great MI6 successes of the war.

Success or not it resulted in Donovan returning to America and convincing Roosevelt that the British needed material and moral support to win the war. It was not totally thanks to Bill Donovan but the Lend-Lease agreement, militarily unimportant to Britain but psychologically crucial, was soon put into place. More importantly, Donovan's advice brought the USA closer to joining in the alliance against Adolf Hitler.

Perhaps equally as significant was the belief of both Stephenson and Donovan, one they resolutely expressed to FDR, that America's best contribution to the war effort in Europe could be made by creating a central intelligence agency for the USA.

It might well have been against all American ideals but it played to FDR's preferences and way of thinking. He agreed that it was time to act and the Office of the Co-ordinator of Information (COI), forerunner of the OSS and the CIA, was established in the summer of 1941. Wild Bill Donovan was to head up the new agency.

It was hardly the most effective of organisations but it was a start. Even so, Bill Donovan wanted more and he called on Stephenson to help give him exactly that. In hindsight it is easy to see why he needed help: 'Donovan had responsibilities but no actual powers and the existing US agencies were sceptical, if not hostile.'[1]

Stephenson sent two staff officers, Admiral John Godfrey and a young fresh-faced lieutenant commander by the name of Ian Fleming, to talk to the president. Quite how effective their intervention actually was remains unclear but at this time America was awash with rumours and fears about fifth column attacks.

Donovan had, in part, created the concerns himself with a series of articles in newspapers, followed up by a pamphlet, which purported to assess the 1940 German victories in France, Norway and Belgium. They were not, said Donovan and his co-writer, Edgar Mowrer, due to superior German generalship or arms but down to efficient fifth column work by the Gestapo. It was, of course, all a fantasy. There was no fifth column, either in Europe or America, but whatever the validity of his claims Wild Bill Donovan now reaped the benefits.

Over the next few months Donovan inundated President Roosevelt with 'black propaganda' that effectively stoked the fires in the White House. Inevitably, it paid off. Within a few months of war breaking out between America and Japan Bill Donovan and the hawks within the US Administration had got their way:

> The major elements of the COI, those concerned with intelligence and special operations, were brought under the control of the Joint Chiefs of Staff and rechristened the Office of Strategic Services (OSS) – a move which Roosevelt approved in a Presidential Order on 11 July 1942.[2]

The primary function of the Office of Strategic Services was to collect and analyse information required by the Joint Chiefs of Staff. However, included almost as an afterthought, it was also to conduct special operations not assigned to any other agencies. The key to the future success of OSS lay in that last objective.

******

J. Edgar Hoover bitterly resented Donovan's sudden elevation to the high table. The OSS, he felt, would soon become a threat to the FBI, which he had built from nothing and cherished like a newborn baby. Not only that, any organisation which maintained strong links with the British – as Donovan's agency clearly did – was bound to be suspect. The FBI's attitude did not bother Wild Bill Donovan who quickly went on to create a persona and a legend to rival Hoover's.

Donovan was brave and maybe even a little crazy. This was the man who, during the final days of the First World War, had rallied his troops and turned looming defeat into stunning victory with a suicidal bayonet charge and the cry 'Come on the fighting Irish, do you want to live forever?' Brave, determined, dedicated, yes; but he was a long, long way from being an ideal manager.

The people he recruited to OSS tended to range from the social elite of New York and Boston to the most bizarre range of misfits ever assembled to serve their country. Mafia hitmen, professional wrestlers, theology professors, Donovan used them all. Small wonder the OSS was sometimes called St Elizabeth's, after the Washington DC lunatic asylum.

The views of the general public, not to mention his military colleagues, did not worry Wild Bill Donovan one jot. As he once declared, he would have put Stalin on the payroll if he thought it would help defeat Hitler.

Donovan's chief sidekick was Stanley Lovell, a man who could easily have passed as the original mad professor. He was in charge of the OSS scientific laboratories where he produced standard secret agent fare like hollow buttons that would hide messages, and bombs that looked like molluscs to attach to the hulls of enemy ships.

He also came up with some of the craziest ideas ever to grace the counter-espionage world. Artificial goat droppings that could be fired onto the North African coast where they would lie on the sand attracting flies and causing disease – that was one of the more sensible ones. Eau de Diarrhoea was a revolting, evil-smelling mixture that in liquid form was sprayed by children onto the uniforms of passing Japanese officers during the campaigns in China. Vials of caustic liquid that would turn to mustard gas in twenty minutes and blind anyone who came into contact with them was perhaps one of his more deadly ideas.

The most fantastic of Lovell's notions concerned Hitler's sexuality. He became convinced that the Führer was straddling the male/female gender line and therefore he proposed injecting female hormones into carrots and beets that would make Hitler's breasts grow and his moustache fall out. Perhaps predictably the idea came to nothing.[3]

The bizarre nature of some of the OSS suggestions did not die when the organisation was dismantled at the end of the war. They carried on into the days of its successor agency, the CIA.

After the humiliation and defeat of CIA-backed mercenaries by Castro's forces at the Bay of Pigs in 1961, Operation Mongoose was put into place. Overseen by Bobby Kennedy, it offered a range of suggestions that were as strange as anything Stanley Lovell could have come up with.

A gift of exploding cigars and a heavily poisoned wet suit that would make Fidel Castro's beard fall out, thus making him less of a man in the eyes of the Cuban people, were just two of the early schemes suggested as part of Operation Mongoose. A variation on the wet suit idea was to lace Castro's diving suit with TB germs. There was also another suggestion that CIA frogmen should plant exploding sea shells on the seabed at Fidel's favourite diving spot.

Perhaps the weirdest idea was for two US submarines to surface at night off Havana and fire star shells over the city. The superstitious Cubans would think it was the second coming of Christ and promptly overthrow Castro. Clearly the OSS did not have a monopoly on madcap ideas; insanity had been passed on to the CIA.[4]

As far as the OSS was concerned Bill Donovan was undoubtedly the guiding force behind its growth and development. In that way he laid the ground for the creation of the larger, more dangerous CIA.

During his tenure in office Wild Bill sent OSS units into every theatre of war he could find. The one area where he was unable to make any advance was the Pacific where General MacArthur saw little point in the organisation and effectively kept them out. In contrast, OSS established close links with both MI5 and MI6, a relationship which survived beyond OSS into the days of the CIA.

That relationship took some hits during the latter stages of the war, particularly at the ground floor level where a degree of disillusionment set in amongst OSS operatives who found it increasingly difficult to accept the more laid-back attitudes of their British comrades. But it survived, that was the crucial point.

By the end of 1944 Bill Donovan was employing almost 13,000 men and women in OSS and the future of an American centralised civilian espionage agency, albeit with strong links to government, looked to be ensured.

One of the great characters of the espionage world, Donovan was a difficult man, but one driven to succeed. Like Vernon Kell and Mansfield Cumming in Britain, the service would not have survived without him. The film director John Ford, who worked closely with him during the Second World War, was later to comment, fondly but succinctly, on the man who helped to create both the OSS and, eventually, the CIA: 'Bill Donovan [...] thought nothing of parachuting into France, blowing up a bridge, pissing in Luftwaffe gas tanks, then dancing on the roof of the St Regis Hotel with a German spy.'[5]

How accurate Ford's description might have been remains a debatable point but his words certainly managed to catch the character of the man.

When the war ended in 1945 the OSS was effectively obsolete and new president, Harry S. Truman, called a halt to its operational life on

20 September 1945. Truman, unlike FDR, had no great love for the world of espionage, but even as the OSS died many people began to realise that in the post-war world of uncertainty and threat a centralised American espionage agency was required.

Despite the death of OSS, Bill Donovan battled hard for some form of centralised spying agency, even advising his former officers to go public about their adventures. This they did. Over the next few years scores of books, comics, even films were produced. It was done with a relish that caught the imagination of the American public who never really let it go.

The members of the now defunct OSS even formed themselves into the Veterans of Strategic Services, an old pal's brigade that kept alive the memory and the concept of their wartime activities. When the time came to create a replacement for the OSS, this veterans organisation filled by men and women of patriotic and nostalgic emotions, particularly those who had worked in the research and analysis section, were available for use by the new department, whatever format it was to eventually take.

Wild Bill Donovan had never really been a spy; he was a fighter, albeit a fighter at his happiest when operating behind enemy borders. His championing of an organisation along OSS lines meant that when the time came and the USA did finally decide to go with a centralised espionage agency, it would be created with covert action as its main function.

Thanks in no small degree to Wild Bill Donovan, in the 1950s and 1960s America would move beyond the role of world policeman. It would become, instead, a world hitman.

******

Like Britain's Special Ops Executive, the OSS had had a mixed war. There were moments of success but many instances of failure when OSS involvement actively hindered progress and caused the deaths of hundreds of resistance fighters in France, Italy and other occupied territories.

Gallons of gung ho spirit could not make up for OSS's greatest weaknesses, in particular a lack of understanding about European culture. Most OSS men had no awareness of what life in occupied territories was actually like, and in combat zones such as France and

China, a total inability to understand the language of the people with whom they would have to work.

Intelligence gathering by OSS was extremely limited, hardly surprising when you consider the characters who had been drawn to enlist and the weaknesses or drawbacks listed above.

Research and analysis of what was provided, thanks to the intellectuals Donovan also employed, was reasonable enough although even their mistakes were always likely – as in one OSS report claiming that the Soviet Union had suffered three-and-a-half million casualties during the war. The actual figure was somewhere in the region of twenty million.[6]

At guerrilla fighting or hit and run campaigns the OSS was far better and far more effective. That was the real strength of the young and headstrong volunteers who had answered Bill Donovan's call.

Now, in the early and uneasy days of peace, with Bill Donovan still campaigning strongly for a central intelligence agency, it was time for the USA to forget about the good and bad points of the war as fought by the OSS. It was time to take action.

After a great deal of manoeuvring and a number of false starts the Central Intelligence Agency was founded under the terms of the National Security Act of 1947. It was ratified by President Harry S. Truman on 26 July of that year.

Based in spacious and luxurious offices at Langley, Virginia, near Washington, and initially headed by its first Director, Admiral Sidney Souers, the new CIA was given a wide range of tasks to perform. These included correlating, coordinating and evaluating intelligence for the security of the country. That was, in President Truman's opinion, its main duty. To other people, however, the core duty, one that governed nearly all of the CIA activities during the Cold War period, was to carry out any other functions as directed by the National Security Council.

That seemingly innocuous addition to the tasks expected of the embryo organisation was the ultimate catch-all, and as a result the CIA was involved throughout the Cold War in a number of surreptitious espionage schemes on behalf of the US government. Some were successful, some ludicrous in their intention and implementation. All were part of the grand CIA schemes for war against the left-wing nations of the world.

The CIA grew quickly and it grew enormously. With officers and managers intent not just on collating intelligence but also on having an input into world affairs, it became difficult to control. It was not long before the CIA was virtually an independent federated state within all the other federated states of the USA. Soon the concept of information gathering disappeared and the CIA became another military arm of the central administration, albeit in essence at least a secret one.

The covert actions of the CIA began with attempts to influence government and living conditions in places like the Ukraine and Poland. There was also work to be done in France and Italy where the communists were finding increased support and were looking like challenging the more traditional political parties. Consequently, the CIA funded anti-communist papers while its operatives successfully wormed their way into trade unions and other political groups.

In July 1953 the CIA charged one of its officers, Kim Roosevelt, with restoring the Shah of Iran to his throne. He had been ousted by the Iranian prime minister and by the Iranian Communist Party. The Anglo-Iranian Petroleum Company had been nationalised and the whole Middle East was in danger of being destabilised. It cost the CIA over $2 million but Roosevelt achieved his aim and the Shah was restored to power.

It was not all undercover work and it was not always successful. Starting in 1949 numerous joint attempts by the CIA and MI6 to drop agents into Albania met with disaster. Dozens of these agents, mostly of Albanian origin, met brutal ends, thanks presumably to the MI6 man in charge of the British involvement, Kim Philby.

The CIA's first really successful intervention in world affairs came in 1954 when President Jacobo Arbenz of Guatemala was deposed, due to their machinations. In line with his decided left-wing ideas, Arbenz had been seizing land owned by the United Fruit Company, a huge foreign conglomerate, and returning it to the rightful owners, the small farmers and fruit growers of Guatemala.

Unfortunately for Arbenz the United Fruit Company was largely American backed and both President Eisenhower and Allen Dulles, by then the new Head of the CIA, had interests, political or financial, in the company. The result was inevitable. Nearly 500 mercenaries trained and funded by the CIA, invaded Guatemala, overthrew Arbenz and his government and replaced them with a regime more favoured by the USA.

The communist President Sukarno of Indonesia also fell foul of the CIA in 1966. As part of the US war against communism wherever it was found, the CIA took the unbelievable step of producing and then distributing a pornographic film starring a Sukarno lookalike. It was a desperate and ridiculous attempt to ridicule and undermine the regime.

Other enterprises were more subtle although ultimately just as unsuccessful. In the mid to late 1960s Operation Mockingbird was the deliberate use of mainstream media such as national newspapers, TV and radio to hammer home the concept of 'a good war' in Vietnam. The growing public dissatisfaction with the war in a country they knew nothing about, the outbreaks of student protests and the burning of draft cards soon showed that this was not one of the more successful of CIA operations.

A far more direct style of intervention led by the CIA was Operation Phoenix which ran between 1965 and 1972. In its crudest form Phoenix was an operation to kidnap, torture or to murder anyone thought to have sympathy with or knowledge of the activities of the Viet Cong. During this time what can only be described as major atrocities were carried out in Vietnam.

The targets were invariably civilians, the CIA assuming that the North Vietnamese forces had infiltrated the civilian population who were now actively helping them in their campaign. Before the end of Operation Phoenix well over 80,000 Vietnamese had been 'neutralised', 26,389 of them killed. From the point of view of the managers and military it was a successful operation but hardly the CIA's most glorious moment.

The Bay of Pigs invasion took place in 1961 and was perhaps the greatest disaster to befall the USA since the War of 1912 when British troops burned the White House. It was a CIA operation from start to finish, a blatant but disastrous attempt by the country's leading counterintelligence agency to inflict American ideals and values on the world.

After years of guerrilla campaigning Fidel Castro had come to power in Cuba at the end of 1959. While never truly communist, his regime provided a significant threat to the increasingly paranoid American nation while the mere fact of his presence in Cuba had a profound effect on the stability of a region on America's doorstep.

The landing at the Bay of Pigs was a CIA-backed invasion, not too dissimilar to the Guatemala affair, in theory at least. Like that enterprise, it was intended that America would remain in the background, funding, training and pulling the strings to achieve the desired result.

THE YANKS ARE COMING

Over 1,000 Cuban exiles were formed into Brigade 2506, named after one of their number killed during the training programme, and put through their paces by CIA and former OSS operatives. They were equipped with American weapons and then sent to attack Castro's island fortress. Badly planned, badly envisaged and launched without the promised US bomber air cover, the exiles had only their enthusiasm and raw courage to see them through. Inevitably, the landings were a total disaster.

The invasion lasted for three days. Several of the invasion ships were sunk and at one stage Brigade 2506's limited air force even managed to attack their own ground forces. Fidel Castro personally oversaw the defence of his island, seizing every opportunity to grab the media limelight.

Ultimately the Cuban exiles were no match for Castro's determined and patriotic militia forces. Most of them were captured or killed, and despite attempts to distance the new Kennedy regime from the chaos, America was made to look like a bullying superpower attempting to take advantage of a smaller, weaker nation.

John F. Kennedy, then in the first year of his presidency, admitted he had been naive and unwary, taking the wrong advice from the wrong people. He put away his James Bond novels and vowed never to blindly follow the advice of the military or his secret service agencies ever again.

The Bay of Pigs disaster was the CIA at its worst and with Khrushchev now believing that Kennedy and his administration were weak and without the backbone to oppose him, led directly to the Soviet installation of missiles in Cuba the following year. Clearly it was not just MI5 and MI6 that were disaster prone.

Chapter Ten

Colder Yet and Colder

'Rule One of the Cold War: nothing, absolutely nothing, is what it seems. Everyone has a second motive, if not a third.'
John Le Carre, 'The Pigeon Tunnel'

The 1950s and 1960s were a time of betrayal and double cross as agents, scientists, army officers and diplomats battled hard with their consciences and their duty. The double crossing went both ways, Soviets betraying their country, British and Americans delivering up secrets with aplomb. There can be no doubt, however, that the USSR was the real expert in the field of running double agents.

The espionage agencies of the Soviet Union had been preparing for years, 'laying in' their moles and sleepers and waiting for the most opportune moment to strike. That moment undoubtedly came after the dropping of the world's first atom bombs on the Japanese cities of Hiroshima and Nagasaki.

Dropping the atom bomb had caught the Soviets by surprise, not because it was unexpected but because of the speed with which the bomb had been produced. Soviet authorities actually knew within days of the decision being taken in 1941 to research, plan and build an atomic weapon, even before Hoover and the FBI, thanks to information passed on by John Cairncross, one of the Cambridge Five who was then Secretary to the Chair of the British Scientific Committee.

It is not difficult to decide on the reason why the 'atom spies' – as a distinct entity – came into existence. That they were ideologically driven goes without saying but they were also men and women who were convinced by the notion of nuclear parity. The idea was a simple one. No single nation should have the monopoly on nuclear weapons. Shared knowledge along with shared possession of such a bomb was one way of preventing nuclear war.

John Cairncross, last of the Cambridge Five, is now widely accepted as the first of the atom spies. Like Kim Philby et al he was recruited as a Soviet agent in the 1930s but left to lie dormant until it was considered safe for him to begin operations. That time came with his release of material on nuclear weapons in 1941.

Cairncross was questioned in 1951 as part of the Burgess and Maclean affair. He was never charged but told to 'keep quiet' and soon moved to the USA where he taught French literature at the North-Western University.

In 1964 John Cairncross admitted spying for the Russians but only in the campaign against Germany, and once again was never charged. After a period in Rome and France when he worked for the United Nations, Cairncross returned to Britain shortly before he died in 1995. Unlike Philby, Burgess and Maclean he did not receive the opprobrium that his treachery probably deserved. By the standards of the other three he remained pretty small fry.

Klaus Fuchs was probably the most important atom spy for the Soviets. A German by birth he fled to Britain when Hitler came to power in 1933 and was educated in England. Undoubtedly a brilliant scientist, his left-wing leanings should have made him a suspect but it appears not.

From 1943 Fuchs was one of the leading scientists on the Manhattan Project and began leaking information to the Soviets soon after taking up his post. Fuchs was one of the few people able to understand the information he was passing on and there is little doubt that he was instrumental in helping the Soviet Union to build their first atomic weapon.

After returning to England in 1946 to work at the Harwell nuclear establishment, Fuchs was uncovered as a spy by the work of the Venona codebreakers. He was arrested by MI5 in February 1950 and while he escaped a charge of treason due to lack of independent evidence he was found guilty of violating the Official Secrets Act. He was stripped of his British citizenship and sentenced to fourteen years in prison. He served nine years before being paroled. After his release he left Britain for Dresden in East Germany.

There were many other atom spies, people like Theodore Hall, the youngest of them all. He was only revealed as a spy long after the others had been sentenced and released. Harry Gold worked as a courier for Klaus Fuchs and was sentenced to thirty years in prison in the wake of the Fuchs affair. He was paroled in 1966 and went to live in Philadelphia where he spent the rest of his working life as a chemist at a local hospital.

Some atom spies were undoubtedly the victims of the communist witch hunts that spread like wildfire through the USA in the 1940s and 50s. One of these was the American film director Irving Lerner. In 1944 he was caught taking photographs of the cyclotron at Berkley University and was arrested for spying. After the war he was blacklisted by Hollywood and the US government.

In light of the later US complaints and accusations that the British security systems leaked like a collection of sieves stacked one on top of the other, it is interesting to see how many of the atom spies were actually American – at least ten compared to just three or four British.

Add in people like George Kovak, a Belarussian and Red Army soldier who infiltrated the US Army to pass on secrets about the detonators used on the Fat Man bomb dropped on Nagasaki, and the balance of guilt hangs very heavily in the direction of the American scientists. The self-satisfied standard bearers of American machismo were never likely to admit that. If anything it took them the other way entirely.

As early as 1946 the arrest and conviction of the British double agent Dr Alan Nunn May, exposed by a Soviet defector in Canada, provided the defensive Americans with enough evidence to restrict the amount of sensitive material they shared with their allies. Alan Nunn May received a sentence of ten years hard labour but his spying undoubtedly laid the ground for the more frosty relationships between Britain and America in the years ahead.

******

The Cold War was a brutal war. Spies and undercover agents knew that they were taking their lives into their own hands when they embarked on missions into enemy territory. Discovery inevitably meant death or, if they were lucky, long terms of imprisonment.

It did not stop with the spies. Even the leaders of the espionage organisations were far from safe. In the western democracies removal from power meant simply dismissal from service or being elbowed aside into other roles. In one-party states like the Soviet Union the threat of a violent end was always strong.

COLDER YET AND COLDER

It has been estimated that seventy-four per cent of the original Central Committee members had been executed, on Stalin's orders, by the beginning of the Great Terror in 1937. The Trial of the Twenty One, a huge purge of Soviet security elite, saw the creation of 'Stalin's Shooting List' and hundreds of previously valued agents going to the firing squads. Stalin himself signed 357 of the death orders.[1]

Sergei Kirov and Leon Trotsky were also 'taken out', shot or killed – with an ice axe in Trotsky's particular case – in order to remove them from the public domain. Trotsky had been in exile for several years but Stalin's agents tracked him down and he was killed by a lone assassin in Mexico City in 1940.

The assassination of Nikolai Yezhov, Head of the NKVD, was another execution that was organised and performed by the State, at Stalin's direction. He had been made Head of the NKVD in 1936 after the arrest, trial and execution – at the orchestration of Yezhov himself – of former chief Genrikh Yagoda.

Nikolai Yezhov was the man responsible for many of the deaths in the Great Purge, and apart from other 'enemies', within a few years had removed many, if not most, of the Old Bolsheviks. These were men and women who still remembered and lamented the 'old days' and who had been members of the Party from before the 1917 Revolutions.

By 1938, however, Yezhov had outlived his usefulness. His deputy, Laventy Beria, was being increasingly favoured by Stalin, and Yezhov could see the writing on the wall, knowing that Beria was plotting his downfall. After all, it was no different from anything he had done with Yagoda.

It was a difficult time for Yezhov. His estranged wife killed herself and finally, consumed by drunkenness and depression, he was relieved of his office.

Over the next few years, after considerable bouts of torture and interrogation, Yezhov confessed to numerous anti-Party traits and in 1940 was shot to death, not by firing squad but by a single pistol shot in a basement room designed for the purpose.

Beria also fell foul of the regime, but in his case the end came in December 1953 after the death of his protector, Josef Stalin.

Beria was perhaps the most feared man in Russia, holding the power of life and death over everyone and anyone. Then the new head man, Nikita Khrushchev, decided that it was time he was removed. Like Yezhov he was shot in private, in the basement of the Moscow Military District Headquarters building: 'General Kozlov shot him in the presence of other generals [...] After the execution Beria's corpse was soaked with petrol and burned on the spot in the cellar.'[2]

Beria apparently fell to his knees and begged for mercy, something he had signally denied his victims over the years. Now he was given the same response by Kozlov – no mercy, no reprieve, just death.

The execution of people like Yezhov and Beria might not have brought much comfort to the Soviet spies but at least they knew they were not alone in the dangerous game of espionage and political intrigue.

******

The most famous of the atom spies, and in some respects the most tragic, were Julius and Ethel Rosenberg. Arguably the Rosenbergs were not atom spies at all but the wave of spy mania that swept America in the wake of the Soviet detonation of an atom bomb on 29 August 1949 demanded at least one scapegoat. In the Rosenbergs America got two.

The American people had been led to believe – by the CIA amongst other agencies – that the Soviet Union would not be in a position to create a nuclear weapon for at least another ten or twenty years. And yet, here they were, suddenly testing an atom bomb in Kazakhstan. The American nation found itself paralysed with the fear of what might happen next. More important was the simple question – how?

If the Soviet scientists did not have the capabilities to create an atom bomb there could only be one explanation – traitors had passed on vital information. J. Edgar Hoover ordered his FBI to leave no stone unturned in the hunt for this new breed of opponent, the atom spy.

The codebreakers of the Venona Project were the catalyst that started the Rosenbergs on the slippery slope that led them to the electric chair. Venona's discovery in 1949 of the name Karl Fuchs in a report on the work of the Manhattan Project at Los Alamos was a seminal moment. By then Fuchs had returned to Britain and the information about his betrayal was passed to MI5. In his confession he implicated his courier, Harry Gold.

Painstakingly, the investigation moved on. Gold was arrested, interrogated and named David Greenglass, an American soldier working as a machinist at the Los Alamos plant, as a fellow spy. It was another rung on the ladder.

As the dominoes began to topple, Greenglass quickly implicated his sister and her husband, Ethel and Julius Rosenberg. He said they were the brains behind the creation of a huge spy ring that had been passing information on the US atom and plutonium bombs to the Soviets. Inevitably, and more than a little gleeful at their success, the FBI swooped. Julius Rosenberg was arrested in July 1950, and Ethel a month later.

The Rosenbergs never admitted their guilt. Included in the list of topics on which they were charged were revealing US radar and sonar capabilities, new jet engine developments and, of course, nuclear weapon designs.

Both Julius and Ethel Rosenberg had been members of the Young Communist League. Julius had even lost a job as an engineer inspector for the Army Signals Corps over his membership. Both were from Jewish-American families, which, just to add to the confusion, led to a charge of anti-Semitism being levelled against the US prosecution teams. They had met while studying at the City College, New York, just before the war.

Now, with the whole of America baying for blood, a guilty verdict was inevitable, no matter how strong the defence might be. Both Rosenbergs were sentenced to death.

There was very little firm evidence against Ethel who had acted more as an administrator than an enemy agent. Julius had undoubtedly built a wide spy ring that included people like his brother-in-law, David Greenglass, his wife, Ruth Greenglass, the courier Harry Gold, and the engineer Morton Sobell. They had certainly passed on secrets to the Soviets. Where the evidence dissolved into shades of grey was in the matter of nuclear weapons.

Neither Julius Rosenberg nor his wife ever worked at Los Alamos. Any information they received on the American atom bomb programme was second-hand, from people like David Greenglass and Morton Sobell. If they did pass on any atom secrets it was information that was already known in the Soviet Union.

There was enormous debate about the guilt or innocence of the Rosenbergs. They were certainly guilty of spying for the Soviets, but whether they deserved the death penalty was another matter. Several Soviet spies who had been found guilty of more obvious acts of treachery were sentenced to imprisonment rather than execution. The Rosenberg accomplice, Morton Sobell, for example, received a sentence of thirty years but was released after serving less than twenty.

Later reports, discovered after the fall of the Soviet Union, appear to indicate that Julius was a carrier and a recruiter, reporting to his contacts Alexander Feklisov and Anatoli Yakovlev, rather than operating as an outright spy. Certainly both at the time and since there has been little evidence to show that he passed on atom bomb secrets.

Whatever he had done, Julius Rosenberg was soon sitting on death row. A worldwide campaign for clemency, supported by the Pope, Albert Einstein and many others, failed to garner a reprieve either for him or for his wife.

The Rosenbergs were executed by electric chair at Sing-Sing Prison in 1953. Apparently it took three attempts to kill Ethel and when the final burst of electricity finished her off smoke was seen to be rising from her scalp.

David Greenglass later admitted to implicating Ethel Rosenberg in an attempt to shield his wife, Ruth. She, rather than Ethel had really typed up the notes of a meeting they had all attended, he stated, but in an attempt to keep her out of the conspiracy he had deliberately blamed his sister. It worked. While Greenglass received a sentence of fifteen years, his wife got away scot-free. They were reunited after his release from prison. He had served just ten years.

A miscarriage of justice or a sacrifice to the baying hordes – either way the Rosenbergs had found themselves in the wrong place at the wrong time. Ten years later and they might well have escaped with prison sentences. The 1950s was a difficult time and now the blood of the American public was well and truly up.

The Korean War was raging and American troops were under all sorts of pressure from Chinese forces. General Douglas MacArthur had just been relieved of his command and Admiral Roscoe Hillenkoetter, the Director of the CIA, had taken the blame for the organisation's failure to report on the Soviet progress towards making their nuclear weapon. He resigned and was replaced by Second World War general and hero Walter Bedell Smith.

The security provided by the atom bomb had been taken away and the Cold War was growing in intensity. Small wonder, then, that Julius and Ethel Rosenberg received no mercy from the US government.

******

It would be all too easy to point the finger at the USA, but it was not just America that was having its security problems. Britain and the Soviet Union also had their share of double agents and spies at this time.

Oleg Penkovsky was perhaps the most infamous and best known of them all. A double agent for the British, he may also have been a triple, working for the KGB. The CIA, at first, wanted nothing to do with Penkovsky when he presented himself as a defector offering information about a wide range of Soviet weapons and missiles.

It was perhaps understandable. Penkovsky was a little too pat, too precise with his information and the CIA, already wracked by the whole idea of moles and sleepers in their ranks, feared it was a set up. And so Penkovsky turned to the British. They accepted the man and his story but doubts about Penkovsky still remain.

His book, *The Penkovsky Papers*, purporting to be extracts from his diary, is clearly something of a false lead, writings cobbled together by people who had a vested interest in ensuring his acceptance by the West. Even so, the book is fascinating and it does provide useful information on the Soviet leadership in the post-Stalin years.

Penkovsky was a senior officer in the GRU, a career soldier with a faultless pedigree. His first meeting with Western spies came in a London hotel on 20 April 1960 when he talked for several hours to two British and two American agents.

The meeting had been arranged by a British businessman-cum-MI6 spy called Greville Maynard Wynne, who had become friendly with the Russians after a series of meetings in Moscow. Greville Wynne was convinced by Penkovsky and now firmly believed that this was a golden opportunity for the security and intelligence services of the UK and USA.

The motives behind Penkovsky's decision to come over to the West were relatively simple. Life in the Soviet Union, and particularly as an employee of the GRU was, as he put it, uncertain. He was dissatisfied with the dangerous 'adventurism' of the regime, in particular his own little part of it: 'The present chief of the GRU, Serov, is not the most brilliant of men. He knows how to interrogate people, imprison them and shoot them. In more sophisticated intelligence work he is not so skilful. His deputy, Major General Rogov, does most of the work.'[3]

Penkovsky longed for the greater freedom of the West. Or did he? There are those who still believe he was a KGB plant, his twofold mission to convince the West that Soviet capabilities in intercontinental missiles was greater than it really was, and to bolster CIA and MI6 confidence and draw them into making mistakes. The other side of the argument was that Oleg Penkovsky was a godsend, the greatest double agent that had ever been.

Either way, over the next eighteen months Oleg Penkovsky provided huge amounts of information, working as a double agent and handing information to his contacts in Moscow or directly to his British handlers during his not infrequent visits to London as part of various trade delegations.

Through Penkovsky the West learned that, despite Khrushchev's boasts about producing missiles 'like sausages', the Soviets were actually well behind the USA in the numbers of missiles available. Also the fuelling and guidance systems for their R12 and R14 missiles were not yet complete and fully operational – and were not likely to be for some time. It was all great news for President Kennedy who had run his 1960 election campaign on the theme of reducing the missile gap between the USA and the Soviet Union.

More importantly, Penkovsky provided the West with plans and descriptions of rocket launch sites on Cuba once the instillation of missiles on the Caribbean island began in 1962. This enabled the CIA to identify and locate a number of rocket sites using the low resolution U2 spy plane photographs they had been given. The images looked, to John and Bobby Kennedy at least, like nothing more serious than a farmer digging out the footings to erect a new barn. It did not take long to disabuse them.[4]

Penkovsky might well have been working for the KGB but his information about the Soviet missiles went some way to averting a nuclear war. Greville Wynne was clear about his honesty, his submerged religious beliefs, and above all, his commitment to the West: 'He was bitter about the Soviet regime. He would weep, quite literally, when he talked about its misdeeds and the sufferings or unhappiness of his friends in the Soviet Union.'[5]

Of course Penkovsky could have been a clever actor. But there is no doubt about the quality of his intelligence and its value in regard to the Cuban Missile Crisis. If it was all a Soviet plot the value of what Penkovsky achieved has to be weighed against the significance of what he and the KGB risked by telling MI6 and the CIA some of the USSR's best-kept secrets.

Sadly for Penkovsky it did not all end well. He was arrested by the KGB on 22 October 1962, just as the Cuban Missile Crisis was coming to a climax. That worked well for President Kennedy, convincing him that Penkovsky's information about the Soviet missiles was genuine. It greatly aided him in calling Khrushchev's bluff, taking the world to the edge of nuclear war but all the while knowing that the Soviets would ultimately back down. It might have been some compensation for Penkovsky who was clearly able to see what now lay ahead of him.

He was tried alongside his friend Greville Wynne. Both men were found guilty. Wynne was sentenced to eight years imprisonment but released after just eighteen months. He was exchanged for the Soviet agent Conon Molody, better known as Gordon Lonsdale, but to the British public it was explained away as a gesture of civility because of his poor health.

Oleg Penkovsky was shot and his body cremated. Even here there are those who disagree, the writer and spy Vladimir Rezun claiming that Penkovsky had been strapped to a stretcher and cremated while still alive – a grizzly warning to other potential double agents.

******

Perhaps one of the most significant but least known Russian defectors at this time was Igor Gouzenko, a cypher clerk from the Soviet Embassy in Ottawa who managed to slip the leash and go over to the Canadians. His moment in the sun was brief but the intelligence he brought with him was exceptionally valuable or disruptive, depending how it was viewed.

Protected by the Canadian Mounties and hidden in an old military training camp on the shores of Lake Ontario, Gouzenko was questioned by Roger Hollis, future Director of MI5. His bank of information was vast and showed that the KGB had been hugely successful in recruiting and turning British and American scientists and agents.

Several Soviet spy rings were smashed by Gouzenko's revelations along with the arrest and conviction of people like Alan Nunn May and Kathleen Willsher. It also became clear that, according to Gouzenko, there was a bank of five moles at the heart of the British intelligence community passing information to the Soviet Union. It was not, as everyone in the intelligence field believed, just Kim Philby, Donald Maclean and Guy Burgess. So who were the 'Fourth' and 'Fifth' men?

An immediate hunt for the missing Soviet agents swung into action. Nobody was above suspicion and even Roger Hollis, head of MI5, soon came under the spotlight. By now he had retired but willingly came forward to answer the questions of the interrogators. Those interrogators – most of whom had their own personal axes to grind at Hollis's expense – concluded that he had indeed been a Soviet agent and was probably part of the Philby ring.

Martin Furnival Jones, the successor to Hollis as Director General of MI5, and Dick White of MI6 analysed and dismissed the report. It was, they said, inconclusive and leaned far too heavily upon circumstantial evidence. Jones and White put the report away and hoped that the matter was now concluded. It was a forlorn hope.

The smear of treachery followed Hollis to the grave. He died in 1973 but the following year MI6 officers approached Prime Minister Harold Wilson with a view to reopening the case. Once again an investigation found that there was no case to answer and that Hollis's reputation was secure.

Far from everything now being over, the row and recriminations rumbled on for years. Allegation was followed by counter allegation, a spiral of fantasy that touched the very heart of British political life. The whole matter had a faintly ludicrous tinge: there was a communist cell at No 10 Downing Street, Harold Wilson was a Soviet agent, the KGB had poisoned Hugh Gaitskell, Wilson's immediate predecessor as leader of the Labour Party, and so on, interminably.

Former MI5 officer Peter Wright, one of the original accusers and investigators of Roger Hollis, could not let it go. From his home in Australia he began to leak information on Hollis and the secret dealings of other MI5 and MI6 staff. By now it was the early 1980s but the interest in espionage had not faded. The press loved it and barely a week went by without lurid headlines about spies and spying gracing the front pages of the morning papers.

What finally emerged from the chaos was public exposure of Anthony Blunt as the fourth member of the Cambridge Five and John Cairncross as the fifth. Blunt had already confessed in April 1964 to spying for the Soviets after being implicated by an American he had tried to recruit in his role as 'talent spotter' for the KGB.

In return for a full confession, when he named at least four other double agents, Anthony Blunt had been given immunity from prosecution. Potential problem-makers like Peter Wright were warned off and the queen, one of Blunt's employers, was notified. Nothing else happened and his life continued as normal. As Professor of Art History at University College, London, and as Surveyor of the Queen's Pictures he led a privileged and comfortable life. However, always something of a prig – a KGB officer called him 'an ideological shit' – Blunt was a clear target for the left-wing press.

By 1979 Blunt had become paranoid in his fear, terrified that a proposed book, *The Climate of Treason*, by Andrew Boyle would threaten his security. Unduly defensive about what Boyle might say, he demanded to see the proofs. Reading Boyle's book now, with hindsight, it is clear what he was implying but in 1979, for the general reader, there was nothing more damaging than the comment that on hearing about the defection of Guy Burgess, the art historian 'took to his bed, sick with anxiety.'[6]

Blunt had damaged nobody but himself with his antics. When in November 1979 the satirical magazine *Private Eye* named him as the fourth member of the Cambridge spy ring, it was clear that some formal acknowledgement was required.

Prime Minister Margaret Thatcher spoke to the House of Commons on 15 November 1979 revealing Blunt as the fourth man in the Cambridge Spy Ring. He was immediately stripped of his knighthood and removed as an Honorary Fellow of Trinity College, Cambridge. A TV 'confession' saw him break down in tears and three years later, in 1983, Anthony Blunt died of a heart attack.

The episode was not quite over. One question still remained – who was the Fifth Man? There were several candidates, ranging from Welshman Goronwy Rees (who *had* once given secrets to the Soviets) to Baron Victor Rothschild. An atom scientist called Wilfred Mann, who had worked at Los Alamos, was also a possibility for a while.

In the end Margaret Thatcher, who like Macmillan found the whole business of spies and double agents reprehensible, was forced to address Parliament again. In 1981 she revealed the identity of the Fifth Man – John Cairncross. Like Blunt, his identity had been known for some time but he and the various espionage agencies had been sworn to silence.

******

The Soviet defector Anatoliy Golitsyn was a notoriously difficult man to pin down and work with, British and American interrogators finding him evasive and incredibly defensive, particularly when he felt his words were not being taken seriously enough. But when his evidence was analysed it was rarely wrong and his denouncements led to the prosecution of several Soviet spies. He played a part in exposing both Philby and Blunt, but his greatest success came with the capture of the British naval officer and spy William John Vassall.

Appointed to the staff of the naval attaché at the British Embassy in Moscow, John Vassall began his spying career in 1954. Lonely, faced by the incessant snobbery of naval and embassy life, he turned for comfort to the homosexual underworld of Moscow. At his trial he alleged that he had fallen into a KGB honey trap, being photographed in compromising positions with several men, and then blackmailed into becoming a spy.

Over the next half dozen years Vassall provided his handlers with a great deal of specialised intelligence on naval technology. It supposedly helped the Soviets to modernise their navy, but after Golitsyn's evidence he was arrested and sentenced to eighteen years in prison. He served just ten.

George Blake was another British naval officer who became a spy – for both MI6 and the KGB. Initially a career officer, Blake's fall from grace was spectacular. He began working for MI6 in 1944, serving in Hamburg where he interrogated U-boat captains, and then Seoul where he gathered information on North Korea. He was turned by the Soviets after being captured during the Korean War and witnessing at first hand the effect of American bombing on civilian targets. He spent three years in captivity where he read Marx and became a communist.

Blake was freed in 1953. He became a case officer in Berlin where he was supposed to interview and persuade Soviet officers to work for MI6. In the event he became a double agent himself. He spent nine years betraying secrets, including Operation Gold, a tunnel into East Berlin that was used to tap Soviet telephone lines.

George Blake was an extremely successful double agent, managing to destroy many of the MI6 operations in Eastern Europe. Dozens of agents were sent into captivity or shot because of him, including P. S. Popov, the top CIA mole in the GRU who was captured and executed in 1960.

Eventually, Blake was arrested on the evidence of the Polish defector Michael Galeniewski and sentenced to a total of forty-two years imprisonment. As the British newspapers gleefully commented, it was one year for every agent he had betrayed.

Blake's fame was ensured when he escaped from Wormwood Scrubs Prison. Assisted by other prisoners who thought the forty-two-year sentence excessive, his escape was the stuff of a *Boys Own* story, involving rope ladders across the wall, safe houses and a dramatic flight across Europe.

George Blake wrote his autobiography *No Other Choice* in 1990. He was due to be paid £60,000 by the publisher but the British government intervened. Blake complained that this was a human rights violation and was granted £5,000 in compensation.

George Blake admitted guilt at his trial but was adamant that he had never betrayed his country. The attribution is unclear – it could belong either to Blake or to Kim Philby – but he supposedly once declared 'To betray you first have to belong. I never belonged.'[7]

******

Somebody once remarked that women were made to be good spies. Something in their make-up and the way that men treat them, gives women the edge when it comes to travelling unsuspected through the mesh of officialdom and the macho male-dominated world of espionage. Women were made to be good spies? It's probably a sexist comment but one that is certainly true.

Melita Norwood was no scientist but as a civil servant and secretary to one of the directors at the Harwell Research station she was regarded by the NKVD and KGB as one of the most valuable agents they possessed, more valuable even than the Cambridge Five.

Norwood was recruited as an agent for the NKVD by the Communist Party of Great Britain in 1937. A member of the Woolwich Spy Ring, she survived an MI5 trawl of 1938 when three members of the ring were arrested. In 1965 she was identified as a security risk but was never arrested or questioned in an attempt to keep MI5's methods secret.

Melita Norwood retired in 1986 and was unmasked thirteen years later in a book by Soviet defector Vasili Mitrokhin. Her neighbours, friends, even her daughter, were astounded by the disclosure. Her spying career was a perfect example of the spy who works tirelessly away for the cause, expecting and receiving little recognition or publicity in return. The 2018 film *Red Joan*, directed by Trevor Nunn and starring Judi Dench and Sophie Cookson, was a loose attempt to tell the story of

Melita. It had little in common with the real story, however, and was not a critical success.

Possibly the most successful of all Soviet spies during the Second World War and the early days of the Cold War was Ursula Kuczynski. A good spy often needs several names and she was also known as Ruth Werner and Ursula Beurton.

Ruth led an eventful and full life. By 1930 she and her husband, the architect and fellow spy Rudolf Hamburger, were in Shanghai where there was plenty of opportunity for Rudolf's business to thrive. That was where her son, Maik, was born and where, with the aid of Soviet master spy Richard Sorge, she began her career as an agent.

Under Sorge's directions she established and ran an effective Soviet spy ring that operated throughout China. The ring flourished, but despite the fact that Ruth Kuczynski had been running the group for some time she was then sent to Moscow for an eight-month training period. It was a strange decision, but it was not one that she or her handlers in the Soviet Union ever regretted.

Ruth became particularly adept at radio work. She learned how to build and operate radio transmitters and receivers and quickly grew to be more than competent in Morse code. Her skills were in demand, so much so that after a further period in China she was despatched to Poland where it was felt that she was needed most.

Before moving to Poland she gave birth to a daughter, the child of an illicit relationship with another Soviet agent. With amazing good grace Rudolf Hamburger accepted the child as his own.

Recalled briefly to Moscow, Ruth discovered that she had been awarded the Order of the Red Banner for her spy work and also, without ever putting on a uniform, been given the rank of colonel in the Red Army. In due course she and her husband were sent to Switzerland where their marriage finally ended. It was just after the conclusion of the Spanish Civil War and Ruth was under instructions to contact the British communist veterans recuperating there.

If possible she was to get one of these British volunteer soldiers to marry her. While she was waiting, beguiling her battle-hardened veterans, Ruth became a short-lived but highly prized member of the famous Lucy spy ring.

A second marriage to the communist Len Beurton, or Brewer as he was sometimes known, enabled her to gain a British passport, and as directed by her masters in Moscow, the couple duly moved to England. They wound up close to Oxford, living in a number of small Oxfordshire villages and finally finishing in Great Rollright where they settled down for nearly twelve years.

It was not long before she was pregnant again and happily fulfilling the role of wife and mother. But wherever they went, Ruth Beurton, as she now was, built and operated radios in order to transmit messages to the Soviet Union. The villagers never knew of her hidden secrets, accepting Ruth and her husband as ordinary members of the community. In fact she was well on the way to becoming one of the most successful agents of all time.

In the years after the Second World War Ruth became the main courier for the atom spies Klaus Fuchs and Melita Norwood. Both Fuchs and Norwood were then working at nearby Harwell, just a fast bike ride away from Ruth's home, and the quantity and quality of their intelligence was, it was later claimed, of unbelievable value to the Soviet Union.

Ruth would take long cycle rides out into the country, complete with her new baby, and there she would meet her contacts. Over the handlebars of their bikes she, Fuchs and Norwood made exchanges without any interference. The baby in the basket of her bike was a perfect distraction for anybody who stopped to talk. As she was to later say, a clothes line full of nappies was the best cover she could ever have dreamed up.

Ruth's father, Rene, a renowned author, academic and economist, was friendly with many left-wing politicians. Unfortunately for them, he also operated as a Soviet spy, happily lending support to his daughter in her task.

He was now living in England, having fled Germany in 1935 and taken refuge in Britain. For most of the war years he and his wife abandoned London and sought refuge from the German bombing campaigns close to Ruth in the Oxford area. When they died soon after the end of hostilities this seemingly respectable old couple were buried in the churchyard at Great Rollright.

Ernest Bevin, Minister of Labour in Churchill's wartime Cabinet, was a friend of Rene and in 1940 he had made a personal intervention to get Ruth's brother, Jürgen Kuczynski, released from internment. Like his father, Jürgen became one of Ruth's agents before joining the United States Air Force in 1942 and rising to the rank of lieutenant colonel. He was never arrested or convicted of spying.

Between them Ruth, Rene and Jürgen built up a wide-reaching spy ring that consisted, amongst others, of a technical officer in the RAF, a locksmith and a specialist in amphibious vehicles. None of them spied for money. Their target, like Ruth's, was Nazi Germany, on behalf of the USSR, which was then of course a British ally.

It was only after 1945, when the enemy changed from Germany to the Soviet Union, that there were any thoughts of treachery and betrayal. By then, of course, it was far too late, the spy ring was established and there was no way out.

Ruth transmitted her messages to Moscow at least twice a month, somehow persuading her landlord, a well-known high court judge, to allow her to erect an aerial on the roof of the house. It seems a strange, even unlikely thing to do in wartime Britain when security, from air raid wardens, MI5 and the police, was at its most intense, but she got away with it.

The inner parts and workings of the radio transmitter were kept hidden inside the teddy bears of Ruth's young children. It was an ingenious hiding place but its effectiveness was never called into question.

After the end of the war Ruth's spy ring continued to operate on behalf of the Soviet Union, but Ruth Kuczynski was no fool. She knew that Klaus Fuchs and her other agents had limited time and that sooner or later MI5 would swoop. She had no intention of spending the next twenty years in jail and when Fuchs was arrested in 1950 she began to make plans to slip out of the country. She eventually left England the day before the Fuchs trial began and settled in the German Democratic Republic.

In time Ruth dropped her allegiance to the Soviet Union, believing implicitly in the ideals of East Germany – a matter of principle rather than politics. She was, after all, a German.

Her best work for the Soviets had been completed by the time she left Britain, the general consensus being that the information she had gathered from Fuchs and passed on to Moscow had speeded up the arrival of the Soviet atom bomb by at least eighteen months. That, in itself, is a stunning tribute and accolade for Ruth Kuczynski.

In retirement Ruth became a full-time writer, working under her new name, Ruth Werner, producing a series of children's books and *Sonya's Report*, her best-selling autobiography. Sonya was her codename, used from the beginning of her career. Along with Richard Sorge she remains perhaps the most successful spy of all time.

Chapter Eleven

A Continuing Fascination

'Mr Bond, they have a saying in Chicago: Once is happenstance, twice is coincidence, the third time it's enemy action.'
Ian Fleming, 'Goldfinger'

Throughout the 1920s and '30s interest in spy fiction grew steadily. Arguably it hasn't stopped growing ever since, morphing from the mindless thuggery of Bulldog Drummond, through the sexist decadence of James Bond to the thinking man's perfect spy, George Smiley.

During the 1920s, with Germany defeated, most spy novelists changed their targets. The Kaiser and his machinations were no longer the issue and attention swung from Germany to the new threat to world peace, the Soviet Union.

John Buchan's *Greenmantle* had lifted spy stories into the higher planes of literature. Now he came up with a new if unlikely set of heroes, the retired grocer Dickson McCunn and the street urchins of the Gorbals Diehards. Set in an old mansion on the Scottish west coast, Buchan's *Huntingtower* took as its theme the rescue of a Russian princess from the clutches of Russian spies. Dickson McCunn might have been no Richard Hannay but the book was an immediate success.

Buchan's work was something of an exception in the early postwar years as spy authors seemed to be more intent on combating the 'Red Menace' than on creating works of art. That did not stop the genre being incredibly popular. And as was the case with the explosion of spy literature in the early twentieth century, there was still a volume of good quality work that stood out.

First-class exceptions to the welter of dross and mediocrity came from the pens of Somerset Maugham, with his Ashenden books, and Alexander Wilson whose *The Mystery of Tunnel 51* gave a surprisingly accurate picture of the first 'C', Mansfield Smith Cumming. Compton

Mackenzie, himself a former agent, produced the first spy satire when he published *Water on the Brain.*

Perhaps the best of the new batch was Eric Ambler. Never a spy himself, and therefore with little knowledge of the hidden intelligence world, Ambler wrote stories that hinged around the gifted amateur entangled in a web of deceit and danger. He wrote several spy books but the best was probably *The Mask of Dimitrios*. Two of his novels, *Uncommon Danger* and *Cause for Alarm* were unusual in that they featured NKVD agents who, rather than hunt them down, actually attempted to help the gifted amateurs.

The approach of war gave spy writers a new focus but it was after the defeat of Nazi Germany that spy writing came into its own once more. After 1945 the Cold War provided a totally new and different focus for proponents of the art. Almost from the beginning two styles began to emerge, the romantic and the realistic.

Desmond Cory fitted easily into the first of those styles with his 1951 novel *Secret Ministry* which featured a government agent and spy who had been given the licence to kill. It was too good an opportunity for Ian Fleming to miss and with the publication of *Casino Royale* the hard drinking, hard womanising James Bond was born. Certainly not a spy, and not even a very good agent – just the original blunt instrument – Bond became hugely popular with the public.

Fleming grew heartily sick of his creation and tried to kill him off in *From Russia with Love*. However, as Arthur Conan Doyle found with Sherlock Holmes, the public demanded his return and the former Naval Intelligence Officer was forced to bring the most famous spy in literature back to life. So popular was Bond that after Fleming's death a whole coterie of quality writers such as Kingsley Amis, John Gardner and Sebastian Faulkes were paid to produce new 007 books.

Two of the most notable spy writers in the realistic field were Graham Greene and John Le Carré. Greene's *The Heart of the Matter*, *Our Man in Havana* and *The Human Factor* were all good quality spy fiction, by turns serious and funny, but none of them ever quite managed to capture the atmosphere and suspense of his masterpiece *The Third Man*.

John Le Carré, of course, remains the master of realistic spy fiction. *The Spy Who Came in from the Cold* was the start, but the Smiley books, *Tinker, Tailor, Soldier, Spy,* and *Smiley's People,* along with the rather more erudite middle book in the trilogy, *The Honourable Schoolboy*, remain as perfect examples of the modern spy writer's craft.

A CONTINUING FASCINATION

In George Smiley Le Carré created a middle-class anti-hero who struggles with the twin problems of ethics and an errant wife. Each day he goes to work at The Circus, as Le Carré named the security service base, in the same way that most men will go to the office or the bank. Smiley has an inherent common sense – except where the relationship between himself and his wife is concerned.

Helen MacInnes was one of the few good quality women writers to try her hand at the spy genre. Her first spy novel, *Above Suspicion*, came out in 1939, but her best-known book remains *Ride a Pale Horse* which rolled off the presses in 1984. There might have been very few women writers but one of the most popular fictional characters of the sixties and seventies was a woman, Modesty Blaze.

Modesty Blaze originated in 1963 as a newspaper comic strip adventure written by Peter O'Donnell and illustrated by Jim Holdaway. The idea of a female agent obviously had an appeal, not unlike the Jayne series of cartoons from the Second World War, and Modesty went on to appear in eleven novels, two short story collections and three films.

The 1970s saw a new departure when writers began to directly combine fact with fiction. Frederick Forsyth, Ken Follett, Desmond Bagley and Gerald Seymour all produced riveting stories based loosely around actual events. Tom Clancey's *The Hunt for Red October*, a combination of classic adventure and the espionage world, was later made into an award-winning film.

It was the growing popularity of TV and films that took spy fiction onto the next level of public appeal. The big screen adaptation of *The Spy Who Came in from the Cold*, starring Richard Burton as a suitably depressed and depressive Alex Lomas, was a magnificent creation, but it was, perhaps, too realistic for the movie watchers of the 1960s and '70s.

The James Bond movies, beginning with *Dr No*, spawned a host of imitators such as the Matt Helm series for actor/singer Dean Martin. *The Wrecking Crew* and other films like James Coburn's *In like Flint* meant that most of the spy movies that were soon dominating the cinema screens had degenerated into vehicles for gadgetry and slick dialogue. Somehow that seemed to reflect the public demand for escapism.

Even the James Bond franchise, realistic and riveting to begin with, soon slipped into the same mode, producing movies where the real interest lay in the latest invention of Q Branch rather than the espionage work itself. It was entertaining, but it was not spy fiction.

Television programmes did attempt to remain more realistic. The *Callan* series, featuring a depressed and disillusioned agent, had a degree of realism that, for a while, succeeded in captivating the nation. Edward Woodward's taut portrayal of the main character was convincing and his foibles, like fighting miniature battles with model soldiers, gave *Callan* an edge that so many other television programmes did not have.

The underplayed BBC series *Spycatcher* tried to give an impression of the work of MI5. It was loosely based on the career of Dutchman Oreste Pinto, regarded by many as the supreme interrogator of the Second World War, and ran for nearly four years in the early 1960s.

The Prisoner, essential cult viewing but still virtually incomprehensible, was filmed at Portmeirion in North Wales and has fascinated critics and aficionados ever since. Even now no one really knows what it was all about. A haven for out-of-date spies, a detention centre run by an unnamed enemy, a rejuvenation centre; you pays your money and you takes your choice.

Exceptionally realistic series like *The Sandbaggers* and *Spooks* were probably the highlights as far as new stories were concerned, but Alec Guinness's portrayal of George Smiley in the TV adaptations of *Tinker, Tailor, Soldier, Spy* and *Smiley's People* remains an iconic image that will hang around the actor's shoulders for ever.

It was too good to last. Hit series like *The Man from U.N.C.L.E.* – hugely enjoyable but about as far from reality as *Flash Gordon* or *Superman* – managed to drag the television version of the spying game down to the same level as the cinema.

The terrorist attacks of 9-11 brought writers and filmmakers back to reality. People like John Le Carré and Freddie Forsyth found what was really a second wind and were soon producing quality work once again, based around the new threat of international terrorism. New writers like William Boyd, whose *Restless* appeared in 2006, added to the rejuvenation of what had become a rather trivialised medium.

Spy novels, films and TV series continue to appear. They continue to hold us in thrall and their popularity will not diminish, not as long as there are active spies and agents in the real world. It might, however, be wise to remember the words of Modesty Blaze in the final strip cartoon of her adventures and then consider that she, like Bond and Smiley and the rest, is probably still out there somewhere, doing what they do best – standing on the wall and keeping us safe: 'No villains, no victims, no blood, sweat and tears [...] We'll take a little break.'[1]

******

If, thanks mainly to Ian Fleming, the early 1950s saw a rejuvenation of interest in the spy novel, it also witnessed numerous disasters in the real world of spying. From the defecting Kim Philby to the exposure of atom spy Klaus Fuchs it seemed as if espionage and its adherents were never off the front pages of the daily newspapers.

The rubric was simple. Who needed spy fiction when spy fact was equally as fascinating? At no time was that a truer statement than during the infamous Buster Crabb affair of 1956.

In April of that year the Soviet cruiser *Ordzhonikidze* arrived in Portsmouth harbour, carrying Soviet leaders Nikita Khrushchev and Nikolai Bulganin. MI5 decided that this was the ideal moment to investigate the ship's anti-submarine equipment. There was only one way – send down a diver and let him explore the bottom of the vessel.

The man chosen to do the job was retired lieuteneant commander Lionel 'Buster' Crabb. He had won the George Medal and an OBE for his work detecting enemy frogmen in Gibraltar during the war but now he was over fifty and nowhere near as fit as he used to be. He had performed a similar operation for MI5 the year before, diving on a *Sverdlov Class* cruiser to examine the technicalities of the ship's incredible manoeuvrability.

The political situation was delicate. Khrushchev and Bulganin were in Britain on an official diplomatic mission, never expecting any sort of covert interest on their ship. Regardless, Buster Crabb dived into Portsmouth Harbour on 19 April 1956 and was never seen again.

Twelve months later, on 19 June 1957, Crabb's headless body was discovered in the waters off Chichester Harbour. According to the Admiralty he had been accidentally killed during trials of new underwater apparatus; the Soviets responded by claiming they had seen a frogman in the water around the *Ordzhonikidze*.

The story was front page news for many months – a war hero killed while clearly carrying out work for MI5. No one really knows what happened but many wild guesses have been made: Crabb was captured and died during interrogation; he was killed by Soviet divers; his body, strapped to the underside of the *Ordzhonikidze's* hull had come loose and been decapitated by the ship's propellers; he was shot by a sentry; he never died but defected.

The Crabb affair caused considerable bad feeling between Britain and the USSR. It was the height of the Cold War and it took very little to get pulses racing. But, perhaps most significantly, the death of Buster Crabb once again emphasised the inadequacy of British intelligence work.

In 1953 Major John Sinclair had been brought in as the new chief to improve things at MI6 while Roger Hollis had recently taken over at MI5. Initially, neither appointment was particularly successful, both men spending more time placating the Americans than in 'cleansing the stables'. It took the arrival of Dick White, along with the gradual increase in efficiency of Hollis, before things finally improved. It was a slow process.

The effect of various MI5/MI6 debacles, in particular the defecting Cambridge spies, took a long time to dissipate. The Americans, quick to accuse but slow to forgive, managed to forget their own inadequacies, but then they were now a superpower and Britain was already firmly lodged in the second division.

The Buster Crabb affair had, at least, given the readers of spy novels something new and real to enjoy. And even Ian Fleming was fascinated. He used the underwater surveillance of enemy ships to create one of the most exciting episodes in his forthcoming Bond novel *Thunderball*.

******

The world moved on and Buster Crabb was eventually consigned to history. In the early '60s it became America's turn to suffer humiliation with the failed attempt to invade Cuba and replace Fidel Castro with a more US-friendly regime.

However, if the Bay of Pigs misadventure in 1961 and the Cuban Missile Crisis of 1962 proved anything it was surely that the art of spying had reached the technological age. Fidel Castro may have stuck to traditional methods, managing to infiltrate his spies into various US agencies and organisations and so prepare himself for what was coming, but it was the American use of U2 spy planes that really broke the mould as far as espionage services were concerned.

A CONTINUING FASCINATION

The U2 was a single seat, single-engined jet aircraft designed to carry out the same tasks as the early biplanes of the First World War. The difference was that the BE2Cs and RE8s from 1914 were able to reach heights of 5-6,000ft, if the weather was fortuitous. The U2s operated almost on the edge of space.

The first U2 spying mission took place in 1955. The high-altitude reconnaissance planes were able to soar to heights of 70,000ft and Allen Dulles, now head of the CIA, was clear that the USA had every right to fly over Soviet territory. It was a debatable point but the fact that the U2s then took photographs of what lay beneath them was certainly not.

By the end of 1959 well over fifty high-altitude CIA reconnaissance missions had taken place over Russia, Vietnam and China. The photographs from these missions furnished Dulles with evidence of Soviet missile capabilities, power plants and regional infrastructure. It would have taken field agents months, if not years to lay their hands on one-tenth of such intelligence.

Then, on 1 May 1960, U2 pilot Gary Powers was shot down by a Soviet surface-to-air missile while flying a high-altitude reconnaissance mission over Russia.

All U2 pilots were issued with lethal suicide devices but for some reason Powers did not use his. Despite having difficulty freeing himself from his oxygen tube, he parachuted to safety when his plane was hit and was quickly captured by Soviet forces.

US President Dwight Eisenhower denied knowledge of the mission, claiming that the aircraft had been a civilian weather machine that had gone off course during a routine flight from Turkey. Eisenhower, knowing that U2 pilots were supposed to kill themselves rather than face interrogation and exposure, assumed that Powers was dead. He was therefore happy to bluff it out.

Khrushchev waited until Eisenhower was so far out along the plank that he could never get back and then played his ace. Gleefully he produced Powers and parts of his surveillance equipment, including a number of illicit photographs of Soviet bases.

Eisenhower had no option but to hold up his hands, apologise and admit defeat. Even so he could not quite resist one final swipe. The Soviets, he declared, should take a look at their own far from perfect espionage history.

CIA operative Gary Powers wasn't the only U2 pilot to be shot down by the Soviets. On 27 October 1962 during the Cuban Crisis Major Rudy Anderson was killed by a Soviet missile, fired by Cuban soldiers. Approaching the Cuban coast at a height of 60,000ft, two SA-2 Sam missiles were fired at his aircraft:

> One of them exploded close behind the aircraft, shrapnel slicing into the cockpit and piercing Anderson's pressure suit. He was, experts later said, probably killed at that point. The U2 broke apart and fell 60,000 feet into Cuban territory, Anderson's body still in the shattered remains of the cockpit.[2]

Powers and Anderson were rarities. Mostly the high-altitude spy planes went about their business, beyond the range of the Soviet anti-aircraft batteries, spying effectively and efficiently for the CIA and the US military.

******

The Gary Powers affair and the death of Rudy Anderson were not the only incidents to rock the espionage world in the early 1960s. There was one scandal that even pop singer Billy Joel wrote about in his song 'We Didn't Start the Fire,' categorising it simply as 'British politician's sex!' His audiences knew exactly what he was referring to.

In 1963 the scandal that effectively ruined a promising political career and hovered around the fringes of the secret spy world suddenly rocked Britain. It made yet more fascinating reading for the general public, proof that beautiful women and Russian spies were not confined simply to the novels of Ian Fleming.

The Profumo Affair was a love triangle that involved John Profumo, then Secretary of State for War in Harold Macmillan's government, the nineteen-year-old model Christine Keeler and Russian naval attaché Captain Yevgeny Ivanov. The society osteopath Stephen Ward – who can be loosely described as Keeler's landlord – was also involved, eventually being charged with living off the immoral earnings of Christine and her friend, Mandy Rice Davies.

A CONTINUING FASCINATION

It turned out to be something of a storm in a teacup. Christine Keeler, a dancer, model and child of the swinging sixties, had become involved with politician Jack Profumo when she met him at Ward's Cliveden Cottage in Buchinghamshire. Ivanov and Keeler also met at one of Stephen Ward's weekend parties in the same house.

A short-lived affair between the model and the politician began but unfortunately at the same time Christine was also sleeping with Ivanov, thereby creating a potential security leak. It came to nothing although MI5 later admitted that they were hoping to use her as a honey trap that might lead Ivanov to defect to the West.

When the affair became public, Jack Profumo, who in March 1963 had appeared before Parliament to deny any impropriety, was forced to recant his statement and resign from the government and as a Member of Parliament. He went on to find a degree of redemption by taking a job at a homeless hostel in south London.

Stephen Ward was found guilty of running Christine and Mandy as prostitutes, but committed suicide before he could be sentenced. Meanwhile Yevgeny Ivanov was whipped back to Moscow by the GRU before the scandal broke.

Christine Keeler was sure that Stephen Ward was acting as a Soviet spy, writing in her book *Secrets and Lies* about various meetings in Ward's house at Wimpole Mews. There, she alleged, she met up with people like George Blake, Anthony Blunt and MI5 chief Roger Hollis: 'It was where I first made coffee for Sir Roger Hollis, the Director General of MI5 and Stephen's fellow spy [...] I saw Hollis and Stephen talking together at Wimpole Mews five times: I saw Hollis and Blunt there three times.'[3]

It's pretty fragile evidence but Christine was convinced. Of course she had an axe to grind and the main protagonists in her story – Ward and Hollis – were already dead. You cannot libel the dead.

Whatever the truth behind all the allegations and finger pointing, the Christine Keeler/John Profumo scandal was as much a story of swinging London in the sixties as it was about spies and spying.

The truth lies buried somewhere but now that Keeler and Profumo have also died it will probably never be known. But as someone once said, 'Why let the truth spoil a good story!' That remains as true about the world of espionage as anything else.

******

While the public fixed its gaze on Profumo, Keeler, the U2 affair and other high profile events, the work of GCHQ went on. In its role of collecting intelligence GCHQ has proved to be one of the most effective departments in the whole of Britain's espionage service:

> Just as the foreign intelligence agency, the Secret Intelligence Service (MI6), is unable to escape the legacy of James Bond, GCHQ remains wedded to its wartime predecessor [...] While the public fixate on spies and special operations, it is GCHQ that provides much of the secret intelligence for government.[4]

If GCHQ in its guise as GC & CS had what can be called 'a good war' it certainly went on to enjoy a good Cold War, and post-1991 a good modern clandestine war against less obvious terrorist and criminal targets.

Britain may well have declined in its status as a major power, but intelligence and intelligence gathering remains one of its strong points, something that is recognised by the USA and by modern-day Russia. That is largely down to the work of GCHQ. The 'Special Relationship' between Britain and the USA has been made stronger by the quality of this information and by an organisation that managed to survive the debacle of the Suez Crisis.[5]

That is not a bad legacy for what began life as a diminutive part of the country's secret service in Room 40 of the Admiralty. 'Blinker' Hall would have been proud.

Chapter Twelve

An End of Spying?

'Spying on people by magic is the same as spying on them in any other way.'

C. S. Lewis

There are many who believe that the spy of old has had his day. The image of the hunted secret agent bent over a radio transmitter in his lonely attic hideout or hunched for warmth behind a fallen tree or snow drift has gone and will never return.

To an extent that is probably true. Nowadays our imaginary spy in the wilds of Russia, in his ramshackle Eastern Bloc apartment or in the desert wastes of Iraq could communicate with base through his wristwatch or his mobile phone. That's if he was even there in the first place.

The advent of new technology has revolutionised the espionage world in much the same way as the creation of MI5 and MI6 managed to do back in 1909. Things that Sidney Reilly or Richard Sorge took as commonplace have changed out of all proportion. The days of spies and agents slipping quietly back and forth across the frontiers of enemy countries have long gone.

When Ian Fleming wrote *From Russia with Love* in 1957 he provided Bond with an attaché case concealing a wide variety of equipment, everything from throwing knives and gold sovereigns to silencers for his Beretta. The case was heavy but Bond carried it through customs and onto the plane for Istanbul with not even the slightest worry that he might be stopped:

> He thought how surprised the ticket clerk at London Airport would have been if she had weighed the case instead of letting it go unchecked as an overnight bag [...] Despite its eight-pound weight, the bag was a convenient way of carrying the tools of his trade, which otherwise would have to be concealed about his body.[1]

Not these days. If he attempted to get that case through airport security now, Bond's luggage would have set off every alarm in the airport. He would have been overpowered by a dozen security men and hauled off to the nearest police station. The Fleming story was fiction but it mirrored real life, and technology had to find some way of circumventing such potential problems.

The way to do that had already begun when Fleming wrote his book. In 1952 President Truman created the National Security Agency to monitor, collect and process foreign and domestic intelligence. While much of its work has always been clandestine it remains the premier intelligence agency in the Western world.

NSA at Fort Meade in Maryland and Britain's GCHQ at Cheltenham work closely together, sharing information and even some aspects of their funding. They both provide signals intelligence, SIGINT, for government use and are vital resources in the modern age. Their methods range from security cameras at airports to rafts of satellite dishes along the coast, all designed to counter threats from Russia, China, even independent criminal gangs.

Despite what might appear as an overtly defensive role, NSA in particular has been known to conduct offensive operations, due primarily to the strong links it has forged with the CIA. NSA has often engaged in the bugging of foreign embassies, close surveillance, and at times even a little judicious breaking and entering.

That said, the organisation is clear that it does not conduct human intelligence gathering. Clearly, as far as NSA is concerned, the day of the traditional spy, armed, equipped and ready to kill is well and truly over.

The modern-day spy is as likely to be a computer geek as he is to be the rough, tough OSS type so beloved by writers of spy fiction. The new spy rarely leaves his or her desk, concentrating on the technology that will bring results. Arguably, there is almost nothing that cannot be done from sitting in front of a computer screen.

Already technology has integrated surveillance cameras with facial recognition systems that allow the identification of individual faces from an information bank of millions, even if they happen to be covered by scarves or balaclavas. All it needs is someone sitting at a computer console to record the identification.

Modern technology has now enabled experts to track and predict the behaviour of suspects simply by their body language. In Japan security

AN END OF SPYING?

cameras in some shops are already predicting and identifying shoplifters simply from their stance.

The use of Artificial Intelligence (AI) to perform the basic or routine tasks of espionage has been one of the great steps forward. It is the stuff of science fiction and you are left marvelling at the evolution of technology over the past ten years when spy devices from the realms of fantasy have moved into the real world.

However, there is a critical question to be asked. Will human judgement be required in the future or is there some remarkable piece of AI lurking in the shadows ready to make the assessment for you? The world is still wondering.

With such incredible advances it is only right that the security services should come under observation and examination. It is difficult to account for a single-party state like the now-rejuvenated Russia or for the deliberately evasive USA, but Britain has at least provided itself with the mechanism to analyse its security networks. The 1994 Intelligence Services Act gave Parliament, through the Intelligence and Security Committee, the power to examine the expenditure, administration and policy of its espionage agencies.

The Act took away the independence enjoyed by the security services since they were established in 1909, but it is the type of oversight that should eliminate risk. Incidents like the 1983 arrest and conviction of Geoffrey Pine of GCHQ for spying should not happen again.

In general, despite the blip over Pine, NSA and GCHQ have received a relatively good press. It would appear that they are the way forward: 'It is said that nothing escapes NSA/GCHQ, that they can even read the number plates on Soviet cars in the KGB car park [...] One British newspaper described the rise of NSA/GCHQ as "Exit Smiley, enter IBM."'[2]

Only historians and the lovers of spy literature – of which there are many – would ever bemoan or debate that point.

******

The 1950s and '60s was an era of independence, a notion that saw the final break up of empires that had existed for hundreds of years.

The French did not enjoy the demise of their empire. French Indo-China became a non-winnable battlefield for them, a battlefield soon passed on to the USA. But the bitterer dispute in Algeria sent shockwaves throughout France. The Algerians fought for their independence and were eventually granted full nation statehood. It was not something that went down well with the French military.

Disgruntled army officers, powered by feelings of betrayal and loss formed themselves into OAS, a secret terrorist organisation, in its own way as ruthless as the Algerians. OAS was dedicated to the elimination of the man who had allowed or even begun the betrayal, President Charles De Gaulle.

There were numerous plots to kill De Gaulle but the French security services managed to infiltrate the OAS and keep the president safe. Even so, for a long while bombs and gunfire were not an uncommon occurrence in French cities. The period was superbly captured in Frederick Forsyth's *The Day of the Jackal* and in the later film by the same name.

The newly created nation of Israel quickly built itself a secret service that within ten years had become the most feared espionage service in the world. The reputation of the Mossad was founded on its operations against Egypt and other Arab nations, but it was the 1959 capture and kidnap of escaped Nazi Adolf Eichmann from his home in Argentina that really made their name.

The activities of Mossad and the French security services were almost traditional in their operations. Electronic surveillance might locate and monitor people like Eichmann but no computer on earth would have been able to lift him out of the country. Larger nations like America, Russia and Britain were moving in the opposite direction – or were they?

From 1980 onwards NSA and GCHQ were monitoring not just people but all sorts of electronic targets. And yet the need for men and women on the ground, good old-fashioned spies and agents, became obvious during the Falkland Islands invasion of 1982.

Before the invasion NSA/GCHQ was regularly monitoring Argentinian military and diplomatic traffic. During the days leading up to the invasion, photographic reconnaissance by aircraft and US satellites provided evidence of a massive build-up of ships and weapons. Even the Argentinian press was trumpeting that the time was near when Las Malvinas would be taken back.

It amounted to a huge knowledge base for the British government. Effectively, they knew all they needed to know about the coming invasion and yet they were still taken by surprise when the Argentinian marines waded ashore on the Falklands. The information was there but nobody trusted it enough to make the necessary moves in defending the islands. A spy on the ground in Buenos Aries, or any other Argentinian city, would have provided exactly the same information and, more importantly, been believed.

What the SIGNIT information lacked was any sign of purpose on the part of the Argentinians. Facts, figures and formations of enemy troops are only useful if the purpose behind those pieces of information is present. That could only have come from the human element, the human factor as Graham Greene might have put it – in other words a spy on the ground.

Technology is a wonderful thing until it goes wrong. And in failing to assess and analyse the information provided by SIGNIT before the Falkland Islands invasion British intelligence sources got it very badly wrong.

******

The disintegration of the Soviet Union in the second half of the 1980s ended on 26 December 1991 when the USSR voted itself out of existence. Declaration No 142-H not only gave self-government to the many republics of the USSR, it also ended the Cold War.

When Mikhail Gorbachev, the last president of the Soviet Union, resigned the day before the Declaration, he passed all the powers of his office, including the Soviet nuclear missile launching codes, to the Russian president, Boris Yeltsin. In a moment of sublime irony the flag of the USSR on the Kremlin was lowered and replaced by the pre-Revolutionary flag of Russia.

While several of the republics immediately forged close links with the new Commonwealth of Independent States and the Russian Federation, others looked to the West. Some of these new nation states, notably those along the Baltic, joined NATO and the European Union.

It was a seismic upheaval, one that was not achieved without cost – riots, assassinations, economic misery. But if the spymasters of the West thought that it meant the end of the Soviet challenge they were greatly mistaken. They had reckoned without Yeltsin's protégée, Vladimir Putin. This former KGB officer and enforcer for the corrupt mayor of St Petersburg rose quickly through the ranks and by 1998 he was head of the FSB. He moved on to become president after Yeltsin.

The FSB, founded in April 1995, took over the role of the KGB – counterintelligence, internal and border security, counter-terrorism and surveillance. Putin's increasingly hostile stance and the assassination of defectors like Alexander Litvinenko and Vladimir Kara-Mursa has been proof positive that continued surveillance of Russian operations is essential.

Whether that surveillance will be carried out by old-fashioned techniques such as men and women patrolling the streets or by increasingly sophisticated electronic cover remains to be seen. Perhaps it will be by a combination of the two?

******

Spy fact and spy fiction, it is sometimes impossible to tell where one stops and the other begins. And that is only becoming truer and more accurate as technology develops.

The spies of 1909 had much in common with Walsingham, the two Cecils and other early spymasters, but so, too, do the computer specialists of the modern age. They gather information, they analyse it and then they pass it on for action. That was no more than what Walsingham did.

It is sometimes argued that spying has had little effect on the outcome of any modern battle or war. That is possibly true but the results of spying have to be measured in millimetres. Spies may not have won wars directly but they have certainly contributed to victories – and defeats.

The examples are obvious. Where would JFK have been without knowledge of the Soviet missile sites, the range and military potential of those weapons on Cuba in 1962? How much longer would the Soviet Union have taken to build its first atom bomb without the help of Klaus Fuchs? Did the work of Alan Turing and the others at Bletchley Park really affect the outcome of the Second World War? The questions are at best imponderables, at worse rhetorical. But they are worth considering.

Spies retain that hint of romance and secrecy that is, by turns, terrifying and deliciously illicit. That is why the genre of spy fiction remains hugely popular.

At the end of the day no computer scientist and no serried ranks of satellite dishes will ever replace James Bond and George Smiley. And as a confirmed and unashamed Luddite I say thank God for that!

Notes

Chapter One: The Second Oldest Profession

1. Anon 'Blackadder: The Whole Damn Dynasty,' Penguin, p128.
2. Buchan, John 'Greenmantle,' Capuchin, p32.
3. Quoted in 'The Second Oldest Profession,' Phillip Knightley, Penguin, p9.
4. Rimington, Stella 'The Spy's Bedside Book,' Arrow, pXIX.

Chapter Two: Spy Fiction and Spy Fact

1. McCormick, Donald 'Who's Who in Spy Fiction,' Sphere, p10.
2. Ibid, p16.
3. Webb, Mike, forward to 'If England Were Invaded,' Bodleian Library, pV.
4. Le Queux, William 'If England Were Invaded,' Bodleian Library, pXVII.
5. Knightly, Phillip 'The Second Oldest Profession,' Penguin, p22.
6. Ibid, p25.

Chapter Three: An Advance into War

1. Knightley, Ibid, p34.
2. mi5.gov.uk/how-spies-operate
3. Ibid
4. sis.gov.uk/our-history.html
5. Hastings, Max 'The Secret War,' Collins, pXVIII.
6. Ibid, p42.
7. McCormick, Donald, Ibid, p21.
8. Knightley, Ibid, p42.

Chapter Four: Conflict Comes at Last

1. Carradice, Phil 'The Accidental Poet,' Meadow Press, p12.
2. McKenna, Marthe 'A Journey to Brussels,' in 'Fifty Amazing Stories of the Great War,' Odhams, pp52-56.
3. Knightley, Ibid, p47.
4. Robertson, Willie, National Archives.
5. 'South Wales Echo', 10 August 1914.
6. Knightley, Ibid, p42.
7. Woodall, Edwin 'Secret Service Days,' in 'Fifty Amazing Stories of the Great War,' Odhams, p370.
8. Peel, C. S. 'The Daylight Raid,' in 'Fifty Amazing Stories of the Great War,' Odhams, p530.
9. Johns, W. E. 'Biggles, Pioneer Air Fighter,' Dean and Sons, London, p69.

Chapter Five: A Host of Spies – the Interwar Years

1. Hastings, Ibid, pXIX.
2. Ibid, p433.
3. www.spartacus.educational
4. Quoted in Knightley, p62.
5. Maugham, W Somerset in 'The Spy's Bedside Book,' Arrow, p18.
6. Hill, George 'The Dreaded Hour,' Cassell, p260.
7. Dukes, Paul 'The Story of ST 25,' Wyman & Sons, p72.
8. Quoted in Colley, Margaret Siriol 'Gareth Jones: A Manchukuo Incident,' pXXI.

Chapter Six: A Gathering Storm

1. Knightley, Ibid, pp97-98.
2. Wighton, Charles & Peis, Gunter 'They Spied on England,' Odhams, p101.
3. Ibid, p102.
4. Carradice, Phil, BBC Wales History Blog, 5 December 2013.

5. sis.gov.uk/our history-html
6. www.wikipedia

Chapter Seven: War!

1. Knightley, Ibid, p113.
2. Hastings, Ibid, pp270-271.
3. Brown, Mike 'Wartime Broadcasting,' Shire, p30.
4. mi5.gov.uk/how-spies-operate
5. Hastings, Ibid, p268.
6. sis.gov.uk/our-history, html
7. Knightley, Ibid, p122.
8. Broke, Alan 'War Diaries,' Phoenix Press, p250.
9. Norris, Kathleen, article in 'Hannes,' March 2019.
10. Norris, Ibid.
11. Norris, Ibid.

Chapter Eight: A Cold, Cold Comfort

1. Fleming, Ian 'From Russia with Love,' Pan, p23.
2. Knightley, Ibid, p179.
3. www.wikipedia
4. Quoted on www.wikipedia
5. Ibid.
6. Le Carre 'The Pigeon Tunnel,' Penguin/Viking, p175.

Chapter Nine: The Yanks are Coming

1. www.wikipedia
2. Knightley, Ibid, p222.
3. Kean, Sam 'The Bastard Brigade,' theatlantic.com/science/archive/2019/07
4. Carradice, Phil 'The Bay of Pigs,' Pen & Sword, Chapter four.
5. Quoted in Kean, Sam 'The Bastard Brigade'.
6. Knightley, Ibid, p240.

Chapter Ten: Colder Yet and Colder

1. simple.wikipdia.org
2. Penkovsky, Oleg 'The Penkovsky Papers,' Collins, pp191-192.
3. Ibid, pp93-94.
4. Carradice, Phil 'The Cuban Missile Crisis,' Pen & Sword, p74.
5. Wynne, Greville 'Personal Statement,' published in 'The Penkovsky Papers'.
6. Boyle, Andrew 'The Climate of Treason,' Hutchinson, p386.
7. Article, www.BBC.co.uk, 12 November 2012 'Double Agent George Blake Celebrates 90th Birthday'.

Chapter Eleven: A Continuing Fascination

1. O'Donnell, Peter & Holdaway, Jim 'Modesty Blaze,' comic strip.
2. Carradice, Phil 'The Cuban Crisis," Pen & Sword, pp73-74.
3. Keeler, Christine 'Secrets and Lies,' Blake, p79.
4. Lomas, Daniel 'Beyond Bletchley,' article in 'History Today,' November 2019.
5. Ibid.

Chapter Twelve: An End of Spying?

1. Fleming, Ian, Ibid, p91.
2. Knightley, Ibid, pp373-374.

Bibliography

Books

Anon 'Fifty Amazing Stories of the Great War,' Odhams, London, 1936.
Anon 'Blackadder: The Whole Damn Dynasty,' Penguin, London, 1999.
Anon 'The Spy's Handbook,' Usborne, London, 2014.
Boyle, Andrew 'The Climate of Treason,' Hutchinson, London, 1979.
Broke, Alan 'War Diaries,' Phoenix Press, London, 2002.
Brown, Mike 'Wartime Broadcasting,' Shire Publications, Oxford, 2018.
Buchan, John 'Greenmantle,' Capuchin Classics, London, 2010, (originally 1917); 'Huntingtower,' Hodder & Stoughton, London, 1922.
Carradice, Phil 'The Accidental Poet,' Meadow Press, Penarth, 2013; 'The Bay of Pigs,' Pen & Sword, Barnsley, 2018; 'The Cuban Missile Crisis,' Pen & Sword, Barnsley, 2017.
Chesney, George & Saki 'The Battle of Dorking and When William Came,' OUP, Oxford, 1998 (originally 1871 and 1913).
Colley, Margaret Siriol 'Gareth Jones: A Manchukuo Incident,' Colley, Newark, 2001.
Corera, Gordon 'Life and Death in the British Secret Service,' W&N, London, 2001.
Dukes, Paul 'Red Dusk and the Morrow,' Biteback, London, 2012 (originally 1922); 'The Story of ST 25,' Cassell, London 1949.
Fleming, Ian 'From Russia with Love,' Pan, London, 1959; 'Goldfinger,' Pan, London, 1961.
Greene, Hugh & Graham 'The Spy's Bedside Book,' Arrow, London, 1957.
Hastings, Max 'The Secret War,' Collins, London, 2015.
Hill, George 'The Dreaded Hour,' Cassell, London, 1936.
Johns, Capt WE 'Biggles, Pioneer Air Fighter,' Dean & Sons, London, undated.

Keeler, Christine 'Secrets and Lies,' John Blake Publishing, London, 2017.
Knightley, Phillip 'The Second Oldest Profession,' Norton, London, 1986.
Le Carre, John 'The Pigeon Tunnel,' Penguin/Viking, London, 2016; 'Tinker, Tailor, Soldier, Spy,' Sceptre, London, 1999.
Le Queux, William 'If England Were Invaded,' Bodleian Library, Oxford, 2014 (originally 1906).
McCormick, Donald 'Who's Who in Spy Fiction,' Sphere, London, 1979.
Penkovsky, Oleg 'The Penkovsky Papers,' Collins, London, 1965.
Taylor, AJP 'The First World War,' Penguin, London, 1963.
West, Nigel 'MI5', Frontline Books, Barnsley, 1981.
Wighton, Carles & Peis, Gunter 'They Spied on England,' Odhams, London, 1958.

Newspapers/Magazines

BBC History Magazine, various dates.
Hannes, March 2019, Vol 12, No 1.
History Today, November 2019, Vol 69, Issue 11.
South Wales Echo, 10 August 1914.

Websites/Blog Pages

BBC Wales History Blogs.
www.bbc.co.uk
mi5.gov.uk/how-spies-operate
simple.wikipedia.org
sis.gov.uk/our-history-html
www.spartcaus.educational
www.wikipedia.org
theatlantic.com/science/archive/2019/07

Index

A

Abwehr, the 101, 103, 119, 122-123, 141
Adams, Donald 104
Alfred the Great 2
Alliance Network, the 130
Ambassador's Plot, the 78-79, 93
Ambler, Eric 17, 186
Anderson, Major Rudy 192
Andre, John 10
Atlantic, the Battle of 133, 135

B

Bates, Ann 10
Bay of Pigs, the 31, 161, 166, 167
Bazna, Elyesa (Cicero) 106
Benes, Edvard 127, 129
Beria, Lowentiy 92, 145, 171-172
Bernhardi, General Friedrich von 34
Berlin Committee, the 84
Best, Captain Sigismund 197, 116-117
Blake, George 155, 180-181, 193
Bletchley Park (CG & GS) 67, 108-109, 122, 133, 134, 136-137, 139
Blunt, Anthony 110, 149, 178-179, 193
Bond, James (fictional character) 4, 40, 82, 167, 186-187, 190, 195-196
Boniface (fake spy) 140
Boyle, Andrew 179
Buchan, John 11, 30-31, 185
Burgess, Guy 110, 149, 150, 151, 153, 155
Brewster, Caleb 9-10

C

Cairncross, John 110, 137, 168, 169, 179
Canaris, Admiral Wilhelm 101, 107, 123
Casement, Sir Roger 65-66
Castro, Fidel 31, 161-162, 166, 167, 190
Cavell, Edith 33-34
CG & GS 109
Cheka, the 76, 79, 80, 86, 89
Childers, Erskine 21, 23
CIA (Central Intelligence Agency) 145, 159, 161-162, 164-167, 174-175, 176, 191-192
Churchill, Winston 30, 39, 75, 77, 81, 117, 126, 131, 133-134, 137-138, 139
Cnockaert, Marthe Mathilde 53-55
Cole, Harold 121
Conrad, Joseph 22, 29
Cory, Desmond 186
Costign, Lewis 8-9
Crabb, Lionel "Buster" 189, 190
Crosby, Enoch 8
Cooper, James Fenimore 19, 20
Cuban Crisis, the 176, 177, 190, 192
Cumming, Captain Mansfield Smith 39-40, 43, 44-45, 51, 53, 66, 69, 75, 86, 88
Curda, Karel 128

D

Dansey, Claude 198
Darragh, Lydia Barrington 9
Davies, Edward Thomas 64
Defence of the Realm Act 64, 114

Dennison, Alistair 134, 139
Dewe, Walthere 53, 129
Donovan, Colonel William "Wild Bill" 158-159, 160-161, 162, 163, 164
Dreyfus, Captain Alfred 13-14, 20
Dulles, Alan 165, 191
Dukes, Paul 85-87, 88-89
Dzerzhinsky, Felix 76, 78-79

E

Edmonds, Colonel James 24-25, 27, 39
Eisenhower, Dwight 165, 191
Elliot, Nicholas 155
Ernst, Karl Gustav 41-42, 63, 67

F

Falkland Islands, invasion of 198, 199
Fischer, Franz 116
Fleming, Ian 4, 31, 40, 159, 186, 190, 195-196
Foreign Office, the 28, 45, 74, 85-86, 124, 147, 148, 150
Fuchs, Klaus 169, 172, 183, 184, 200

G

Gabcik, Jozef 127-128
Garcia, Juan Pujol (Garbo) 140
GCHQ 194, 196, 197, 198
Giskes, Major Herman 120
Gleiwitz Incident, the 118-119
Goebbels, Joseph 91, 102, 119
Goertz, Herman 103
Gold, Harry 169-170, 172-173
Goring, Hermann 101, 102
Grand, Colonel Lawrence 108
Greene, Graham 186, 199
Greenglass, David 172-173, 174
Golikov, FI 145-146
Golitsyn, Anatoly 154, 179-180
Gouzenko, Igor 177

H

H Haldane, RB 24, 26, 27
Hale, Nathan 7

Hall, Admiral Reginald "Blinker" 45, 67, 68, 133
Hall, Theodore 169
Hess, Rudolf 102, 146
Heydrich, Reinhard 101, 119, 127, 128, 131
Hill, George 82-83
Himmler, Heinrich 101, 102
Hiss, Alger 149
Hitchcock, Alfred 31
Hitler, Adolf 3, 91, 97, 101, 114, 135, 146, 161
Hollis, Roger 178, 190, 193
Hoare, Samuel 125
Hoover, J Edgar 153, 155, 157, 160, 172

I

Intelligence Services Act (1994) 197
Inverlair Lodge (Detention Centre) 132
Ivanov, Captain Yevgeny 192, 193

J

Jesus of Nazareth 2, 155
Joel, Billy 192
Joint Intelligence Committee 124
Jones, Gareth 91
Joyce, William (Lord Haw-Haw) 121
Judas Iscariot 2

K

K Keeler, Christine 192-193
Kell, Captain Vernon 38-39, 41, 42, 63, 66, 69, 74-75, 117
Kennedy, John F 31, 167, 176, 177
Kennedy, Robert 31, 161, 176
Kerensky, Alexander 72, 73, 84
KGB, the 76, 110, 111, 152, 154, 155, 175-177, 180
Khrushchev, Nikita 151, 167, 171, 176, 191
Kim (novel) 21, 22
Kings and Queens
    Czar Nicholas 11 72, 73
    Elizabeth 1 3

INDEX

George V 88
Kaiser Wilhelm 11 12, 13, 23, 54
Mary, Queen of Scots 2-3
Kipling, Rudyard 21, 23, 96
Kirov, Sergei 171
Klop, Lt Dirk 116-117
Knox, "Dilly" 67,134
Kovak, George 170
Kruger, Karl 61-62
Kubis, Jan 127-128
Kuczynski, Jürgen 183
Kuczynski, Rene 183
Kuczynski, Ruth 182, 184

L

La Dame Blanche 51-52, 53
Lambrecht, Dieudonne 52, 53
Le Carre, John 14, 186
Le Queux, William 13, 24, 25-26, 27, 29
Lenin, Vladimir 76, 78-79, 89, 95
Lidice 128-129
Lockhart, Robert Bruce 79, 93-94
Lody, Carl Hans 64
Lovell, Stanley 161

M

MacLean, Donald 110, 149, 150, 151
MacInnes, Helen 187
Macmillan, Harold 153-154
Masterman, JC 122
Mata Hari 55-57, 58, 71
Maugham, W Somerset 30-31, 83-84, 85
Menzies, Colonel Stewart 109, 123, 124, 126-127, 135
MGB (Ministry for State Security) 144, 145
MI5 (previously MO5) 38, 39, 41, 42, 45, 66, 74-75, 105, 117, 122-124, 141, 154
MI6 (previously SIS) 38, 42, 129, 130-140, 141, 152, 154, 165
MI9 121, 125
Modesty Blaze (cartoon character) 187, 188-189
Montgomery, Bernard 136

Moses (patriarch) 2
Mossad, the 198

N

ND, the (Geheime Nachrichtendienst) 46
Nikolai, Major Walther 36
Norwood, Melita 181, 183
NSA (National Security Agency) 196, 197, 198

O

OGPU, the 80, 89-90, 92
Okhrana, the 37
Official Secrets Act (1910) 28, 42
Olsen, Olaf Reed 130
Operation Mongoose 31, 161
Operation Phoenix 166
Ordzhonikidze (Soviet Cruiser) 189, 190
OSS (Office of Strategic Services) 159, 160-161, 162-163, 164
Owen, Arthur 194-106, 122
Ozaki Hotsumi 111, 147

P

Penkovsky, Oleg 175-176, 177
Petite, Gabrielle 51, 52
Petrie, Sir David 117, 122, 123, 140
Philby, Harold "Kim" 100, 110-111, 150-151, 152-156
Pine, Geoffrey 197
Ping Fa, the 17
Popov, PS 180
Powers, Gary 191, 192
Profumo, John 192, 193
Project Sussex 130
Putin, Vladimir 199, 200
Pyrene Company, the 46, 158

Q

Q Branch (Bond films) 188

R

Ransome, Arthur 94, 95, 96
Redl, Colonel Alfred 58, 59-60

Reilly, Sidney (Ace of Spies) 76, 77-78, 79, 80-81, 92, 93
Ribbentrop, Joachim Von 102, 109
Riddle of the Sands, the 21, 22
Rimington, Stella 13
Roberts, Eric 123
Rohm, Ernst 101
Rosenberg, Ethel 172, 173, 174
Rosenberg, Julius 172, 173, 174
Room, The 158
Roosevelt, Teddie 157
Roosevelt, Franklin Delano 157, 158, 160
Rutland, Frederick 113, 114

S
Savinkov, Boris 92
SD (Sicherheitsdienst) 101, 107, 118, 123
Service Clarence 129
Shippen, Peggy 10
Sidney Street, Siege of 30
Sinclair, Major John 190
Sinkov Mission, the 138, 139
SMERSH 143-144, 145
Sobell, Marlon 173, 174
SOE (Special Operations Executive) 126-127, 128, 130, 131-132, 152
Sorge, Richard 111-112, 147, 182
Spy, the (novel) 19
Spy Films/TV programmes 31
Spy Rings
   Cambridge Five 4, 110, 111, 149, 169, 178, 179
   Culper Spy Ring 7, 9
   Karl Ernst Spy Ring 41, 42, 63
   Lucy Spy Ring 146, 147
   Woolwich Spy Ring 181
Stalin, Josef 40, 89-90, 91, 112, 142, 143, 145-146, 171
Stasi, the 144, 145
Stephenson, Colonel Bill 158-159
Stevens, Richard 116, 117
Stretton, Wilbert 46-47
Strong, Anna Smith 4-5

T
Thatcher, Margaret 179
Tilney, Richard 61-61
Tottenham Outrage, the 30
Trotsky, Leon 78, 82, 89, 93, 171
Truman, Harry S 162-163, 164
Trust, The 80, 92
Turing, Alan 135, 138
Twenty Committee, the 122

U
U2 Spy Planes 176, 191-192
Ultra Intelligence 133, 137, 140, 152

V
Vassal, William John 180
Venona Project, the 150, 169, 172
Venlo Village 116
Verdun, the Battle of 52, 58, 68

W
Walsingham, Francis 2-3
Ward, Stephen 192, 193
Washington, George 7
Welchman, Gordon 135
White, Sir Richard "Dick" 154, 178
Wilson, Alexander 185
Wilson, Harold 178
Wire of Death, the 63
Woodhall, Edwin 69-70
Wright, Peter 178
Wynne, Greville 175, 176, 177

Y
Yagoda, Genrikh 171
Yeltsin, Boris 199
Yezhov, Nikolai 171
Yoshikawa, Takeo 114, 115

Z
Zimmermann Telegram 68
Zinoviev Letter 79-80
Z Organisation 108